HUMAN RESOURCE MANAGEMENT

HUMAN RESOURCE MANAGEMENT

Key Concepts and Skills

P. B. Beaumont

SAGE Publications

London • Thousand Oaks • New Delhi

© P. B. Beaumont 1993

First published 1993, Reprinted 1994 (twice)

 SAGE Publications Ltd
6 Bonhill Street
London EC2A 4PU

SAGE Publications Inc
2455 Teller Road
Thousand Oaks, California 91320

SAGE Publications India Pvt Ltd
32, M-Block Market
Greater Kailash – I
New Delhi 110 048

British Library Cataloguing in Publication data

Beaumont, P. B.
  Human Resource Management: Key Concepts
  and Skills
  I. Title
  658.3

  ISBN 0–8039–8814–1
  ISBN 0–8039–8815–X pbk

Library of Congress catalog card number 93–85035

Typeset by Megaron, Cardiff, South Wales
Printed in Great Britain by The Cromwell Press Ltd,
Broughton Gifford, Melksham, Wiltshire

To Pat, our respective parents
and, of course, Piers

CONTENTS

ACKNOWLEDGEMENTS

Over recent years I have worked closely with Andrzej Huczynski on a number of in-company HRM teaching and training programmes. This has been both an interesting and pleasurable experience and I am grateful for all he has taught me in the course of this work, much of which is reflected in the content and approach of this book. A number of particularly helpful discussions with Tom Kochan are also gratefully acknowledged. Thanks also go to the numerous organizational members who were so willing to discuss with me a variety of HRM issues and items which I have drawn on to provide much of the illustrative material presented here. Feedback from a number of students in both Britain and the United States has been particularly helpful in getting much of the material here into its final form. Finally, I am, as always, grateful to my long-suffering secretary, Eithne Johnstone, for her tolerance, good humour and efficiency in dealing with my numerous requests for just one more final revision.

The table on pages 20–1 is reprinted from Randall S. Schuler and Susan E. Jackson, 'Linking Competitive Strategies with Human Resource Management Practices', *Academy of Management Executive*, 1 (3), August 1987, pp. 209–13; by permission of the *Academy of Management Executive*. The table on pages 39–42 is reprinted by permission of *Harvard Business Review*, 'From Control to Commitment in the Workplace', by Richard F. Walton (March–April 1985); copyright © 1985 by the President and Fellows of Harvard College; all rights reserved. The table on pages 134–5 is reprinted from David W. Lacey, Robert J. Lee and Lawrence J. Wallace, 'Training and Development', in Kendrith M. Rowland and Gerald R. Ferris (eds.), *Personnel Management*; copyright © 1982; by permission of Allyn and Bacon. The table on pages 169–70 is compiled from information taken from IDS Study No. 462, *Employee Attitude Surveys*, July 1990; it is reprinted by permission of Incomes Data Services.

INTRODUCTION

THE IMPACT OF HUMAN RESOURCE MANAGEMENT

In the 1980s (and into the 1990s) the term 'human resource management' (HRM) came to be increasingly used by both practitioners and researchers. This particular term challenged and frequently replaced the previously popular terms 'personnel management' and/or 'industrial relations'. Moreover students in colleges and universities appeared to respond relatively positively (at least in terms of enrolment numbers) to courses with the former title, whereas courses concerned with industrial relations matters did not have anything like the same pulling power that was apparent in the 1970s. Furthermore, 1990 saw the launching in Britain of two new journals concerned with human resource management issues.

The above changes were held to be the result of changes in organizational practice. That is, certain key changes in the environmental context of the 1980s, particularly in the product market area, triggered a number of changes in management and organizational practice that pointed in the human resource management direction. The individual changes most frequently cited in this regard included the increased priority attached by senior line managers to human resource management issues, the retitling of personnel management departments (i.e. a name change to human resource management), and the reduced priority attached to collective bargaining and joint consultative arrangements relative to more individual employee-orientated practices and arrangements designed to enhance motivation, commitment and organizational identification. For example, a survey of the concerns of chief executives in Britain for the 1990s reported that fully 84 per cent of them placed human resource management issues among their top three concerns (*The Times*, 6 March 1990).

At the same time, however, a relatively critical body of academic literature concerning human resource management has emerged. In essence this literature has raised the following sorts of questions about human resource management developments. How extensive are actual developments along these lines? Do they derive from a coherent, long-run management strategy in individual organizations? Are they anything more than personnel management with a new name? Do they contribute to organizational effectiveness, *ceteris paribus*? Are they anti-union? Are they essentially limited to the operation of new plants or greenfield sites?

There are, as yet, few definitive answers to these (and other) questions concerning the role and impact of human resource management in advanced industrialized economies. However, they are important questions and I will be considering them at various points during the course of this book (particularly the final chapter) by making reference to certain key research findings, drawn particularly from work done in Britain and the United States. At the same time, however, it is essential to stress that this book is very much designed as a teaching text. Its primary purpose is to provide a set of both skills- and knowledge-based information and material that will be of use to (current and future) practitioners in dealing with a range of human resource management issues that they will inevitably confront in their working lives. The material presented derived from essentially two sources, namely a teaching module for third year MBA students in both Britain and the United States and, secondly, a variety of individual teaching and training courses provided for a range of employees in individual organizations.

These origins are important in the sense that both the range and the nature of the material presented here are explicitly designed for students and practitioners likely to hold *line management* positions in organizations. This reflects my belief that the majority of existing human resource and personnel management texts are designed for specialists in the subject area, whereas the vast majority of students and practitioners involved in management education and training courses are line managers. The latter are, for obvious reasons, not interested in hearing and learning about, for example, all the details of government employment legislation, or the latest techniques in manpower planning or forecasting work; these are the concerns and tasks of the human resource management specialists in organizations. Instead they are primarily interested in the techniques ('the dos and don'ts') of dealing with the range of human resource management issues which they will inevitably have to confront as part of their line management responsibilities. In general I have attempted to provide two sorts of material here: first, knowledge-based material that will allow, for instance, senior line managers to make an informed input to decisions such as whether some form of performance-related pay system is appropriate to their particular organizational circumstances; and second, skills-based material such as the appropriate interpersonal approach for conducting a useful performance appraisal interview.

These origins have also substantially influenced the manner of presentation of the material here. Each chapter has a reasonably common format in which I have presented a good deal of information in tabular form for teachers. The text also includes a number of short vignettes, which have been drawn from research, training, interviews and discussions carried out in actual organizations over a number of years. These are set out in box form in the text. They have a number of different purposes. In some instances they are simply illustrative examples designed to put a little 'flesh' on the bones of the discussion in the text. In other cases they can provide the basis of small group discussions, while in others they are explicitly set out as role play exercises, etc. The Appendix to the book also contains a set of questions which can be variously used for discussion, essay or assignment purposes.

The topics covered in the chapters which follow are those which, in my judgement, are of most direct relevance and interest to line managers. However, the selected topics presented do fall within the selection, appraisal, rewards and development sub-headings of strategic human resource management as viewed by Fombrun, Tichy and Devanna,[1] and within the four human resource management policy areas of employee influence, human resource flow, reward systems and work systems, listed by Beer and Spector.[2]

Currently there are three sorts of books available to teachers and practitioners in HRM. The first are the specialist books for HRM professionals which usually have a strong orientation towards knowledge (i.e. content or environment) rather than skills. The second are the critical reviews of HRM developments (i.e. it's not all that common, we need more research, it's anti-collective bargaining), and the third are the 'popular' management books which are long on anecdote and prescription and short on evidence and analysis. Although books of all three types are plentiful on my shelves, I found none of them particularly useful when contemplating the task of preparing and presenting material for MBA classes or in-company training sessions. Accordingly in writing this book I set myself the rather ambitious (many would say foolhardy) task of trying to produce something rather different. Primarily I wanted to present material that was essentially geared to the practitioner (i.e. skills- and techniques-orientated), but at the same time had some foundation in empirical research. The material presented overwhelmingly comes from the US and British literature and experience. The reasons for this are, firstly, that HRM has its origins overwhelmingly in US experience and research. Secondly, for many of the topics discussed, it is the US literature that has the strongest empirical foundations. I would argue (admittedly with some qualifications for particular topics) that this research base does not limit the applicability of many of the techniques discussed simply to these cultural environments. The skills and techniques involved in conducting a good performance appraisal interview are very largely the same whether the organization concerned is based in London, Detroit or Oslo.

A PERSONAL VIEW OF HRM

A standard joke about HRM teachers and researchers is that they are individuals in search of a subject area. Accordingly it seemed only appropriate to set out at this early stage my own view of the subject area to be discussed. In order to do this it is useful to start with some of the criticisms which have been made of HRM.

One can, for instance, argue that many of the critics of HRM are reading too much into the term. In other words, it can be viewed as simply a generic term for the full range of employee–management relations issues (including collective bargaining) that arise in an individual organization. This seems to me not an unreasonable usage of the term, although it does run the risk of missing out the most important, distinctive message that is contained in the human resource management literature.

To many individuals the key message of the HRM literature is the need to establish a close, two-way relationship between business strategy or planning and HRM strategy or planning. And yet research in both Britain and the USA has clearly demonstrated that such a linkage rarely exists to any sizeable extent or depth across a wide range of organizations. This finding does not, however, particularly surprise me, at least at present. The establishment of a business strategy is not the result of a one-off, straightforward, mechanical decision-making process; i.e. it is very much an iterative process embedded in a highly political, intra-management decision-making process. Besides, business strategies are rarely and not easily changed. Many organizations in advanced, industrialized economies are only now beginning to confront the awkward reality that keeping down wage costs and raising productivity are no longer sufficient conditions for competitive success. The world market place is increasingly interdependent and competitive and places a particular premium on quality, innovation, speed of delivery, etc. In any case, developments in finance markets leading to hostile takeover and merger attempts have frequently necessitated short-term responses which have blown off course attempts to reformulate longer-term strategy. In short, I think rather unreasonably high standards are frequently applied in tests of whether HRM exists in many organizations at the present time.

The essential absence of this two-way linkage does not convince me that the HRM literature has offered little in the way of new insights or has no grounding in actual organizational experience. It is in fact this literature based on the practical experience of the 1980s and early 1990s which has above all else demonstrated the key importance of a 'new' variable in shaping the nature of employee–management relations in many organizations, namely how an organization seeks to compete effectively in the product market. This theme is pursued at some length in Chapter 1, although here it is worth noting that the fact that matters such as training are no longer discussed and analysed as discrete, self-contained subject areas, but rather are covered in a larger conceptual framework whose centrepiece is the nature of competitive strategy, is an important advance brought about in substantial measure by the HRM literature.

In summary, I personally view HRM as a useful generic term and one which contains a key message which accords well with the practical experience of recent times. At the same time I accept that much of the relevant literature is highly descriptive and prescriptive in nature (indeed there is frequently considerable confusion as to whether individual commentators are engaged in the process of describing or prescribing) and contains some very naive assumptions about the processes of organizational change and strategy. For example, the nature of environmental turbulence is arguably double-edged as regards the formulation of strategy. Difficulties in the product market may provide the stimulus or incentive to reformulate strategy, but these same difficulties pose problems for the formulation and implementation of a new strategy. Equally, the literature fails to recognize the significance of intra-management, political processes in seeking to reformulate competitive strategies. A smooth, easy transition to a close two-way relationship between business strategy and HRM strategy was never a realistic possibility over a limited time frame for most organizations, and the relative absence of an internally coherent package of HRM policies and practices in many individual organizations should occasion little surprise at the present time. Instead, one is more likely to observe an essentially piecemeal, *ad hoc* move in the HRM direction over the course of time. The very fact that a personnel director in a leading company is more interested in talking about training for a total quality management programme or the selection criteria for establishing multi-disciplinary product development teams, rather than changes in the level of collective bargaining, is indicative of thinking and moves along these lines.

Does the above imply that a coherent human resource management strategy, which is closely linked to the nature of larger competitive strategy, will gradually emerge via a learning curve? In many cases I suspect that this will occur as organizations learn (via negative experience) that simply changing one element of the human resource management policy mix, for instance, will not produce the results and benefits they anticipated or hoped for. This being said, the speed with which individual organizations, and indeed national systems, move along the HRM path is likely to be highly variable. For instance, individual organizations which are embedded in national systems characterized by the extensive use of a low-wage competitive strategy, relatively decentralized labour–management systems, and strong financial pressures and influences which place a premium on short-run operating results seem the least likely to move (if at all) rapidly along these lines.

Indeed, even in the US system, which initiated the human resource management phenomenon, there still remain important obstacles to the more widespread adoption and institutionalization of the approach. Such obstacles include, for instance:

1   the need for senior line managers to set realistic and tangible expectations for the HR professionals in their organizations, provide the opportunities and resources to realize these expectations and reward line and staff managers in ways that reinforce a new strategic role for HRM;

2   the removal or clarification of certain uncertainties in the system: for instance, if traditional collective bargaining arrangements continue to decline, what are useful and viable alternative mechanisms for direct and indirect employee representation and participation? .

3   the need for the government to establish a national HRM strategy that assists and complements the adoption, institutionalization and diffusion of a coherent HRM strategy in individual organizations.

In summary, it seems difficult to write off human resource management as simply another fad in a long list of short-term management fads. There is simply too much going on in individual organizations that is part of the HRM approach.[3] Equally, however, it is apparent that there are important unresolved issues and debates (frequently of a highly 'political' nature) both within and external to individual organizations that will need to be played out before the rhetoric and organizational reality of HRM are more closely aligned.

THE PLAN OF THE BOOK

The first two chapters of the book are concerned with macro-level issues. In Chapter 1 I consider the origins of human resource management, its key messages and its alleged differences from traditional personnel management. I also introduce the subject area of competitiveness debates in order to illustrate important national system differences in the approach towards HRM. Chapter 2 concentrates on organizational culture and the associated issue of organizational change. As well as considering the nature of organizational culture I am particularly interested in the question of how culture can be changed as part of a larger programme of organizational change.

The micro-subject areas of particular interest to line managers are then surveyed in Chapters 3–8. In Chapter 3 I examine the recruitment–selection decision, concentrating on the limitations of the traditional interview approach and then considering the potential value of testing and assessment centres as alternative or complementary instruments in the selection process. Chapter 4 looks at the process of employee appraisal, paying particular attention to the appropriate skills required in the conduct of the interview process; a short appendix to this chapter discusses the nature of employee counselling, a technique that is useful in the context of employee appraisals but also in a number of other functional HRM areas.

Chapter 5 is concerned with reward and payment systems and there I look at the various pluses and minuses of different reward systems, paying particular attention to the increased interest in performance-related payment systems, profit-sharing and pay for knowledge schemes. Career management and development is the subject of Chapter 6, where I look at various approaches designed to help align individual and organizational needs in this area, and identify some of the important career-related issues facing organizations at present.

In Chapter 7 I examine the subject of employee–management communication by looking at the increased attention being given to this area, via various mechanisms such as team briefing and employee attitude surveys. Chapter 8 looks at the related areas of employee participation and team working, with particular attention to quality circles, the total quality management approach and the call for team working arrangements to be spread from the shopfloor into certain white collar–professional areas.

The choice of this particular set of micro issues for coverage and treatment here essentially reflects my judgement that they are of particular interest and relevance to practising line managers. At the same time, however, I have tried to ensure that the details of the coverage are consistent with the main messages emerging from the contemporary HRM literature; witness, for instance, the attention given to performance-related pay. I have also attempted, albeit often briefly, to inject the strategic orientation of the current HRM literature into the discussion of these specific subject areas. In other words, I have frequently asked in what ways, for instance, traditional selection devices need to be changed in order to try and ensure that more attention is given to the current and future strategic needs of the organization, rather than simply recruiting for the requirements of an individual job.

The final chapter of the book returns to the macro-level by identifying and discussing some of the leading criticisms, reservations, worries, etc. about the theoretical literature and organizational practice of HRM. This chapter also considers some of the likely future directions in which HRM will move.

REFERENCES

1   Charles Fombrun, Noel M. Tichy and Mary Anne Devanna, *Strategic Human Resource Management*, Wiley and Sons, New York, 1984, pp. 43–50.
2   Michael Beer and Bert Spector (eds.), *Readings in Human Resource Management*, Free Press, New York, 1985, pp. 3–4.
3   John Storey, *Developments in the Management of Human Resources*, Blackwell, Oxford, 1992.

1

COMPETITIVE STRATEGY AND HUMAN RESOURCE MANAGEMENT

INTRODUCTION

This chapter essentially introduces the subject of human resource management. I shall examine some of the alleged differences between human resource management and the previous practice of personnel management. And second, I shall discuss the question of in what sense human resource management can be considered strategic. The latter in particular involves a consideration of key product market changes which are forcing organizations to rethink the way in which they need to compete effectively in the market place.

In the course of this chapter, a good deal in the way of research findings and recommendations for change will be drawn from US sources of literature. This is because, firstly (as mentioned in the Introduction), the notion of human resource management originated in the USA in the 1980s, hence there is considerably more relevant literature to draw on there than is the case for other advanced industrialized economies. Second, I believe (though admittedly not all commentators would agree) that many of the questions (if not all the answers being offered) about human resource management in the US contain a number of potentially important lessons for other countries. Finally, it is interesting to pose the question, why did HRM first emerge in the USA and not elsewhere? This is not a question that can be definitively answered, although the tradition of decentralized and autonomous operations of individual organizations (permitting relatively more organizational choice in employment matters) and the relatively close business school–business community interactions (resulting in an applied, rather than theoretical, teaching approach) are arguably part of the story.

THE ORIGINS OF HUMAN RESOURCE MANAGEMENT

The concept and practice of human resource management are widely held to have evolved out of the prior area of personnel administration.[1] The essence of this evolutionary process is that employees are now viewed as a valuable resource (rather than a cost to be minimized) which, if managed, rather than administered, effectively from the strategic point of view, will contribute significantly, *ceteris paribus*, to organizational effectiveness, and thus will be a source of competitive advantage to the organization concerned. A number of rather more *specific* differences between human resource management and personnel administration are mentioned in the US literature. Those most frequently mentioned include the following: (1) the early practice of employment forecasting and succession planning has broadened into a concern with establishing a more explicit (two-way) linkage between human resource planning and the larger organizational strategy and business planning of the organization; (2) the traditional, central concern of the personnel function (in a unionized organization) with negotiating and administering a collective agreement has expanded into a wider notion of 'workforce governance' in which non-collective bargaining mechanisms (e.g. quality circles) are important in permitting employee involvement and participation in work-related decisions; (3) the traditional concern with the job satisfaction of individual employees initially led to an interest in the broader notion of 'organizational climate' which has further evolved into a focus on the notion of 'organizational culture'; (4) the idea of selection, training, performance appraisal and compensation decisions being heavily centred on the role of individual employees (with their detailed individual job description) has given way to the belief that effective team or group working is the route through which effective performance is achieved; and (5) the relatively narrow focus of training on the teaching and learning of individual job skills has been broadened into a concern with developing (via both training and non-training means) the full, longer-term potential of individual employees.[2]

As is obvious from the above terminology, the predominant theme which is held to differentiate human resource management from its predecessor, personnel administration, is a broadening or widening notion. The leading advocates of human resource management, who are typically behavioural scientists in the USA, see it essentially as an organization-wide 'philosophy' which is much broader, more orientated to the long run and less problem-centred than personnel administration.³ In short, to such individuals human resource management is something quite new and different. A rather different interpretation has come from some of the older, institutionally orientated collective bargaining researchers in the United States. To such individuals human resource management is simply the latest stage of development in a line of management research and practice which began with the human relations movement of the 1940s and 1950s. For example, Strauss has compared the messages of the original human relations literature with that of the organization development and change models of the 1960s and 1970s.⁴ He noted some differences between them, such as a movement from a concentration on blue collar workers to a concentration on management personnel, a movement from an interest in the social needs of workers to an emphasis on the achievement of 'self-actualization' and a change from seeking to eliminate conflict to seeking to draw out the joint problem-solving potential of conflict. At the same time, however, he argued that both bodies of literature were subject to essentially the same sorts of criticisms, namely that they ignored external, economic variables, were anti-union or ignored unions, were potentially manipulative approaches, and sought to have the organization operate as a harmonious, co-operative system which would act as virtually a community surrogate. The US human resource management literature cannot be criticized for ignoring external, economic variables (see the next section) unlike these alleged predecessors, although the other three sets of criticisms are still frequently made of it. The latter criticisms will be touched on at various points in the book, particularly in the final chapter.

By way of a short summary, Table 1.1 sets out the differences in the *textbook* treatment of human resource management and the *observed (organizational) practice* of personnel management which have been highlighted by one British commentator; the emphasis here highlights the fact that one is not strictly comparing like with like.

Why did human resource management come into vogue in the 1980s? The answer to this question typically makes reference to the following influences: (1) the increasingly competitive, integrated characteristics of the product market environment; (2) the 'positive lessons' of the Japanese system and the high performance of individual companies which accord human resource management a relatively high priority; (3) the declining levels of workforce unionization, particularly in the US private sector; (4) the relative growth of the service, white collar sector of employment; and (5) the relatively limited power and status of the personnel management

Table 1.1 *Stereotypes of personnel management and human resource management*

	Personnel management	Human resource management
Time and planning perspective	Short-term, reactive, *ad hoc*, marginal	Long-term, pro-active, strategic, integrated
Psychological contract	Compliance	Commitment
Control systems	External controls	Self-control
Employee-relations perspective	Pluralist, collective, low-trust	Unitarist, individual, high-trust
Preferred structures/systems	Bureaucratic, mechanistic, centralized, formal defined roles	Organic, devolved, flexible roles
Roles	Specialist/professional	Largely integrated into line management
Evaluation criteria	Cost-minimization	Maximum utilization (human asset accounting)

Source: David E. Guest, 'Human Resource Management and Industrial Relations', *Journal of Management Studies*, 24 (5), 1987, p. 507.

function in individual organizations due to its inability to demonstrate a distinctive, positive contribution, *ceteris paribus*, to individual organizational performance.[5] In short, it is viewed as a change or development driven by fundamental environmental changes (particularly in product market conditions) to which the traditional concerns, orientations and 'power' of the personnel management function could not adequately respond.

ADVERSE IMPLICATIONS FOR THE PERSONNEL FUNCTION?

Does the above suggest essentially negative implications for the future of the personnel management function in individual organizations? In other words, is this specialist staff function likely to be increasingly squeezed between line managers assuming a greater interest in and responsibility for HRM matters and the particular expertise of outside consultants being periodically drawn on, as and when circumstances demand (the latter being one part of organizational moves along the lines of increased numerical flexibility)? Perhaps the worst case scenario (from the personnel function point of view) is that personnel will remain responsible for collective employment issues (i.e. collective bargaining) and that line managers, together with external consultants, will concentrate on the growing package of measures for the individual employee; the adverse implications for organizational performance from such a division of labour are potentially very considerable. Alternatively, can the function essentially adapt to the demands of HRM, absorb it and possibly even champion it as an internal agent of change? There are differing views concerning these questions and possible scenarios,[6] with the reality likely to be considerable variations both between and within different national systems; in the USA the larger size and greater specialization of labour within the personnel function of many organizations compared to other national systems has meant that a sub-unit or part of the function (behavioural science-trained organization development specialists) could internally 'champion' HRM, in conjunction with line management colleagues. The ability of the personnel management function in any individual organization to adapt successfully to the demands of HRM will be heavily influenced by its existing level of power, resources, status and influence within the organization. In general the personnel management function has been traditionally conceived of as a 'boundary spanning' unit, designed to insulate the technical core of the organization from sources of environmental uncertainty, notably tight labour market conditions, government employment legislation and regulations and union power.[7] These three sets of factors, which are basically exogenous to the control of the personnel function, have largely helped explain why the resources, status and influence of the function in individual organizations have been so highly variable.

Arguably the personnel function is better placed to manage the demands of HRM in certain national systems than in others. For instance, in organizations in Japan, training managers are nearly universal, while 'personnel departments . . . are seen as key departments, likely to be manned, not by a company's more sluggish and unimaginative elements, but by some of its brightest and most ambitious spirits, many of whom have a good chance of ending up as Board members'.[8] In contrast, in Britain, for instance, research during the 1980s has variously revealed that: (1) only a small minority of strategic decisions, as viewed by the senior managers concerned, are

Box 1.1　*What's happening to personnel management?*

1　This long-established heavy engineering organization has taken on something like 600 extra staff in the last two years. Both a benefits manager and a training manager have been recently appointed and new policy initiatives include the carrying out of an employee attitude survey and a training and development audit, the latter arising out of the prior practice of succession planning.

2　In this civil service department the establishment officer (responsible for personnel management) has been retitled the director of personnel, and the number of staff in the personnel function has increased from 25 to 30. Following the Cassells report on personnel management in the civil service, the main initiatives in this department have been department-level responsibility for recruitment, a review of the appraisal process, increased concern with poor work performance (i.e. a reduced probation period), closer monitoring of equal employment opportunities for women and minorities, and much more emphasis on training, particularly centred around the notion of managerial competencies.

3　This plant with some 250 employees is part of a large computer manufacturing organization. The organization has recently merged with another company. The merger, together with competitive problems in the industry, has resulted in a corporate restructuring programme which has scheduled the plant concerned to cease manufacturing operations and become a servicing outlet only, with only some 120 staff. Against this background, the personnel manager at the plant has left and not been replaced; an OD (organizational development) manager (responsible for training and development to promote cultural and attitudinal change in the workplace) in the period 1988–90 was transferred to an engineering management role and all OD activities have since been suspended; and a training scheme in interpersonal skills for shopfloor supervisors, which was started in 1989, has been discontinued as a result of the supervisory grades being eliminated from the organizational structure – the individuals concerned have been redeployed or made redundant and their responsibilities have been assumed by (non-trained) shopfloor team leaders.

Box 1.1 *continued*

4   This passenger transport company is part of a nationalized industry group scheduled for privatization in the future. The company currently employs some 1,200 staff. Following the 1986 Transport Act, which deregulated local bus services, the central personnel management function at the group level has been of declining influence in the strategic and day-to-day operations of the company. Admittedly a group-wide performance appraisal scheme has recently been introduced, but national-level collective bargaining arrangements no longer exist, with pay and conditions being currently determined at the company level. Furthermore, line managers' responsibility for a wide variety of 'manpower matters' at the company level has recently been enhanced. Although the personnel officer at the company level reports more regular interaction with his line management colleagues, it is generally held that the marketing department (at the company level) is increasingly influential as a result of the more competitive operating environment and the flatter organizational structures which have been introduced.

5   This large regional council has been Labour-controlled from 1986, since when a strong political commitment has been given to the introduction and operation of equal employment opportunities policies and procedures. These pressures led to a review of staffing levels in the central personnel department, which resulted in the creation of five new posts. This increased staffing has facilitated the introduction and revision of personnel policies and procedures in a number of areas, such as flexible working hours, disciplinary procedures, new technology, etc. At the same time, however, the central government's compulsory competitive tendering initiatives have stimulated much more senior officer concern with notions of 'efficiency', 'commercialism', 'value for money', 'customer sensitivity', etc. This, in turn, has led to some questioning of the value or contribution of central services departments, such as the personnel function. In response, 'service-level agreements' have been developed and implemented; these define the level and nature of the service which a 'user' department will 'buy' from a central support function like personnel (they attempt to allocate the costs of central services more fairly in relation to the needs of the user, rather than by reference to the number of staff in each department). From 1992 the personnel unit will be operating such agreements with all departments.

personnel–industrial relations ones, at least as traditionally defined; (2) only approximately one in three organizations have specialist, personnel directors; and (3) only a minority of establishments have full-time, qualified individuals responsible for personnel management matters.[9] However, within any single national system, broad system-wide predictions about the direction of changes in the position of the personnel management function are likely to be fraught with dangers. Box 1.1 helps to make this point.

IN WHAT SENSE STRATEGIC?

As the term 'human resource management' has replaced the term 'personnel management', the prefix 'strategic' has been increasingly attached to it. An examination of the literature suggests there are at least three ways or senses in which the term 'strategic' has been used. The first concerns the employee coverage of human resource management practices.

Traditionally in unionized organizations a sharp distinction was drawn between the employment practices which concerned blue collar or shopfloor employees, and those which concerned white collar or non-manual employees. In the former case the personnel management function concentrated on the negotiation and administration of the collective agreement, while in the latter case there were more individual-employee-centred practices, such as performance appraisal and succession planning. In contrast to this sharp distinction, human resource management seeks to have much more of a comprehensive, common *all-employee* coverage. This can manifest itself in a number of ways such as the introduction of single status or harmonized terms and conditions of employment, the spreading of performance appraisal arrangements to blue collar workers or the recruitment of production workers on the grounds of not so much their immediate employment skills, as their trainability and flexibility, and hence potential for longer-term development. These examples are all in the direction of blue collar workers becoming more like white collar workers. However, some developments might go in the other direction. For example, it has been suggested in the USA that the positive lessons of team working arrangements among production workers in the 1980s may well be spread to white collar employees in the future in view of the increasing concern about white collar productivity and performance levels.[10]

A second sense in which the term 'strategic' has been applied to human resource management concerns the organizational level at which key, relevant decisions are made. This particular usage of the term follows from the distinction drawn between (1) the *strategic* level (of managerial work) which deals with policy formulation and overall goal setting; (2) the *managerial* level, which focuses on the processes by which the organization obtains and allocates resources to achieve its strategic objectives; and (3) the *operational* level, which is concerned with the day-to-day management of the organization.[11] This particular perspective, which above all emphasizes the level of decision-making which gives a sense of longer-run direction to an organization, has a number of important implications. First, it suggests that if human resource management matters are to be of strategic significance in organizations, in the sense of where the relevant decisions are made, then, almost by definition, senior line managers will need to be extremely important in these decision-making processes. And secondly it recognizes, at least implicitly, that the performance of the human resource management system of any organization is strongly influenced (for good or bad) by senior management decisions which will not necessarily be viewed as exclusively, or even largely, human resource management ones taken by staff specialists.[12]

The third and most popular usage of the term 'strategic' concerns the need for an explicit (two-way) linkage between the *substantive* nature of human resource management decisions and the *substantive* nature of the external, competitive strategy of the individual organization. In this regard, Beer and Spector have commented as follows:

> A business enterprise has an external strategy: a chosen way of competing in the market place. It also needs an internal strategy: a strategy for how its internal resources are to be developed, deployed, motivated and controlled. There are several implications to the strategic perspective. One is that the external and internal strategies must be linked. Each strategy provides goals and constraints for the other. A competitive strategy based on becoming the low-cost producer may indicate different approaches to compensation and employment security than a competitive strategy that depends on product innovation. The very idea of an internal strategy implies there is consistency among all the specific tactics or activities that affect human resources. Hence the need for practices to be guided by conscious policy choices to increase the likelihood that practices will reinforce each other and will be consistent over time.[13]

It is this third usage of the term 'strategic' which has generated so much discussion, disagreement and controversy about both the short-term and longer-term contribution and staying power of human resource management. Admittedly there is growing consensus that business strategies are rarely and not easily changed in individual organizations, particularly if one subscribes to the view that organizational decisions are embedded in social, political processes, rather than being rational or (completely) environmentally determined.[14] In contrast there is much less consensus among academics as to, firstly, how one should study and observe the processes of strategy formulation and reformulation and, secondly, what are the relevant categories or types of business strategy which individual organizations can and do pursue in the product market. In many ways the 1980s (and early 1990s) have been an apparently confusing period in which individual organizations have pursued a rather mixed set of activities which, in the view of many commentators, have not added up to a coherent strategy. For instance, the theme of product or service quality has been much talked about in management circles, although this has been accompanied by restructuring moves which have typically involved downsizing, lay-offs, redundancies, etc. In short, it would appear that actual organizational practice in many cases has not involved a discrete choice between different ways of seeking competitive advantage, but rather has involved multiple efforts to improve competitive performance by reducing labour costs and increasing quality, flexibility and adaptability. For instance, the Ford Motor Company in the USA in the 1980s has sought to respond to competitive problems and difficulties by:[15]

1   reducing its workforce by some 42 per cent from its peak level of employment in the 1970s;

2   negotiating a collective agreement with the United Automobile Workers (UAW) that introduced profit-sharing and new employment security provisions for senior workers permanently laid off because of technological change, plant closing or other corporate restructuring actions;

3   endorsing and expanding its commitment to working with the UAW to promote employee involvement, statistical process control and quality improvement efforts;

4   establishing mutual growth forums for communicating with worker and union leaders at plant and corporate levels;

5   greatly expanding its training and education programmes;

6   changing the managerial and technical structures of the organization in order to facilitate the development and operation of cross-functional, new product development teams; and

7   revamping relations with suppliers by reducing the number of suppliers, developing longer-term contracts, and working more closely with suppliers to improve levels of cost, quality and service delivery performance.

The widely held view that there needs to be an explicit, complementary relationship between the internal human resource management strategy of individual organizations and their external product market or larger business strategy has led to the formulation of a number of typologies of product market strategies and their (desirably) associated human resource management strategies and practices. For example, Schuler and Jackson have identified: (1) an innovation strategy designed to gain competitive advantage (i.e. develop products or services different from those of competitors); (2) a quality enhancement strategy (i.e. enhance product and/or service quality); and (3) a cost-reduction strategy (i.e. be a low-cost producer).[16] The patterns of employee role behaviour and human resource management policies held to be associated with these particular business strategies are set out in Table 1.2.

I shall return to the implications of this typology (which certainly warrants empirical examination, refinement and development) later in the chapter. For the moment, however, we need to note that there has been relatively little systematic empirical research designed to identify the nature and determinants of the human resource management policy mix of individual organizations. Some potentially useful conceptual discussions of the issue have put forward a number of general and specific hypotheses,[17] but these have rarely been taken up and tested in empirical work. There has also been some useful conceptual discussion of the factors associated with organizations adopting certain individual human resource management practices. For example, a recent examination (in the 1980s) of the employment security commitment of DEC (Digital Equipment Corporation) suggested that this particular human resource management practice has variously resulted from the values of senior executives which underpinned the organization's culture, a compatible relationship with the organization's competitive strategy which emphasized speed of response to the market, and its location within a larger, coherent package of human resource management policies.[18] A further line of possible conceptual development concerns the use of product or

Table 1.2   *Employee role behaviour and HRM policies associated with particular business strategies*

Strategy	Employee role behaviour	HRM policies
Innovation	A high degree of creative behaviour	Jobs that require a close interaction and co-ordination among groups of individuals
	Longer-term focus	Performance appraisals that are more likely to reflect longer-term and group-based achievements
	A relatively high level of co-operative, interdependent behaviour	Jobs that allow employees to develop skills that can be used in other positions in the firm
	A moderate degree of concern for quality	Compensation systems that emphasize internal equity rather than external or market-based equity
	A moderate concern for quantity	Pay rates that tend to be low, but that allow employees to be stockholders and have more freedom to choose the mix of components that make up their pay package
	An equal degree of concern for process and results	Broad career paths to reinforce the development of a broad range of skills
	A high tolerance of ambiguity and unpredictability	
Quality enhancement	Relatively repetitive and predictable behaviour	Relatively fixed and explicit job descriptions
	A more long-term or intermediate focus	High levels of employee participation in decisions relevant to immediate work conditions and the job itself
	A moderate amount of co-operative, interdependent behaviour	

Table 1.2 *continued*

Strategy	Employee role behaviour	HRM policies
		A mix of individual and group criteria for performance appraisal that is mostly short-term and results-orientated
	A high concern for quality	A relatively egalitarian treatment of employees and some guarantees of employment security
	Modest concern for quantity of output	Extensive and continuous training and development of employees
	High concern for process	
	Low risk-taking activity	
	Commitment to the goals of the organization	
Cost reduction	Relatively repetitive and predictable behaviour	Relatively fixed and explicit job descriptions
	A rather short-term focus	Narrowly designed jobs and narrowly defined career paths that encourage specialization, expertise and efficiency
	Primarily autonomous or individual activity	Short-term results-orientated performance appraisals
	Moderate concern for quality	Close monitoring of market pay levels for use in making compensation decisions
	High concern for quantity of output	Minimal level of employee training and development
	Primary concern for results	
	Low risk-taking activity	
	Relatively high degree of comfort with stability	

Source: Randall S. Schuler and Susan E. Jackson, 'Linking Competitive Strategies with Human Resource Management Practices', *Academy of Management Executive*, 1 (3), August 1987, pp. 209–13.

Table 1.3 *Critical human resource management activities at different organizational or business unit stages*

Human resource management functions	Life cycle stages			
	Introduction	Growth	Maturity	Decline
Recruitment, selection and staffing	Attract best technical/prof-essional talent	Recruit adequate numbers and mix of qualified workers. Management succession planning. Manage rapid internal labour market movements	Encourage sufficient turnover to minimize lay-offs and provide new openings. Encourage mobility as reorganiza-tions shift jobs around	Plan and implement workforce reductions and reallocation
Compensation and benefits	Meet or exceed labour market rates to attract needed talent	Meet external market but consider internal equity effects. Establish formal compensation structures	Control compensation	Tighter cost control
Employee training and development	Define future skill requirements and begin establishing career ladders	Mould effective management team through management development and organizational development	Maintain flexibility and skills of an ageing workforce	Implement retraining and career consulting services

Table 1.3 *continued*

Human resource management functions	Life cycle stages			
	Introduction	Growth	Maturity	Decline
Labour/employee relations	Set basic employee relations philosophy and organization	Maintain labour peace and employee motivation and morale	Control labour costs and maintain labour peace. Improve productivity	Improve productivity and achieve flexibility in work roles. Negotiate job security and employment adjustment policies

Source: Thomas A. Kochan and Thomas A. Barocci, *Human Resource Management and Industrial Relations*, Little, Brown, Boston, 1985, p. 104.

organizational life cycle theory (which typically identifies the four stages of start up, growth, maturity and decline) in order to help identify an individual organization's *priorities* in the human resource management area over time. Table 1.3 indicates one view of how such priorities may change over time.

THE COMPETITIVENESS–HUMAN RESOURCE DEBATE IN AMERICA

Like all advanced industrialized economies in the 1980s, the USA has operated in a relatively turbulent product market environment characterized by increased global competition, the shortening of product life cycles, a greater differentiation within product markets and a growing emphasis attached to the importance of product quality and innovation. The relatively poor performance of the American economy in responding and adapting to these changes has led to the establishment of a number of productivity or competitiveness commissions which have investigated the reasons for this poor performance and recommended a number of lines of change or reform.[19] These commission reports, as well as various academic publications,[20] have frequently put forward the general proposition that the USA must pursue a comparative advantage through a greater development and fuller utilization of its human resources. For present purposes, however, I wish to highlight a number of individual, more specific findings, comments and recommendations, which are of some considerable interest in their own right, and may also offer some potentially useful lessons and insights for other advanced industrialized economies.

The first point concerns the increased recognition of the limits of the low-wage (cost-reduction) competitive strategy as a viable, longer-term option for the American economy.[21] This strategy is seen to have two serious limitations. First, in an environment of increased global competition it is simply not possible for American industry to constrain or lower wage costs to anything like the level which would make them competitive with those in developing countries. And secondly, an exclusive or large-scale reliance on a cost-reduction strategy is likely to undermine substantially any human resource management developments initiated to enhance competitive performance, particularly those centring around employee involvement.

Secondly, there is considerably more to a successful competitive strategy for an organization based in an advanced industrialized economy than a set of measures designed simply to enhance the level and growth of labour productivity. Although increasing productivity is important as a basis for real wage growth, the concept of productivity needs to be considerably expanded beyond simply the notion of output per hour. This point is well made by one Commission study in the USA:

> Productivity is only one of the factors that affect the performance of a company. Success may depend as much or more on the quality of a firm's products and on the service it provides to its customers both before and after the sale. The firm's response time may be as important as the cost and quality of its products ... Hence, while trends in labour and multi-factor productivity may be the best available indicators of how well the nation's production system is performing, they cannot be relied upon exclusively for monitoring economic progress or for charting a future course ... To account for all these important yet not conventionally measured factors, the Commission adopted the term *productive performance* as a broader measure of economic vitality. The productive performance of a firm or an industry is compounded of its productivity and of various other factors that tend to be ignored in most economic statistics, like quality, timeliness of service, flexibility, speed of innovation, and command of strategic technologies.[22]

Given the rapidly changing nature of the product market environment of the 1980s which faced individual organizations in advanced industrialized economies (and assuming such characteristics remain a feature of the 1990s) what sort of firms appear to have adapted and responded most successfully? The Commission cited above examined this particular question, and suggested that 'best practice' firms were characterized by: (1) a focus on simultaneous improvement in cost, quality, and delivery; (2) closer links to customers; (3) closer relationships with suppliers; (4) the effective use of technology for strategic advantage; (5) less hierarchical and less compartmentalized organizations for greater flexibility; and (6) human resource policies that promote continuous learning, team work, participation and flexibility.[23] The Commission particularly stressed that these features were very much a cohesive, integrated package, as opposed to a menu from which individual selections could be made.

The key messages or terms in the human resource management literature are a strategic focus, the need for human resource policies and practices to be consistent with overall business strategy, and the need for individual components of a human resource management package to reinforce each other, while the individual components of the package should particularly emphasize team work, flexibility, employee involvement and organizational commitment. This is a very different message to the traditional demands on the human resource or industrial relations systems of countries like Britain and the United States which largely centred on collective bargaining arrangements. The traditional demands on these collective bargaining arrangements from both employers and policy-makers (the latter giving tangible expression to the 'social or public interest' in industrial relations) were that if you ensured a relatively low level of strike activity and wage increases moved essentially in line with productivity then the arrangements were relatively successful and little more could (and should) be asked of them. The product market environment of the 1980s has changed this situation in that these traditional demands still need to be met, but at the same time the human resource management system must also meet the new demands for team work, flexibility, participation and commitment at the level of the individual employee and indeed throughout the entire organization.

What is the likelihood of such demands being met? The American literature offers two observations in this regard. The first is that the need for flexibility, team working, motivation, participation, etc. is more compatible with (in the sense of being both needed for and reinforced by) a competitive strategy that emphasizes product innovation and/or product quality (see Table 1.2);[24] in contrast, a competitive strategy very largely emphasizing low wages and cost containment has less need for and ability to bring about such patterns of employee role behaviour. The second observation concerns the so-called 'integration' hypothesis, which is largely derived from Japanese human resource management practices.[25] The essence of this hypothesis is that: (1) individual human resource management innovations (e.g. introduction of quality circles) are unlikely to survive over time and have a positive impact on organization performance, whereas (2) the integration of arrangements for employee participation, work design and the introduction of new technology, etc. in a way which adds up to a consistent, coherent package are likely to be much more successful.

BEYOND THE DEBATE IN THE USA

As was emphasized earlier, some of the points made in the US competitiveness reviews and reports of the 1980s appear to have important implications for individual organizations in a number of advanced industrialized economies. This is obviously the case in Britain, where Michael Porter pointed to the failure to upgrade the quality of human resources as 'in many ways the most fundamental problem for the nation's economy . . . .'[26] The issue of industrial training is a useful microcosm of the larger HRM debate as an examination of it helps to make two key points, namely (1) the nature of the dominant competitive strategy adopted by individual organizations in individual countries will facilitate or constrain the extent of training, and (2) the level of training both influences and is, in turn, influenced by other, complementary measures in the human resource management policy mix.

The long-standing concern about the deficiencies of vocational education and training in Britain compared to the position in other countries has been substantially heightened in recent years by the appearance of certain figures on the training expenditure of British employers compared to those elsewhere. For example, one estimate suggests that British firms only devote some 0.15 per cent of turnover to training compared to 1–2 per cent in Japan, France and West Germany.[27]

Admittedly any such statistics need to be treated with considerable caution as individual firms rarely have good standardized data on training expenditures, while there is also the problem of measuring the extent of informal, on-the-job training. Nevertheless, a number of matched comparisons of organizations in Britain and Germany have indicated that the German organizations enjoyed productivity differentials which were associated with a better trained and more flexible workforce.[28] The leading reasons why British employers have historically under-invested in training are typically held to be the comparatively poor levels of management education, relatively short time horizons due to the strength of immediate financial objectives and the nature of competitive strategy.[29]

The employer-led TECs (Training and Enterprise Councils) which came into being in 1991 are an attempt to break out of a self-reinforcing network of relationships which has trapped Britain in a 'low-skills equilibrium'.[30] This will, however, be far from easy to accomplish if training is viewed and acted upon as essentially a discrete, self-contained activity. Both the nature of competitive strategy and the other elements of the HRM policy mix are all-important facilitators of, or constraints upon, moves towards enhanced workforce training. For instance, a recent review of training in the USA compared to Japan and (West) Germany concluded that average employment tenures in Japanese and German organizations were considerably greater than in US organizations.[31] These length-of-service differentials encouraged greater investment in training in Germany and Japan compared to the USA (because employers in the former systems can recoup the benefits of training), with these greater tenures being derivative from the larger competitive strategies and HRM policy mixes of the Japanese and German organizations. At the same time one should not under-play the significant role of training in helping to establish these mutually reinforcing linkages within the HRM policy mix and between it and the larger competitive strategy of the organization. As one recent review of the German situation has concluded:

> A system of VET (vocational education and training) is far more than merely an instrument for the production of technical skills . . . the German system creates not only a distinct social structure in business organizations but also a host of behavioural and attitudinal patterns. These shape interactions in labour markets and in the field of employment, in industrial relations and work organization, and even in the area of technological innovation. These various social consequences of the German skill structure constitute strong 'push' and 'pull' factors which, together with recent changes in the market environment and in technology, have led managements to adopt new

production concepts. These have enabled enterprises in many industries to maintain or improve their competitive position in world markets.[32]

Similarly in the case of Japan it has been noted that the relatively high levels of investment in training are reinforced by a number of other features of their human resource management systems at the level of the individual organization. These features include extensive employee–management consultation, wage payments geared (at least in part) to overall organizational performance, a strong commitment to employment security and the use of manufacturing and technology strategies which critically depend on a highly motivated, skilled and flexible workforce, etc. The strongest and most clear-cut evidence that (1) flexible production strategies strongly drive the level of workforce training, (2) training is an integral part of an organization's larger human resource management system, and (3) the effective integration of the production and human resource management system results in positive productivity and product quality differentials comes from a study of motor vehicle manufacturing plants across a number of countries.[33]

In summary, both negative (i.e. Britain) and positive (i.e. Japan and Germany) evidence from different national systems provides considerable support for the leading messages of the HRM literature, namely the all-important linkage between competitive strategy and HRM strategy, with the latter involving a set of mutually reinforcing arrangements and practices.

WILL ONE-WAY BECOME TWO-WAY?

Arguably the most clear-cut message of organizational experience in the 1980s and 1990s is that the way in which individual organizations seek to compete in the product market has a major impact (for good or bad, intended or unintended) on the human resource management practices and arrangements of the organizations concerned. Box 1.2 provides a simple illustration of how a change in the range of business activities has adversely affected internal communications in one organization.

There is clear evidence of the existence of a one-way relationship between business strategy and HRM practices and arrangements, running from the former to the latter. But what of the key message in the HRM literature, namely the need for establishing a close, two-way

Box 1.2   *The HRM impact of business growth and diversification*

The organization concerned is a relatively long-established one which produced essentially a single product. Traditionally the structures and processes of management there were highly task-orientated, with a strong inbuilt resistance to change. As the product with which the organization is traditionally associated reached the decline stage of its life cycle, the organization diversified in the mid to late 1970s into the manufacture of gas turbines for a variety of industries. And in the early 1980s this manufacturing capability was extended into the full range of tasks and stages associated with the power generation industry. It became in effect a 'total power contractor' offering a full set of project management skills and capabilities for the power generation industry. Most recently it has also diversified into the water industry with a separate division for this being created; this particular division has grown rapidly in staff numbers and currently accounts for nearly a third of total turnover. The organization's activities are over-whelmingly concentrated in a highly competitive set of foreign market places (four main competitors from various countries) where margins are relatively low; the manufacturing division of the organization is very much at the low value-added end of its full set of operations.

Following a period of declining employee numbers, the organiza-tion has grown from some 900 employees in the mid-1980s to the current figure of around 1,500. Moreover, the employment mix at the organization has changed quite substantially. For instance, there is now a much higher proportion of white collar staff there than was traditionally the case, and the diversification into the water industry has resulted in the employment of chemical engineers there for the first time. These internal changes need to be seen in the larger context of the organization having been acquired in the mid-1980s by a large conglomerate which sets explicit objectives for the individual organization and monitors them closely.

This broader set of business activities, together with the associated growth of (heterogeneous) employee numbers, led to some concern among certain senior managers that the organization was not as internally cohesive as it had been in the past (with its single-product focus). There were two dimensions to this belief or concern. The first was that the organization now had three distinct sub-cultures (centring around the manufacture of gas turbines, the water industry division and the project management division) which, because of different orientations, training, employment backgrounds, etc., did

Box 1.2 *continued*

> not always communicate well on a lateral basis (i.e. across divisions, departments, etc.). The second dimension was that some of the older managers, with their historically strong task orientation, who occupied largely middle management positions in a number of divisions consititued something of a barrier to vertical communication, delegation of decision-making, management development, etc.
>
>   These concerns received considerable support from the results of an employee attitude survey conducted with the assistance of outside consultants in 1991. The results suggested some staff dissatisfaction with the extent and nature of communications below the senior management level, and across departments. These findings were also highly consistent with the results of an internal training needs analysis which pointed to the need for more knowledge and understanding of relationships with suppliers, communications, career development and succession planning. These two sets of findings have resulted in the annual training budget being doubled in size, and a substantial capital allocation being given to the training function for the establishment of a new facility. The intention is that a series of inter-related training and communication-centred initiatives over time will be the centrepiece of an organization development and change exercise targeted at internal management processes rather than at organizational structures.

relationship between business strategy and HRM strategy? As indicated in the Introduction, survey evidence in a number of countries currently reveals the relative lack of such a relationship.[34] For instance, a recent US study has said that 'recent surveys suggest that at least some level of integration has been achieved by between 20 and 45 per cent of medium-sized and large firms. More intensive case studies support these figures, but call into question the depth of integration in many cases.'[35] From this fact it seems clear that rhetorical calls for human resource managers to become partners with line managers in order to achieve such an integration are likely to be inadequate to the task. What then are the prospects for such a move in this direction?

There are a variety of opinions as to the likelihood of change. The most optimistic scenario is that the pressure of product market circumstances, combined with internal evidence of existing HRM deficiencies (as revealed by an HRM audit), will inevitably push many organizations in this direction. A second, more pessimistic view is that such a change will only occur in a relatively small sub-set of organizations characterized by special circumstances, such as those with an already well regarded personnel management function whose senior members have considerable line management experience (flagging the importance of 'political' influences and considerations in internal decision-making processes).[36] And yet a third view is that some set of public policy instruments and measures will be essential to bring about change along these lines. Obviously only time will tell which of these (and other possible) scenarios will be the more accurate description of reality, but what is clear is that considerably more than rhetoric will be needed to effect such a sought-after change.

REFERENCES

1   Thomas A. Mahoney and John R. Deckop, 'Evolution of Concept and Practice in Personnel Administration/Human Resource Management', *Journal of Management*, 12 (2), 1986, pp. 223–41.
2   Ibid., pp. 229–34.
3   Edgar H. Schein (ed.), *The Art of Managing Human Resources*, Oxford University Press, New York, 1987.
4   George Strauss, 'Human Relations – 1968 Style', *Industrial Relations*, 7, May 1968, pp. 262–76.
5   David E. Guest, 'Human Resource Management and Industrial Relations', *Journal of Management Studies*, 24 (5), September 1987, p. 504.
6   See, for example, Derek Torrington, 'Human Resource Management and the Personnel Function', in John Storey (ed.), *New Perspectives on Human Resource Management*, Routledge, London, 1989, pp. 56–66.
7   P. B. Beaumont, *Change in Industrial Relations*, Routledge, London, 1990, Chapter 4.
8   David Cairncross and Ronald Dore, 'Employee Training in Japan', Office of Technology Assessment, Washington DC, 1989, p. 9, quoted in Thomas A. Kochan and Paul Osterman, 'Human Resource Development and Utilization: Is there Too Little in the US?', Mimeographed Paper, Sloan School of Management, MIT, 1990, p. 29.
9   Beaumont, *Change*, Chapter 4.
10 Thomas A. Kochan, 'Adaptability of the US Industrial Relations System', *Science*, 240, 15 April 1988, p. 291.
11 Charles Fombrun, Noel Tichy and Mary Anne Devanna, *Strategic Human Resource Management*, Wiley, New York, 1984, p. 42.
12 Beaumont, *Change*, p. 75.
13 Michael Beer and Bert Spector (eds.), *Readings in Human Resource Management*, Free Press, New York, 1985, pp. 5–6.
14 See Jeffrey Pfeffer, *Organizations and Organization Theory*, Pitman, Boston, 1982.

15   Cited in Thomas A. Kochan, 'Looking to the Year 2000: Challenges for Industrial Relations and Human Resource Management', Mimeographed paper, Sloan School of Management, MIT, 1988, p. 13.

16   Randall S. Schuler and Susan E. Jackson, 'Linking Competitive Strategies with Human Resource Management Practices', *Academy of Management Executive*, 1 (3), August 1987, pp. 207–19.

17   See, for example, V. V. Murray and D. E. Dimick, 'Contextual Influences on Personnel Policies and Programs: An Explanatory Model', *Academy of Management Review*, 3 (4), October 1978, pp. 750–61.

18   Thomas A. Kochan, John Paul MacDuffie and Paul Osterman, 'Employment Security at DEC: Sustaining Values amid Environmental Change', Working paper: Management in the 1990s, Sloan School of Management, MIT, June 1988.

19   See, for example, Cuomo Commission Report on Trade and Competitiveness, *The Cuomo Commission Report*, Simon and Schuster, New York, 1988.

20   See, for example, Roy Marshall, *Unheard Voices: Labor and Economic Policy in a Competitive World*, Basic Books, New York, 1987.

21   Thomas A. Kochan and Robert B. McKersie, 'Future Directions for American Labor and Human Resources Policy', *Relations Industrielles*, 44 (1), 1989, pp. 231–3.

22   Michael L. Dertonzos, Richard K. Lester and Robert M. Solon, *Made in America: Regaining the Productive Edge*, MIT Press, Cambridge: Mass., 1989, pp. 32–3.

23   Ibid., p. 118.

24   Thomas A. Kochan and Robert B. McKersie, 'Human Resources, Organizational Governance and Public Policy: Lessons from a Decade of Experimentation', Mimeographed paper, Sloan School of Management, MIT, March 1990, pp. 12–16.

25   Thomas Kochan, Joel Cutcher-Gershenfeld and John Paul MacDuffie, 'Employee Participation, Work Redesign and New Technology: Implications for Public Policy in the 1990s', Paper prepared for the Commission on Workforce Quality and Labor Market Efficiency, US Department of Labor, May 1989.

26   Michael E. Porter, *The Competitive Advantage of Nations*, Macmillan, London, 1990, p. 498.

27   Cited in D. Finegold and D. Soskice, 'The Failure of Training in Britain: Analysis and Prescription', *Oxford Review of Economic Policy*, 4, 1988, p. 23.

28   See, for example, H. Steedman and K. Wagner, 'A Second Look at Productivity, Machinery and Skills in Britain and Germany', *National Institute Economic Review*, November 1987.

29   E. Keep, 'Corporate Training Strategies: The Vital Component?', in John Storey (ed.), *New Perspectives on Human Resource Management*, Routledge, London, 1989, pp. 109–25.

30 Finegold and Soskice, 'Failure of Training', p. 23.
31 Kochan and Osterman, 'Human Resource Development', pp. 33–5.
32 Christel Lane, 'Vocational Training, Employment Relations and New Production Concepts in Germany: Some Lessons for Britain', *Industrial Relations Journal*, 21 (4), Winter 1990, pp. 247–8.
33 John Paul MacDuffie and Thomas A. Kochan, 'Does the US Underinvest in Human Resources? Determinants of Training in the World Auto Industry', Paper presented at the Academy of Management Meeting, 1991.
34 See, for example, D. Quinn Mills, 'Planning with People in Mind', *Harvard Business Review*, July–August 1985, pp. 997–1005.
35 Thomas A. Kochan and Lee Dyer, 'Managing Transformational Change: The Role of Human Resource Professionals', Working paper, Sloan School of Management, MIT, April 1992, p. 14.
36 Paul F. Buller, 'Successful Partnerships: HR and Strategic Planning at Eight Top Firms', *Organizational Dynamics*, Autumn 1988, pp. 27–43.

2

ORGANIZATIONAL CULTURE AND CHANGE

INTRODUCTION

Discussions of the notion of organizational culture figure prominently in the strategic human resource management literature. In essence it is argued that an organization's external competitive strategy needs to be complemented and reinforced by an appropriate organizational culture which is itself shaped by and consistent with a coherent mix of human resource management policies.

The notion of organizational culture is not entirely new. For example, as we saw in the previous chapter, some individuals have seen it largely as an extension and broadening of the earlier concepts of workforce 'morale' and 'organizational climate'. Secondly, some of the early human relations literature, particularly the writings of Elton Mayo, tended to emphasize the need for a co-operative, integrative organization providing employees with a sense of stability and identity that was no longer being adequately provided by other institutions in other aspects of their lives.[1] This theme has been echoed in some of the more recent writings on organizational culture.[2] And finally the type of organizational culture which is seen by many commentators to be most appropriate to the rapidly changing product market environment of the 1980s and 1990s appears to have considerable similarity to the 'organic' management system of Burns and Stalker[3] (formulated in the 1960s) in which a strong individual employee–organization identification process is so prominent.

This being said, there is no denying that the subject of organizational culture was one of the 'hot' management areas of the 1980s. There have arguably been two reasons for this state of affairs. The first is the economic success of Japanese organizations in which human resource management skills and practices, in particular the ability to establish and maintain a co-operative, team-based organizational culture, are seen to have played a vital role. The second is the 'companies of excellence' type of literature, in which it is argued both that successful leadership skills are more 'soft' (than 'hard') management skills, involving the ability to motivate and draw out commitment from individual employees, and that there is a positive correlation between strong organizational cultures (largely embodied in chief executive officers who view human resouces as the organization's leading source of competitive advantage) and organizational performance.[4]

Admittedly the companies of excellence literature has been subject to a range of relatively strong academic criticisms.[5] Furthermore, there are individuals who have questioned the general applicability of the notion of culture (with its foundations in anthropology) in understanding the activities and performance of organizations.[6] Nevertheless, recent years have witnessed considerable interest among researchers and practitioners in the subject of organizational culture. Specifically, practitioners have become increasingly interested in the questions of how an organizational culture is created, institutionalized or changed, whereas researchers have tended to focus more on matters such as how the concept is most appropriately measured and studied. These will be among the leading themes pursued in this chapter.

THE DEFINITION AND ELEMENTS OF CULTURE

The substantial volume of literature on organizational culture contains a variety of definitions. Two definitions, however, appear to come reasonably close to what many people understand by the term:

> The customary or traditional ways of thinking and doing things, which are shared to a greater or lesser extent by all members of the organization and which new members must learn and at least partially accept in order to be accepted into the service of the firm.[7]

> The simplest way to think about the culture of any group or social unit is to think of it as the sum total of the collective or shared learning of that unit as it develops its capacity to survive in its external environment and to manage its own internal affairs. Culture is the solutions to external and internal problems that have worked consistently for a group and are, therefore, taught to new members as the correct way to perceive, think about, and feel in relation to those problems.[8]

These definitions highlight three leading characteristics of the concept of organizational culture, namely that it is shared, learned and transmitted. The notion of organizational culture has in fact become an increasingly popular metaphor for seeking to understand organizations, in that 'the organization is now seen to reside in the ideas, values, norms, rituals, and beliefs that sustain organizations as socially constructed realities'.[9]

However, according to Morgan the cultural metaphor (and indeed all the individual metaphors used) provides only a *partial* way of analysing and understanding organizations. In his view the notion of culture as 'an ongoing, pro-active process of reality construction' has both strengths and limitations for looking at organizations. For instance, the cultural metaphor may yield important, useful insights concerning organizational leadership, organization–environment relations and organizational change, but he also suggests that:

> The insights generated by the culture metaphor have sent many managers and management theorists scurrying to find ways of managing corporate culture. Most are now aware of the symbolic consequences of organizational values, and many organizations have started to explore the pattern of culture and subculture that shapes day-to-day action. On the one hand this can be seen as a positive development, since it recognizes the truly human nature of organizations and the need to build organization around people rather than techniques. However there are a number of potentially negative consequences.[10]

The two potentially negative consequences of such an approach cited by Morgan are (1) the attempt to manage corporate culture in a manipulative way that makes it a tool of ideological (management) control and (2) the mistaken belief on the part of management that culture is a mechanistic phenomenon which can be easily managed, controlled or changed by senior management. Schein[11] has also highlighted a number of mistakes that need to be avoided in thinking about culture, including the following:

1   Do not oversimplify culture, as it goes beyond slogans, behaviour patterns, and values to basic assumptions.
2   Do not limit your thinking about the areas of culture content, as it goes beyond human relations into fundamental concepts of reality, truth, social structure and organization design, how decisions are made, and so on.
3   Do not assume that culture change is easy.
4   Do not assume that more culture or stronger culture is better; it depends on the stage of evolution of the company and its current state of adaptiveness.

Table 2.1   *The key elements of corporate culture*

1   The business environment

2   Values (i.e. basic concepts and beliefs of an organization)

3   Heroes (i.e. individuals who personify the values of the culture and provide role models for emulation)

4   Rites and rituals (i.e. indicators of what the organization stands for and the sort of behaviour expected of employees)

5   The cultural network (i.e. the primary, but informal, means of communication within the organization which carries the values, etc.)

Source: Adapted from Terrence Deal and Allen Kennedy, *Corporate Cultures*, Penguin, London, 1988, pp. 13–15.

There is no denying that senior management values will often figure prominently in the creation and maintenance of organizational cultures, at least in certain organizations. Indeed one of the few relatively consistent themes in the research-based literature on organizational culture concerns the extremely important, formative influence of the organizational founder or early senior managers of organization in creating cultures.[12] However, the fact that such values are not the sole element of corporate culture is what makes the management of culture so difficult to understand. Table 2.1 sets out the views of one set of commentators concerning the principal elements of a corporate culture.

Academic writers like Schein have gone beyond the contents of Table 2.1 to argue that culture in an organization exists at three levels.[13] These are artefacts (visible behavioural manifestations), values (some of the reasons behind some of the behaviour) and learned underlying assumptions, with the latter essentially being the driving force behind the first two levels; the latter level is the most important, but also the most difficult to identify and hence change.

THE HRM DIMENSION

Where does HRM fit into this picture? The general line of argument typically advanced in the literature is that the human resource management policy mix is both an important determinant and reinforcer of the nature of organization culture. This proposition is frequently illustrated by reference to a small number of case studies of

Table 2.2   *Ouchi's Theory Z*

Japanese organizations	American organizations
Life-time employment	Short-term employment
Slow evaluation and promotion	Rapid evaluation and promotion
Non-specialist career paths	Specialized career paths
Implicit control mechanisms	Explicit control mechanisms
Collective decision-making	Individual decision-making
Collective responsibility	Individual responsibility
Holistic concern	Segmented concern

Source: Adapted from William Ouchi, *Theory Z*, Addison Wesley, Reading, Mass., 1981.

well-known organizations (e.g. Hewlett-Packard),[14] or more broadly by a comparison between US and Japanese organizations. The best-known exposition along the latter lines is Ouchi's Theory Z, which characterized and contrasted certain key HRM features of Japanese and US organizations along the lines of Table 2.2.[15]

Ouchi went on to recommend (in America) the adoption of a Type Z organizational form (i.e. a modified American one) involving long-term employment, consensual decision-making, individual responsibility, slow evaluation and promotion, implicit informal control with explicit formalized measures, moderately specialized career paths and a holistic concern. The other well-known approach is that of Richard Walton, who focuses explicitly on the issue of trying to obtain workforce commitment (which is central to much of the HRM literature), advocates the need for a coherent and consistent set of HRM measures to achieve this state of affairs, and recognizes the inevitable reality of moving in this direction only via a transitional stage or series of steps. Table 2.3 sets out the package of HRM measures that Walton identifies as being important in trying to move from a workforce control to a workforce commitment strategy or culture; many of the individual HRM measures listed in this table are among the leading items discussed in subsequent chapters.

Table 2.3   *Human resource management practices for moving from workforce control to commitment*

	Control	Transition	Commitment
1 Job design principles	Individual attention limited to performing individual jobs	Scope of individual responsibility extended to upgrading system performance, via participative problem-solving groups in QWL, EI and quality circle programs*	Individual responsibility extended to upgrading system performance
	Job design deskills and fragments work and separates doing and thinking	No change in traditional job design or accountability	Job design enhances content of work, emphasizes whole task and combines doing and thinking
	Accountability focuses on individual		Frequent use of teams as basic accountable unit
			Flexible definition of duties, contingent upon changing conditions
2 Performance expectations	Measured standards define minimum performance		Emphasis placed on higher 'stretch' objectives which tend to be dynamic and orientated to the market place
	Stability seen as desirable		

Table 2.3 *continued*

	Control	Transition	Commitment
3 Management organization: structure, systems and style	Structure tends to be layered, with top down controls	No basic changes in approaches to structuring control or authority	Flat organizational structure with mutual influence systems
	Co-ordination and control rely on rules and procedure	A few visible symbols change	Co-ordination and control based more in shared goals, values and traditions
	More emphasis on prerogatives and positional authority		Management emphasis on problem-solving and relevant information and expertise
	Status symbols distributed to reinforce hierarchy		Minimum status differentials to de-emphasize inherent hierarchy
4 Compensation policies	Variable pay where feasible to provide individual incentive	Typically no basic changes in compensation concepts	Variable rewards to create equity and to reinforce group achievement: gain sharing, profit-sharing
	Individual pay geared to job evaluation		Individual pay linked to skills and mastery
	In downturn, cuts concentrated on hourly payroll	Equality of sacrifice among employee groups	Equality of sacrifice

Table 2.3 *continued*

	Control	Transition	Commitment
5 Employment assurances	Employees regarded as variable cost	Assurances that participation will not result in loss of job; extra efforts to avoid lay-offs	Assurances that participation will not result in job loss; high commitment to avoid or assist in re-employment; priority for training and retraining workforce
6 Employee voice policies	Employee voice allowed on relatively narrow agenda; attendant risks emphasized.	Addition of limited *ad hoc* consultative mechanisms; no change in corporate governance	Employee participation encouraged on wide range of issues; attendant benefits emphasized; new concepts of corporate governance
	Methods include open-door policy, attitude surveys, grievance procedures and collective bargaining in some organizations	Additional sharing of information	Business data shared widely

Table 2.3 *continued*

	Control	Transition	Commitment
7 Labor–mana-gement relations	Adversarial emphasis on interest conflict	Thawing of adversarial attitudes; joint sponsorship of QWL or EI; emphasis on common fate	Mutuality; joint planning and problem-solving on expanded agenda
			Unions, managers and workers redefine their respective roles

* QWL   quality of working life
   EI   employee involvement
Source: Richard F. Walton, 'From Control to Commitment in the Workplace', *Harvard Business Review*, 85 (2), March–April 1985, p. 81.

ORGANIZATION CULTURE: TYPES, STRENGTH AND NATIONAL SETTING

What about the different types of organizational culture? This theme has not attracted a great deal of systematic empirical research. The obvious exception here is the older work of Burns and Stalker, referred to earlier in the chapter, which distinguished (on the basis of some research work on the electronics industry in Britain) between a 'mechanistic' and 'organic' management system. The latter was viewed as the most suitable for operating in a rapidly changing product market environment, with its essential feature being the close individual employee–organization identification process involved; the contrast was between mechanistic (workforce control) and organic (workforce commitment). A number of the more 'popular' management books offer listings along these lines. For instance, Deal and Kennedy[16] identify a tough-guy macho culture, a work hard/play hard one, a bet-your-company culture and a process culture, while Handy[17] talks about club, role, task and existential cultures. However, Deal and Kennedy went on to comment that companies with very strong cultures – i.e. the companies that intrigue us most – fit this simple mould hardly at all. These companies have cultures that artfully blend the best elements of all four types – and blend them in ways that allow these companies to perform well when the environment around them changes, as it inevitably does.[18]

This general proposition in the popular management literature, namely that there is a positive correlation between organizational performance and the strength of an organization's culture, has come in for considerable academic criticism and questioning. For instance, I noted earlier Schein's view that the search for a strong culture may be doomed to failure (given the present circumstances of an individual organization), or may even be counterproductive (if achieved) given the likelihood of the need for further adaptation to environmental change; in other words, a strong culture (which is viewed as the source of previous organizational success) will constitute a strong barrier to any attempt at organizational change necessitated by changing environmental circumstances. Furthermore some academics are giving increased attention to the issue of locating individual organizational cultures in their larger national settings. According to some commentators the cultures of individual countries are considerably more powerful and stable than those of individual organizations,[19] a view which is likely to have considerable implications for organizations engaged in an increasingly global set of operations. The research underpinning such views is very much associated with European academics, such as Hofstede and Laurent (whose work will be more fully discussed in the concluding chapter), who have documented, via surveys in various multinational companies, the existence of important national differences in the nature of management assumptions. The information in Box 2.1 gives some indication of one organization's thinking along these lines.

STUDYING AND MEASURING ORGANIZATIONAL CULTURE

Both academics and practitioners are slowly coming to some limited degree of agreement that, first, the notion of organizational culture is elusive and not easily measured and, secondly, that it is essentially a contingency-based concept. That is, there is no one particular organizational culture that is best suited to all organizations in all circumstances. In keeping with the first observation, it is apparent that

---

Box 2.1   *Thinking about national cultures*

This British organization is establishing an international joint venture (IJV) with a French organization. Knowledge of the relatively high failure of IJVs due to 'people problems', combined with the practical need to handle the contracts of management transferees to the joint venture operation, has resulted in the establishment of a human resource management working group (the first one established) across the British and French organizations. This group has been meeting on a monthly basis, alternating between France and Britain, over something like eight months; its membership typically consists of 6–8 individuals from the respective HRM departments.

The working group commissioned a two-day workshop on organization and national culture which was presented by an 'academic expert' in the British organization and was then repeated in the French one. The workshop presentation stressed that the IJV cannot and should not seek to establish a corporate culture that can transcend or supplant the effects of differing national cultures. In essence it was argued that there are countries with a Blue Culture (e.g. USA, Sweden), which involves fundamental assumptions, values and behaviour with the emphasis on doing things, time as money and time management (e.g. planning, punctuality, etc.). In contrast there are countries with a Green Culture (e.g. Middle East) where the emphasis is much more on the value of relationships, networking arrangements, etc. In the former, management activities are sequential, whereas in the latter they are simultaneous. Britain is viewed as a Blue/Green culture and France a Green/Blue one.

The purpose of the workshops, subsequent meetings (with academic support), and a cultural audit of the two organizations, is to seek an understanding and appreciation of each other's culture, rather than attempt to change the culture of either.

---

academics are increasingly urging and adopting a mixed methodology approach in the study of organizational culture. This may, for instance, involve the combined usage of obtrusive observation, self-administered questionnaires and personal interviews to fill out the picture.[20] Furthermore, a number of practitioner-orientated techniques have been devised for assessing the nature of organizational culture, and these are increasingly being combined as packages of assessment measures. Table 2.4 contains a brief outline of three such approaches.

Table 2.4   *Practitioner techniques for assessing organizational culture*

Technique	Description
An iterative interviewing process involving outsiders and insiders	The outsiders enter the organization and experience certain puzzles and surprises. These observations are shared with insiders, with their meanings being jointly explored. This iterative process results in a written description of the assumptions underlying an organizational culture
Survey instrument	This may be used to identify any difference between the actual and desired culture. One such instrument asks organizational members to respond to 28 standard norm pairs concerning actual and desired norms to achieve high performance
	Possible cultural gaps in the areas of task support, task innovation, social relationships and personal freedoms are examined
Describing culture in terms of key managerial behaviours	Individual and group interviews generate specific normative statements about how managerial tasks are performed and how relationships are managed in an organization. This data is used to assess the cultural risk of trying to implement organizational changes to support a new strategy

Source: Based on Thomas G. Cummings and Edgar F. Huse, *Organization Development and Change*, West Publishing, St Paul, Minn., 4th edition, 1989, pp. 425–7.

CULTURAL AND ORGANIZATIONAL CHANGE

The increased attention given to the notion of organizational culture has been useful in alerting both academics and practitioners to the fact that organizational change (at least of any substantial scale) will involve considerably more than simply changing organizational structures etc.[21] This being said, there is considerable debate as to whether changing an organization culture is feasible, and what are likely to be the most powerful levers in affecting such a change.[22] In essence, difficulties in bringing about cultural change stem from the importance of the deeper elements of culture (i.e. values and basic assumptions) in that,

> Because these deeper elements represent taken-for-granted assumptions about organizational life, members do not question them and have a difficult time envisioning anything else. Moreover, members may not want to change their cultural assumptions. The culture provides a strong defense against external uncertainties and threats. It represents past solutions to difficult problems. Members may also have vested interests in maintaining the culture. They may have developed personal stakes, pride, and power in the culture and may strongly resist attempts to change it.[23]

Nevertheless a number of prescriptive lists for changing organization culture have been put forward, particularly in various popular management books. For instance, Deal and Kennedy have suggested that an organization variously needs to position a 'hero' in charge of the process, recognize a real threat from outside, make transition rituals the pivotal elements of change, provide transition training in new values and behaviour patterns, bring in outside consultants, build tangible symbols of the new directions, and insist on the importance of security in transition.[24] Other lists of guidelines emphasize the need for a clear strategic vision, top management commitment, symbolic leadership, supporting organizational changes (such as in HRM), selection and socialization of newcomers and termination of deviants, and ethical and legal sensitivity.[25]

To some commentators the inevitable difficulties of successfully carrying through a full-scale programme of cultural change are such that it should only be attempted after less ambitious and costly measures of change have been tried. At the same time Schein has argued that cultural change does not always involve large-scale programmes of change in crisis situations.[26] Instead an organization should recognize that the need for, nature of and instruments involved in, cultural change will vary according to the stages of the product or organizational life cycle.

In order to illustrate some of the leading issues, themes and uncertainties involved in cultural and organizational change, the rest of this chapter will concentrate on respectively the new plant or greenfield site 'solution' to change and the 'turnaround' approach in an established organization. For obvious reasons particular attention will be given to the HRM dimension.

NEW PLANTS AND ORGANIZATIONAL CULTURE

A number of commentators have highlighted the fact that new plants or greenfield site operations tend to be disproportionately associated with relatively innovatory human resource practices and arrangements, which reflect a conscious attempt to break quite sharply with the working practices and culture of older, established plants in the company's set-up.[27] In Britain, for instance, the new Pilkington plant established at St Helens in the early 1980s had an explicit human resource management statement which included the following components: (1) increased site commitment; (2) better co-operation between trade unions; (3) well-trained employees who fully understand their role in the works as a whole; (4) flexible employees — able to do a wide range of tasks; (5) management style based on openness and employee involvement; (6) responsibility pushed down the hierarchy, (7) removal of status differences which cannot be justified; (8) a simple, effective and easily understood reward system and (9) elimination of payment for overtime.[28] More recently, the Pirelli greenfield site plant in South Wales has been cited as an organization operating with an explicit HRM philosophy (i.e. employee commitment, co-operation and team work) which influenced and was reinforced by a mix of policies which emphasized and encouraged training, flexibility and single status.[29]

The combination of a competitive strategy based on product innovation or quality enhancement with a new, greenfield site operation is a very powerful one, which is frequently associated with a relatively high priority being given to human resource management and a conscious attempt to establish (and maintain) a particular organizational culture. It is in such organizations that one is most likely to find relatively well developed internal labour market arrangements (in matters of promotion, training and career development), flexible work organization systems, contingent compensation practices, high levels of employee and work group participation in task-related decisions, and extensive internal communications arrangements, all of which are held to constitute a comprehensive and coherent human resource management package. Furthermore, such organizations frequently operate with an explicit mission statement. Box 2.2 sets out the statement of one such new plant in Britain.

Box 2.2   *New plant philosophy or culture statement*

1   *Continuous development of management or culture statement*

Using progressive management methods, the company should develop a highly motivated, flexible, professional and cohesive team. Management should create an open and participative environment which encourages the continuous development of the company and its employees.

2   *Effective product development*

A consistent and competitive standard of quality (upper quartile) product should be designed and continuously developed, to meet the present and future market requirements, through co-operation between customer and paper mill.

3   *Application of quality*

The concept that everyone is responsible for the quality of the product as well as for the quality of his/her performance will be applied and developed.

4   *Use of high technology for effective production*

There should be constant review and assessment of 'state of the art' technology in all areas and it should be applied, where appropriate, to ensure the company is among the most effective lightweight coated paper companies in Europe.

5   *Service and marketing/sales effectiveness*

5.1   Progressive long-term relationships with key customers should be developed for mutual benefit.

5.2   A high standard of service should be established using effective communications.

5.3   The image of a professional paper producer and effective business partner should be developed.

Box 2.2 *continued*

6   *Security of sufficient resources*

The availability of good quality fresh timber should be guaranteed. Availability of all other raw materials and consumables must be guaranteed in all circumstances. A supportive local infrastructure should be developed.

7   *Community relations*

7.1 The company should create and maintain a positive environmental image.

7.2 It should be an attractive and socially responsible employer and community member.

7.3 Connections with specialist institutions should be made.

Obviously there is, as the discussion of this chapter has indicated, much more to the task of creating or changing an organizational culture than simply the production of a statement such as that above. To many commentators a formal mission statement is only a relatively superficial artefact of organizational culture. There is, however, no denying that establishing a sense of mission (rather than simply issuing a statement of it) is an increasingly prominent feature of attempts to establish an organizational culture in new and existing organizations (*Financial Times*, 11 October 1991).

It is widely held that the ability to bring about organizational and cultural change in new plants is relatively substantial because 'new organizations simply have a number of advantages when it comes to creating high involvement systems. They can start with a congruent total system; they can select people who are compatible; no-one has a vested interest in the *status quo*; and it is possible to do the whole organization at once so the participative island disease is avoided.'[30] In many cases it is hoped that the establishment of a new organizational culture in a new plant or greenfield site will constitute a role model for the rest of the multi-plant organization, with a process of diffusion being encouraged to spread from the new to the old. In fact there is only limited evidence of this occurring. Rather there is much more likelihood that the new plant will stand as a discrete, self-contained entity in the larger company set-up, remaining quite isolated from the culture of the rest of the organization.[31] This indifference or even hostility to the new plant in the larger organization set-up clearly points to the limitations of this partial approach to the task of bringing about a change in organizational culture.

SEEKING TURNAROUND IN AN ESTABLISHED ORGANIZATION

A long-standing conceptual view of the processes of organizational change involves a three-stage model, whereby the organization: (1) seeks to change or unfreeze existing practices and arrangements; (2) undergoes a period of experimentation in which a new set of practices and arrangements are tried and tested; and (3) institutional-izes or refreezes the new arrangements as the standard mode of operation.[32] A number of more recent discussions of the organiz-ational change process follow roughly similar lines, emphasizing, for example, the development of concern, the acknowledgement and understanding of the problem, planning and acting, and stabilizing change.[33] This sequential, staged sort of approach does, however, run the risk of viewing the processes of organizational change as rather more mechanical, predictable and ordered than tends to be the case. Indeed the reality of large-scale organizational and cultural change is a relatively complex, messy process in which problems and difficulties are frequently encountered and solved (if at all) in a rather unstructured, *ad hoc* manner. Students of organizational change have, for instance, frequently highlighted the fact that the larger the scale of proposed change the more likely it is there will be consolidated opposition to it, with the result that it may well fail.[34] Furthermore, standard organization development and change models invariably stress the key role of senior management in initiating a change process, but for this to be carried through successfully from the unfreezing to the refreezing stage requires that strong, consistent linkages be established with lower level operational managers.[35]

In large-scale, turnaround situations in which 'cultural trans-formations' are sought, a wide variety of change tools have frequently been utilized: for example, the issuance of new mission statements, structural change, education and training programmes, new com-munication packages, pay system changes, replacement and promotion of personnel, attitude surveys to identify constraints, desired changes, etc., consultants, leadership by executives committed to change, etc.[36] The key questions involved in such attempts are (1) which of these instruments of change are individually the most powerful and (2) what is the order in which they should be used for maximum effectiveness? These all-important questions tend to divide individual commentators and there is only limited systematic research on them to inform actual practice. For example, some individuals have argued that reward systems are a particularly powerful instrument for bringing about organizational and cultural change.[37] In contrast, others have argued that:

> In the early stages efforts are made to persuade people to change attitudes and behaviour voluntarily. This is done through philosophy statements, communication and education. It is often insufficient to affect behaviour, so new behaviour is 'forced' by various structure and system changes. Those who are able to change get to keep their jobs and the best get promoted. It is this judicious management of replacements and promotions that is the key instrument of change, not, in my view, monetary rewards . . . In most cases change in behaviour precedes changes in attitudes and values. Top managers use their power to orchestrate this process, changing structure and promoting supporters. Consultants, philosophy statements, education, and communication are the ways in which messages about expected new behaviour are sent. Of course, new behaviours will become institutionalized only if a critical mass of new managers can be placed in key positions.[38]

Box 2.3 illustrates one organization's attempt at cultural change which has particularly emphasized the role of new senior management personnel.

Although there has always been, as we have seen, a great deal of disagreement about which are the most powerful individual levers of change and the order in which they should be used, there was for a long time considerable consensus to the effect that organization change needed to be an organization-wide process led by senior management. However, even this has been questioned in recent years, with one prominent publication arguing instead for much more of a bottom up, sub-unit approach in initiating organizational change.[39] Specifically, this particular publication is highly critical of top down attempts to change organization culture, of starting the process of change by changing formal organizational structures and systems, and of introducing major new elements in the HRM policy mix. All of these are viewed as having limited potential impact, and in some cases even being counterproductive. Instead the authors favour initially basing change in new, small and relatively isolated sub-units of the organization and then taking various measures to

Box 2.3   *Cultural change via new senior management personnel*

The organization concerned is an engineering one which currently employs some 1,440 people. It has a strong commitment to R&D, and employs a substantial number of trained engineers. Historically the organization has been described as having a paternalistic, role- (rather than task-) orientated culture. The turnaround situation occurred in the late 1980s and involved a fundamental change in business strategy and a resulting programme of cultural change in which a re-vamped HRM strategy was prominent. A proposed merger (which stimulated an enhanced divisional concentration), an enforced change from cost-plus pricing to competitive tendering arrangements (in its major customer relationship), a change in the product mix (with significant implications for the skill mix of the workforce) and an upgrading of the manufacturing technology (from a modular to a systems company) were the key triggers of change in the business strategy area.

These, in turn, led to a re-orientation of the human resource management strategy in which two particular changes were prominent: first, an increase in training expenditure (from £200,000 per year in 1987 to £500,000 in 1988), but with much more emphasis on managerial (75 per cent of expenditure in 1988), as opposed to technical, training; and secondly, a sizeable headcount reduction in the organization, with the workforce being reduced from some 2,200 in 1988 to 1,440 in 1991 (projected to be down to 1,000 in 1992).

A key instrument of organizational and cultural change was the injection of new senior management personnel who were explicitly recruited as internal agents of change. For example, only three of the original twelve board members in the mid-1980s are still with the company; the board has been reduced to seven members with three of these (Finance, HRM, Production) being newcomers to the company. Admittedly the present CEO has been in the organization for some considerable time, although he was always considered something of a 'maverick' within the older, senior management ranks.

institutionalize and spread these initiatives throughout the rest of the organization.

HRM AND ORGANIZATIONAL CHANGE

Although in this chapter I have frequently emphasized the limited empirical grounding of much of the descriptive and prescriptive literature concerning organizational culture, it is important to recognize that the cultural metaphor has helped raise the priority given to 'people issues' in change situations relative to the traditional approach of changing formal structures. As a result there has been increased recognition of the strategic linkage between human resource management practices and policies in helping to create, reinforce and change organizational cultures.

This being said, there is both controversy ('it is manipulative') and uncertainty (which HRM policy levers should be changed, at what level, and in what manner) as to how such a linkage should be managed. Furthermore, in the early 1990s there is the very real possibility of a strong backlash, particularly in the USA, against the notion of culture being central to the practice of organization change as the pressures of recession and finance markets are translated into cost-cutting and employment reduction exercises in individual organizations (*Business Week*, 1991).

REFERENCES

1 Elton Mayo, *The Human Problems of an Industrial Civilisation*, Macmillan, New York, 1933.
2 See, for example, W. G. Ouchi and Jerry B. Johnson, 'Types of Organizational Control and their Relationship to Emotional Well-Being', *Administrative Science Quarterly*, 23, June 1978.
3 T. Burns and G. M. Stalker, *The Management of Innovation*, Tavistock, London, 2nd edition, 1968.
4 T. J. Peters and R. H. Waterman, *In Search of Excellence*, Harper and Row, New York, 1982.
5 See Michael Hitt and Duane Ireland, 'Peters and Waterman Revisited: The Unended Quest for Excellence', *Academy of Management Executive*, 1 (2), May 1987, pp. 91–8.
6 V. Lynn Meek, 'Organizational Culture: Origins and Weaknesses', *Organisation Studies*, 9 (4), 1988, pp. 453–73.
7 Eliott Jacques, *The Changing Culture of a Factory*, Tavistock, London, 1951, p. 251.
8 Edgar H. Schein, 'Organizational Culture: What it is and How to Change it', in Paul Evans, Yves Doz and André Laurent (eds.), *Human Resource Management in International Firms*, Macmillan, London, 1989, p. 58.

9   Gareth Morgan, *Images of Organization*, Sage, Beverly Hills, Calif., 1986, p. 14.

10   Ibid., p. 138.

11   Schein 'Organizational Culture', p. 81.

12   Edgar H. Schein, 'The Role of the Founder in Creating Organizational Culture', *Organization Dynamics*, Summer 1983, pp. 13–28.

13   Schein 'Organizational Culture', pp. 60–1.

14   Stanley Harris, 'Hewlett-Packard: Shaping the Corporate Culture', in Charles J. Fombrun, Noel M. Tichy and Mary Anne Devanna, *Strategic Human Resource Management*, Wiley, New York, 1984, pp. 217–33.

15   William Ouchi, *Theory Z*, Addison Wesley, Reading, Mass., 1981.

16   Terrence Deal and Allen Kennedy, *Corporate Cultures*, Penguin, London, 1988.

17   Charles Handy, *Gods of Management*, Pan, London, 1985.

18   Deal and Kennedy, *Corporate Cultures*, p. 108.

19   André Laurent, 'A Cultural View of Organizational Change', in Paul Evans, Yves Doz and André Laurent (eds.), *Human Resource Management in International Firms*, Macmillan, 1989, pp. 83–94.

20   W. Jack Duncan, 'Organizational Cultures: "Getting a Fix" on an Elusive Concept', *Academy of Management Executive*, 3 (3), August 1989, pp. 229–38.

21   Morgan, *Images of Organization*, pp. 137–8.

22   P. Frost, L. Moore, M. Louis, C. Lundberg and J. Martin (eds.), *Organizational Culture*, Sage, Beverly Hills, 1985, pp. 95–156.

23   Thomas G. Cummings and Edgar F. Huse, *Organization Development and Change*, West Publishing, St Paul, Minn., 4th edition, 1989, p. 428.

24   Deal and Kennedy, *Corporate Cultures*, pp. 175–6.

25   Cummings and Huse, *Organization Development*, pp. 428–30.

26   Schein, 'Organizational Culture', pp. 65–80.

27   P. B. Beaumont and B. Townley, 'Greenfield Sites, New Plants and Work Practices', in Valerie Hammond (ed.), *Current Research in Management*, Pinter, London, 1985, pp. 163–80.

28   Derek Norman, 'How a New Plant Made Pilkington Reflect on its IR Structure', *Personnel Management*, 15 (8), August 1983, p. 22.

29   David Yeandle and Jon Clark, 'Personnel Strategy for an Automated Plant', *Personnel Management*, June 1989, pp. 51–5.

30   Edward G. Lawler, 'Increasing Worker Involvement to Enhance Organizational Effectiveness', in Paul S. Goodman (ed.), *Change in Organizations*, Jossey-Bass, San Francisco, 1982, p. 307.

31   Richard E. Walton, 'Establishing and Maintaining High Commitment Work Systems', in J. Kimberly and R. Moles (eds.), *The Organizational Life Cycle*, Jossey-Bass, San Francisco, 1980.

32   K. Lewin, 'Group Decision and Social Change', in E. G. Maccoby, T. M. Newcomb and E. L. Hartley (eds.), *Readings in Social Psychology*, Holt, Rinehart and Winston, New York, 1958, pp. 197–211.

33 A. V. Johnston, 'Revolution by Involvement', *Accountancy Age*, 7 (36), 17 September 1975, p. 11.

34 J. G. March and J. P. Olsen, 'Organizing Political Life: What Administrative Reorganization tells us about Governing', *American Political Science Review*, 77 (2), 1983, pp. 281–96.

35 Andrew Pettigrew, *The Awakening Giant: Continuity and Change in ICI*, Basil Blackwell, Oxford, 1985, p. 476.

36 Michael Beer, 'Revitalizing Organizations: Change Process and Emergent Model', *Academy of Management Executive*, 1 (1), February 1987, p. 54.

37 Jeffrey Kerr and John W. Slocum Jr, 'Managing Corporate Culture Through Reward Systems', *Academy of Management Executive*, 1 (2), May 1987, pp. 99–108.

38 Beer, 'Revitalizing Organizations', p. 54.

39 Michael Beer, Russell A. Eisenstat and Bert Spector, *The Critical Path to Corporate Renewal*, Harvard Business School Press, Boston, Mass., 1990.

3

THE SELECTION DECISION

INTRODUCTION

In this chapter I consider the first of the 'micro' issues in the human resource management area likely to confront line managers, namely recruiting and selecting new employees. I look first at the general areas of planning recruitment and assessing the selection process. The chapter then examines, in turn, the limitations of the traditional job interview process and some suggestions for improving its effectiveness, the use of testing procedures in the selection decision and finally the use and effectiveness of assessment centres for selecting (very largely) managerial personnel.

Obviously the selection decision has always been important as the vehicle for obtaining, at least in principle, the appropriate 'person–job fit' which will, when aggregated, contribute in turn towards organizational effectiveness. However, at least three themes in the HRM literature would appear to have enhanced the potential importance of the selection decision in individual organizations in the current operating environment. First, certain significant demographic trends and changes in the labour market environment confronting organizations, such as declining birth rates, an ageing population, an increasingly educated workforce and the increased participation of women, are making for a less homogeneous workforce which is placing a premium on the 'effective management of diversity'. And at the very least this has meant that the criterion of fairness has become of increased importance in the selection decision. Secondly, the HRM literature emphasizes the need for a multi-skilled, flexible workforce in which team working arrangements are particularly prominent. This has meant that the selection decision is less about matching an individual employee to the fixed requirements of an individual job at a single point in time. As a consequence, immediate skills and employment background are of rather less importance relative to willingness to learn, adaptability and willingness/ability to work as part of a team. (This is undoubtedly an important factor driving the increased use of employment testing, a subject covered later in this chapter.) And thirdly, as indicated in Chapter 1, the leading single theme in the HRM literature is the need to establish a close two-way relationship between competitive strategy/business planning and HRM planning. As a consequence, some academic commentators have discussed the notion of *strategic selection* in which three concerns are particularly prominent, namely the design of a selection system that supports the overall organizational strategy, the monitoring of the internal flow of personnel to match emerging business strategies and the need to match key executives to business strategies.[1] (This concern or aim is arguably a factor in the increased use of assessment centres for the selection of senior management personnel, a subject discussed later in this chapter.)

PLANNING FOR RECRUITMENT

Before any applicants for a job are interviewed, any organization about to engage in the recruitment and selection process needs to undertake a number of important steps. These prior steps, in which the HRM specialists in the organization are likely to be particularly prominent (relative to line managers) include the forecasting of human resource needs, the specification of individual job requirements and the identification and use of appropriate recruitment channels. The first two of these prior tasks have been particularly prominent areas of discussion in the strategic human resource management literature of the 1980s.

There have been numerous articles arguing the case for (and benefits of) a more integrated relationship between competitive strategy and human resource planning, while others discussed the various statistical and forecasting techniques that could be utilized in such a comprehensive planning process.[2] However, as noted in both the Introduction and Chapter 1, the relatively limited linkage that has occurred to date in this subject area is well known, with the nature of the steps necessary to bring about improvement in this regard being actively debated, at least in certain quarters of organizational decision-making; one suspects, as suggested in Chapter 1, that organizations which have moved and will move most rapidly in this direction are those where existing HRM professionals (staff management) have had some prior experience in line management positions (thus 'smoothing' the internal political processes of decision-making) and/or those organizations that have experienced substantial 'costs' as a result of the absence of such a linkage. As to the second matter, the traditional basic purpose of job analysis has been to provide an up-to-date and accurate job description which will indicate the sort of qualifications and experience to be used in advertising the position. This, as indicated earlier, is likely to be an important area of current change in many organizations as a result of changes in technology and in contemporary thinking about the 'ideal' arrangements for organizing work. The combination of 'scientific management' thinking, the practice of collective bargaining and use of job evaluation techniques has historically resulted in a system of work organization which involved a hierarchy of narrowly designed and highly specialized job tasks to each of which was attached 'the (pay) rate for the job'.

This traditional system of work organization, with its important implications for individual job descriptions and job analysis, has been variously challenged (although certainly not supplanted) over time by individual experiments in job rotation, job enlargement and job enrichment in the 1960s, the concept of socio-technical design systems (with its emphasis on autonomous or semi-autonomous work groups) and, most recently, by flexible work organization systems. The latter (particularly in new plant operations) typically involve a reduction in the number of individual job classifications, team working arrangements and the integration of responsibility for quality control into production jobs.[3] Such changes have important implications for individual job descriptions and job analysis. For example, in one high technology organization I have been following quite closely there has been, since the mid-1970s, a sustained movement away from low-volume, long cycle-time production to a position of high-volume, short-cycle production. As a consequence, production employees in the manufacturing area have increasingly taken on tasks and responsibilities previously associated with non-manufacturing, support groups of employees. The result has been a large-scale re-analysis and rewriting of job descriptions in recent years in the manufacturing area, both for existing employees and any employees who are to be newly recruited.

Finally, there is the question of the choice of appropriate recruitment channels for advertising posts and obtaining applicants. The main points here are: (1) the human resource management literature puts a great deal of emphasis on the need to have well-developed internal labour market arrangements (as regards promotion, training, and individual career development) which would suggest that many openings can and should be filled internally, particularly if employees were originally hired with a view to their longer-term development potential; (2) different channels of recruitment are favoured and used for different grades and levels of employees; (3) the various potential channels of recruitment tend to yield different sorts of information (i.e. extensive or intensive) about applicants; and (4) the value of different channels of recruitment can be assessed by comparing their costs to their *yield* (i.e. number hired/number of applicants for each particular channel) and *retention* ratios.[4]

ASSESSING THE SELECTION PROCESS

In this section I briefly note some of the leading concepts and measures which are relevant in assessing the success of any selection procedures for employees. Firstly, the basic aim of the selection process is to try and minimize both *false positive* and *false negative* errors. In the former case the selection process predicts success in the job for an applicant, who is therefore hired, but the applicant fails, whereas in the latter case an applicant who would have succeeded in the job is rejected because the process predicted failure. As the latter case is essentially unobservable to the organization concerned, it tends to be the costs of false positive errors that are of most concern to organizations engaged in the recruitment and selection of employees. Secondly, the concepts of *validity* and *reliability* have traditionally figured prominently in discussions of the success of selection procedures. The process of validation asks whether a significant statistical relationship exists between a predictor (e.g. interviewer rating of an applicant) and a criterion measure of successful performance on a job (e.g. a measure of work behaviour or work outcome); it is important to note here that the particular measure of work performance/success utilized may have serious implications for validation tests, although in the selection literature predictors are always discussed in much more detail than criteria. A measure obviously cannot be valid unless it is also reliable, and the concept of reliability concerns the consistency of a measure over time or between different measures of the same concept or behaviour. Some discussions of validity frequently go further and distinguish between (1) *criterion*-related validity (i.e. can a significant relationship be demonstrated between the predictor and some measure of work behaviour or performance?); (2) *construct* validity (i.e. can the selection process measure the degree to which an applicant has certain psychological traits or constructs which are inferred from job for the position?); and (3) *content* validity (i.e. a selection process has this type of validity if it representatively samples significant parts of the job for which the applicant has applied). To these traditional concerns about validity and reliability in the selection process has been added a concern about equity and fairness, largely as a result of the passage of anti-discrimination and equal opportunities legislation and regulations. Some commentators have also added applicability (i.e. the extent that the selection method can be applied across the full range of jobs and applicants) and the cost of implementing the method.[5] (In practice, however, the research literature is dispro-portionately concerned with the validity issue.)

THE INTERVIEW: LIMITATIONS AND POSSIBLE CHANGES

In general the most common predictors used in the selection process are interviews, tests (of various types), the information contained in letters of application and on application forms, and references obtained from previous employers. The interviewing process is widely used (largely, one presumes, for reasons of low cost and high applicability) and heavily relied upon in the ultimate selection decision, despite the fact that a consistent stream of research over an extended period of time has indicated that its reliability and validity is, to say the least, far from impressive.[6] The failings of the interview have been found to derive from the processes by which interviewers make judgements. That is, people (i.e. interviewers) are essentially not good at the task of processing information. Table 3.1 sets out a list of some of the leading findings.

There is also the danger highlighted by some researchers that interviewers may tend to 'over-sell' the organization to applicants they are particularly keen to attract, and hence may not convey particularly accurate or realistic job information in the course of the interview;[7] the result may be relatively high turn-over rates. As the essentially negative message centring around Table 3.1 has been increasingly absorbed in management circles, organizations can react (and have done) in a number of ways. Although there is no question of the interviewing process being dispensed with, organizations may, firstly, seek increasingly to supplement it by, for example, the use of occupational testing; this is an approach considered in the next section. Secondly, they may seek to reform or improve the interviewing process by introducing certain organization-wide changes into the relevant processes. A third possibility is that

Table 3.1 *Limitations of the selection interview process*

1 *First impressions, favourability and order of information*

(a) Early information has a disproportionate influence on the final outcome.

(b) The order of information, as well as its favourability, is critical in decision-making (favourable information early and later in the interview are particularly influential).

(c) Interviewers make their decisions very quickly (an average of four minutes from the beginning of the interview is a widely cited, although not widely replicated, statistic).

2 *Stereotypes*

(a) The search for information and decision-making are heavily influenced by applicants being compared with an ideal applicant stereotype.

(b) The stereotype and the related concept of implicit personality theory are a substitute for seeking specific information from the applicant.

3 *Trait attributions*

The belief that past behaviour is a good predictor of future behaviour omits mediating influences and circumstances.

4 *Other effects and biases*

(a) The preceding applicants create a context in which the current applicant is evaluated (this 'contrast' effect can result in serious under- or over-rating).

(b) The applicant's non-verbal behaviour can have a significant impact on evaluations.

(c) The 'halo effect' can result from an over-generalization of one 'outstanding' characteristic (for good or bad) of an applicant.

(d) Negative information is sought out and given undue emphasis.

Source: Adapted from Milton D. Hakel, 'Employment Interviewing', in Kendrith M. Rowland and Gerald R. Ferris (eds.), *Personnel Management*, Allyn and Bacon, Boston, 1982, pp. 135–41.

individual interviewers can and will begin to change the way in which they conduct interviews, even in the absence of any explicit organization-wide changes to interviewing procedures and arrangements. There are numerous guidelines for an improved interviewing technique and Table 3.2 sets out one such list of recommendations.

Numerous self-help or guidance books on best practice interviewing techniques essentially make similar points.[8] Such voluntary

Table 3.2   *Recommendations for interviewers*

---

1   Prior to the interview develop a 'game plan' for it.

2   The game plan should specify what is to be covered in the interview (i.e. build rapport, obtain information, provide information, answer questions).

3   Base the game plan on relevant job information.

4   Initially communicate the game plan to the applicant.

5   Follow a common format for all applicants.

6   In general avoid leading and closed questions.

7   Try to help put the applicant at ease.

8   Seek to provide a specific and realistic description of the job and organization.

9   The conduct of the interview should ensure that the applicant does the majority (i.e. 75 per cent) of the talking.

10   Develop active listening skills.

11   Develop the skills both to observe and provide non-verbal communication.

12   Record your observations during and at the end of each interview.

13   Be aware of current legal and ethical issues surrounding the interviewing process.

14   Obtain feedback on the subsequent job performance of individuals interviewed.

Source: Adapted from David C. Gilmore, Gerald R. Ferris and K. Michele Kacmar, 'The Nature of Employment Interview Decisions', in Gerald R. Ferris, Kendrith M. Rowland and M. Ronald Buckley (eds.), *Human Resource Management: Perspectives and Issues*, Allyn and Bacon, Boston, 2nd edition, 1990, pp. 126–7.

changes on the part of individual interviewers can arguably, however, be strengthened and reinforced by certain organization-wide changes in the interviewing process. The most frequently mentioned changes along these lines include (1) multiple interviews, (2) training interviewers in the necessary skills, and (3) the use of a standardized or common interviewing format and assessment measure. For example, one attempt to develop a structured interviewing technique (to raise its psychometric properties) suggests that it should be based on the following steps: develop questions based on job analysis, ask the same questions of each candidate, anchor the rating scales for scoring answers with examples and illustrations, have an interview panel record and rate answers, consistently administer the process to all candidates, and give special attention to job relatedness, fairness and documentation in accordance with testing guidelines.[9] Research concerning the effectiveness of such changes is still far from complete, although the verdict on the evidence to date is that only relatively marginal improvements in validity are likely to result.[10] As a consequence both researchers and, increasingly, practitioners have concluded that the information obtained from selection interviews needs to be supplemented by information obtained by other means. Psychological testing is one of the increasingly favoured supplementary means, and it is to this subject that I turn in the next section.

PSYCHOLOGICAL TESTING: THE ANSWER?

Psychological testing involves a very heterogeneous set of instruments which are frequently categorized under the headings of intelligence tests, ability and aptitude tests, and interest and personality tests. The latter are the most controversial, as we shall see, although they are frequently viewed as growing in popularity and usage. Undoubtedly the best-publicized use of personality testing in recent times has been in new plants where a workforce is to be recruited from scratch, a background of employment experience in the particular industry is not deemed to be particularly relevant or even (in some cases) desirable, there are large numbers of applicants relative to the positions available, and the competitive strategy, technology and work design systems place a premium on flexible work operations. Box 3.1 describes the recruitment–selection process in one such organization.

In this particular greenfield site there were over 10,000 applications and some 2,500 individuals were called for interview and testing purposes, which resulted in a final selection figure of approximately 300. This particular organization used Cattells 16 PF test which is designed to measure the normal dimensions of personality. It provides sixteen basic scores, fifteen personality traits plus a measure of 'intelligence'. (Various combinations of these 'primary' scores give 'second order' factors, or broader groupings of personality characteristics. There are fuller and shorter versions of the test.) Table 3.3 sets out the personality traits measured by this particular test.

The report from which Table 3.3 is extracted went on to list the following broad assumptions of individuals using the 16 PF for personnel selection.[11]

1   The 16 PF gives a more or less useful description (depending on the practitioner's experience or point of view) of an individual's personality in the form of traits.

Table 3.3   *Personality traits measured by the 16 PF test*

Reserved, detached v. Warm-hearted, outgoing
Dull v. Bright (intelligence factor)
Affected by feelings v. Emotionally stable
Accommodating, submissive v. Assertive, dominant
Sober, serious v. Enthusiastic, happy-go-lucky
Expedient v. Conscientious, rule-abiding
Shy v. Socially bold
Tough-minded v. Tender-minded, sensitive
Trusting v. Suspecting
Practical v. Imaginative
Forthright, unpretentious v. Astute, shrewd
Self-assured v. Apprehensive, anxious
Conservative v. Radical
Group-dependent v. Self-sufficient
Low self-image v. High self-image
Relaxed v. Tense

Source: M. A. Pearn, R. S. Kandola, R. D. Mottram and Pearn Kandola Associates, *Selection Tests and Sex Bias*, Equal Opportunities Commission Research Series, HMSO, London, 1987, p.119.

2   Skilled interpretation of this description can help predict an individual's job preferences and satisfactions, probable style of operation, aspects of the job they are likely to perform well, or less well, and their likely contribution in terms of team work.

3   16 PF is most useful when combined with other information such as past record, and with achievement and aptitude test results.

4   The pattern of personality it indicates is reasonably consistent over time once maturity has been reached.

5   While some occupations may have a 'typical personality profile', there is room for a wide range of individual differences, particularly the higher up the management ladder you look.

There is considerably more to psychological testing than simply the 16 PF test; one publication in the late 1980s, for example, noted that there were more than 5,000 psychological instruments available in the English language.[12] It has been aptly observed that 'there is probably no subject more controversial in occupational psychology than the merits and demerits of personality assessment'.[13] For instance,

---

Box 3.1   *Psychological testing for a new workforce*

Advertisements in the press for operator grades specified a profile of mid-20s to mid-30s, a good basic education, and process/textile/coal industry experience. The local Job Centre initially handled all applications; those which were deemed suitable were passed to the personnel/line management of the organization for screening and then candidates were called for interview. The recruitment team interviewed an average of twenty candidates a day, four days a week, over a period of a month. At the end of a day each candidate should have been seen by at least five people – two line supervisors, one psychologist, one personnel management representative and one other psychologist who administered a test.

Candidates were asked to arrive at 8.30 a.m. and as they arrived were allocated randomly to one of the slots numbered 1 to 20. Following a brief introductory talk the candidates were introduced to the interviewing team. After this the people numbered 11–20 were taken to another room to take part in a series of timed aptitude tests. In the meantime the group remaining were set off on a series of untimed personality tests and launched into the interview pro-gramme. At lunchtime the groups would swap round and the morning test group would go through the interview programme and the morning interview group would go through the aptitude testing programmes.

The types of tests used covered aptitude, mechanics, matrices, numeracy, verbal, computer (memory and reaction time) and personality tests, notably the 16 PF. The aims of the tests were to assess the willingness of the applicants to learn new skills (trainability) and work flexibly, and to predict their likely patterns of on-the-job behaviour.

At the end of each day, with all this test information and reports from each interviewer available, full-scale review meetings were held at which each candidate was discussed in turn. Their test results were put forward and each interviewer would pass comment and an attempt was made to reach a consensus decision as to whether the applicant should be hired.

---

a number of industrial psychologists have long argued that there are likely to be serious limitations to the validity and reliability of personality and interest tests in the selection decision because of the possibility of applicants faking the answers.[14] In fact a review of the available evidence in the USA has suggested that ability and aptitude tests have only a modest degree of predictive accuracy concerning job performance, with personality tests being even less successful in this regard;[15] their predictive performance is, however, considerably better than that of the interview process.[16] In keeping with these findings, the increased use of personality (as opposed to aptitude) tests by organizations in Britain is currently associated with considerable controversy and disagreement concerning their validity as predictors of job performance (*The Times*, 5 September 1991).

The use of selection tests has also raised a number of important issues concerning the potential for discrimination, as well as certain broader ethical concerns. In the USA, for instance, the use of selection tests initially declined after the passage of civil rights legislation in the 1960s, although their usage is apparently on the increase in more recent times. There has in fact been much discussion and controversy in the United States as to whether such tests have an adverse impact on the selection of minorities;[17] federal government guidelines have specified that such tests, to be acceptable for equal opportunity purposes, must be criterion, content and construct valid. And in Britain a research publication by the Equal Opportunities Commission has also raised the issue of whether the use of such tests can adversely impact on the selection of women;[18] a considerable range of variation in organizational practice was observed in choosing tests, applying the test procedures, interpreting the results, being aware of equal opportunities implications, etc. More broadly, there have been a number of concerns expressed about the ethics of selection testing. For instance a code of practice issued by the Institute of Personnel Management in Britain emphasized the need to use (only) chartered occupational psychologists, provide feedback to applicants, and observe confidentiality, as well as ensuring compliance with equal opportunities legislation.[19] Indeed, the British Psychological Society announced in early 1991 the establishment of a quality assurance scheme for occupational testing, with a statement of competence in such testing to be issued only to individuals who have completed an approved training course or who are registered with one of the main test publishers.

In general it has been argued that the process of employee selection is particularly important when a job's base rate of success is low (i.e. relatively few employees reach an acceptable level of job performance), a job is of particular importance in an organization and the selection ratio for a job (i.e. the number of applicants selected relative to the total number of applicants) is low.[20] For these reasons it is unlikely (and indeed undesirable) that a uniform or common set of selection procedures will characterize all job levels in an individual organization. This perspective leads to the next section where I discuss the role and effectiveness of assessment centres for the selection (and promotion) of managerial personnel.

MANAGEMENT ASSESSMENT CENTRES

Management assessment centres, whose origins are frequently held to lie in the British War Office Selection Boards during World War II, have been variously used to select candidates for a given job, identify individuals with the longer-term potential for senior management positions, and assess the training and development needs of individuals. In selecting candidates for management positions the procedures involved in assessment centres typically seek to measure and identify the potential for effective management performance by reference to the dimensions of leadership, organizing and planning, decision-making, oral and written communication skills, initiative, energy, analytical ability, resistance to stress, ability to delegate, flexible behaviour, human resource management skills, originality, control, self-direction and overall potential.[21] The tests and exercises involved in an assessment centre to assess potential along these lines are frequently some combination of those set out in Table 3.4.

The alleged strengths of assessment centres (or at least well designed and administered ones) are the variety of techniques used, the assessment of candidates together, the use of multiple assessors and the basing of assessments on several dimensions. In order to try and maximize the potential advantages of an assessment centre a number of design issues or a sequence of processes need to be given detailed attention. Table 3.5 contains a checklist of the individual issues or processes most frequently mentioned.

The research on assessment centres, which has overwhelmingly been conducted in the USA, has focused on the reliability and stability of assessment results, their predictive validity, the acceptability of the processes to participants and organizations, and equity and equal opportunity themes. It is not difficult in the literature to find relatively favourable discussions of the success of assessment centres. For example, one recent publication summarized some existing research which suggested that the probability of selecting an 'above average performer' on a random basis was 15 per cent, a figure that rose to 35 per cent using appraisal and interview data and to 76 per cent using assessment centre results.[22] Furthermore a recent meta-analysis

Table 3.4   *Tests and exercises in a management assessment centre*

---

1   *The in-basket simulation* (usually considered the most important)
     The candidate is asked to dispose appropriately of an accumulation of memos, reports, notes of phone messages, letters, etc. by writing letters, notes, self-reminders, agendas for meetings, etc.

2   *The leaderless group discussion*
     Participants are given a discussion question and have to arrive at a group decision.

3   *Management games*
     Participants are required to solve problems, either co-operatively or competitively.

4   *Individual presentations*
     A short, oral presentation has to be made on a given topic or theme.

5   *Objective tests*
     These are paper and pencil tests of mental ability, personality, interests and achievement.

6   *Projective tests*
     These are not common, although some organizations use, for instance, sentence completion tests to get at behavioural characteristics such as originality and the need for achievement.

7   *Interview*
     An interview between a participant and at least one assessor is likely to cover general background, past performance, interests and motivation.

8   *Other techniques*
     Written exercises, creative writing assignments, mock interviews or dealing with an awkward phone conversation may be included here.

Source: Adapted from Ann Howard, 'An Assessment of Assessment Centers', in Gerald R. Ferris, Kendrith M. Rowland and M. Ronald Buckley (eds.), *Human Resource Management: Perspectives and Issues*, Allyn and Bacon, Boston, 2nd edition, 1990, pp. 158–9.

conducted in the USA, which was based on some 50 existing assessment centre studies, supported the widely held contention that assessment centres have predictive validity, with this validity being significantly enhanced the more assessment devices were used, when psychologists were used as assessors and when assessor ratings were supplemented with those provided by peer groups.[23]

At present, the biggest research question centring around assessment centres is not whether they have predictive ability, but rather exactly *why* they do. For instance, one recent review of assessment centres concluded:

Table 3.5   *Key processes in establishing and operating an assessment centre*

---

1   Organization-wide commitment to the importance of the centre
2   Job analysis to identify the behaviours relevant to the performance of the jobs concerned and the grouping of behaviours into an appropriate number of dimensions
3   A determination of the number and types of exercises to measure these particular dimensions of behaviour
4   The selection and training of assessors
5   The standardization of assessment procedures to try and ensure reliability and validity
6   The development of administrative procedures to ensure a manageable flow of the essential accompanying paperwork
7   Establishment of procedures for ensuring a controlled, confidential dissemination and usage of assessment information

---

Source: Adapted from Virginia R. Bochin, 'Assessment Centers and Management Development', in Kendrith M. Rowland and Gerald R. Ferris (eds.), *Personnel Management*, Allyn and Bacon, Boston, 1982, pp. 337–44.

> The fact is – we don't know why ACs work so well. It's an increasingly derided tradition for psychologists to conclude every research paper by saying 'More research is needed.' But sometimes more research really *is* needed: analysis of AC validity is a prime candidate. If we knew which elements of the AC contribute to its success we could improve its predictive accuracy still further, or reduce the AC's length and expense, or perhaps achieve both at once.[24]

There have been a number of different views and reasons put forward to account for the validity results emerging from assessment centres, some of which are more positive than others. However, in pursuing research into the 'why of assessment centre success' it is likely that individuals will need to take on board the following suggestions:[25]

1   There may be a pronounced opportunity for criterion contamination with assessment centre evaluations. This is because the superior who provides a subjective assessment of a subordinate's performance may know of the subordinate's performance in an assessment centre and be influenced by it.

2   The assessors in the assessment centre may give higher evaluations to those individuals who, in their judgement, are most likely to fit and get on in the organization concerned.

3   Assessment centre evaluations seem to predict most accurately promotability in an organization, but are rather less successful in predicting more objective criteria.

OVERALL EFFECTIVENESS AND STRATEGIC SELECTION

In this concluding section my aim is two-fold: firstly, to summarize briefly some of the leading findings concerning the effectiveness of individual selection instruments and devices; and secondly to highlight some possible developments in the direction of organizations adopting more of a strategic approach towards employee selection. As to the first matter, the leading results of one recent review article[26] pointed to the following conclusions:

1   An examination of research results concerning eleven different selection methods indicated that there was no one method that was high on validity, fairness and applicability, and low on cost (i.e. a series of trade-offs was involved).

2   The single method that came closest to meeting the above standards was biographical information, which was high on validity and applicability and low on cost, but only moderate on fairness.

3   In terms of validity, those which scored high were work samples, biographical information, peer assessments and assessment centres.

4   Interviewing was low on validity, moderate on fairness, high on applicability and low on cost.

5   Personality tests were moderate on validity, high on fairness, low on applicability and moderate on cost.

6   Assessment centres were high on validity, high on fairness, low on applicability and high on cost.

What about strategic selection? In the introduction to this chapter I indicated that some commentators are urging that needs deriving from the nature of larger competitive strategies and longer-term human resource planning considerations should be increasingly injected into the selection decision-making process relative to the traditional desire to obtain a close (individual) person–job fit at a single point in time. Moreover there are single organization case studies, particularly of greenfield sites, where such an orientation has been attempted.[27] However, what about the larger potential of some of the individual selection devices discussed here to operate in such a way? It is apparent, for instance, that the use of assessment centres in selection decisions has begun to spread beyond managerial grades to other groups of employees, such as sales staff and supervisors.[28] Does this suggest that the assessment centre may become a leading instrument for injecting strategic considerations into the selection decision-making process, at least for key personnel? To certain individuals it has the potential to be operated in this way, although questions remain about its cost, more general applicability (beyond management grades) and whether its alleged tendency to identify 'clones' may not be counterproductive for the future. It is also apparent that team working needs on the shopfloor have stimulated the increased use of psychological testing, particularly in greenfield sites. Moreover it is likely that conversion to team working arrangements on 'brownfield sites' will stimulate (and has done) the use of peer group involvement in the selection process.

These are all interesting individual changes in the approach to selection which cumulatively over time may point in the direction of a more strategic orientation towards the selection decision. However, the pace of movement in this direction will only be accelerated by senior line managers viewing the selection process as much more than simply achieving an individual person–job fit at a point in time.

REFERENCES

1   Charles Fombrun, Noel M. Tichy and Mary Anne Devanna, *Strategic Human Resource Management*, Wiley, New York, 1984, pp. 43–6.

2   Lee Dyer, 'Human Resource Planning', in Kendrith M. Rowland and Gerald R. Ferris (eds.), *Personnel Management*, Allyn and Bacon, Boston, 1982, pp. 52–77.

3   Thomas Kochan, Joel Cutcher-Gershenfeld and John Paul MacDuffie, 'Employee Participation, Work Redesign and New Technology: Implications for Public Policy in the 1990s', Paper prepared for the Commission on Workforce Quality and Labor Market Efficiency, US Department of Labor, May 1989, pp. 14–18.

4   Thomas A. Kochan and Thomas A. Barocci, *Human Resource Management and Industrial Relations: Text, Readings and Cases*, Little, Brown, Boston, 1985, pp. 165–72.

5   Paul M. Muchinsky, 'Personnel Selection Methods', in Cary L. Cooper and Ivan T. Robertson (eds.), *International Review of Industrial and Organization Psychology 1986*, Wiley, Chichester, 1986, pp. 38–9.
6   Milton D. Hakel, 'Employment Interviewing', in Kendrith M. Rowland and Gerald R. Ferris, *Personnel Management*, Allyn and Bacon, Boston, 1982, p. 134.
7   J. P. Wanous, *Organizational Entry: Recruitment, Selection and Socialization of Newcomers*, Addison-Wesley, Reading, Mass., 1980.
8   See, for example, Jack Gratus, *Successful Interviewing*, Penguin, Harmondsworth, 1988.
9   Michael A. Campion, Elliott D. Pursell and Barbara K. Brown, 'Structured Interviewing: Raising the Psychometric Properties of the Employment Interview', in Tim O. Patterson (ed.), *Human Resource Management: Readings and Cases*, Houghton Mifflin, Boston, 1990, pp. 118–33.
10 Richard D. Arvey and James G. Campion, 'The Employment Interview: A Summary and Review of Recent Research', *Personnel Psychology*, 35, 1982, pp. 281–322.
11 M. A. Pearn, R. S. Kandola, R. D. Mottram and Pearn Kandola Associates, *Selection Tests and Sex Bias*, Equal Opportunities Commission Research Series, HMSO, London, 1987, p. 118.
12 John Toplis, Vic Dulewicz and Clive Fletcher, *Psychological Testing: A Practical Guide for Employers*, Institute of Personnel Management, London, 1987, p. 7.
13 Pearn et al., *Selection Tests*, p. 117.
14 Ernest J. McCormick and Joseph Tiffin, *Industrial Psychology*, George Allen and Unwin, London, 6th edition, 1975, pp. 181–7.
15 N. Schmitt, R. Z. Goodins, R. A. Noe and M. Kirsch, 'Meta-Analysis of Validity Studies published between 1964 and 1982 and the Investigation of Study Characteristics', *Personnel Psychology*, 37, 1984, pp. 407–22.
16 N. Schmitt and R. A. Noe, 'Personnel Selection and Equal Opportunity', in C. L. Cooper and I. Robertson (eds.), *International Review of Industrial and Organizational Psychology*, Wiley, Chichester, 1986.
17 See, for example, Dale Yodder and Paul D. Straudshar, 'Testing and EEO: Getting Down to Cases', in Gerald R. Ferris, Kendrith M. Rowland and M. Ronald Buckley (eds.), *Human Resource Management: Perspectives and Issues*, Allyn and Bacon, Boston, 2nd edition, 1990, pp. 133–40.
18 Pearn et al., *Selection Tests*, p. 117.
19 Personnel Management Factsheet No. 24, *Psychological Testing*, December 1989.
20 Thomas H. Stone and Noah M. Meltz, *Personnel Management in Canada*, Holt, Rinehart and Winston, Toronto, 1983, pp. 139–40.

21 Ann Howard, 'An Assessment of Assessment Centres', in Gerald R. Ferris, Kendrith M. Rowland and M. Ronald Buckley (eds.), *Human Resource Management*, Allyn and Bacon, Boston, 1990, p. 157.

22 Ibid., p. 165.

23 Barbara B. Gaugler, Douglas B. Rosenthal, George C. Thornton and Cynthia Bentson, 'Meta-Analysis of Assessment Center Validity', *Journal of Applied Psychology*, 72 (3), 1987, pp. 493–511.

24 Mark Cook, *Personnel Selection and Productivity*, Wiley, Chichester, 1988, p. 170.

25 Muchinsky, 'Personnel Selection Methods', pp. 58–9.

26 Ibid., pp. 60–2.

27 P. B. Beaumont and L. C. Hunter, 'Competitive Strategy, Flexibility and Selection: The Case of Caledonian Paper', in Brian Towers (ed.), *The Handbook of Human Resource Management*, Blackwell, Oxford, 1992, pp. 392–403.

28 Personnel Management Factsheet No. 22, *Assessment Centres*, October 1989.

4

APPRAISING EMPLOYEES

INTRODUCTION

The process of appraising individual employees is viewed as one of the central planks of strategic human resource management for two reasons. Firstly, it is argued that the grounds (i.e. criteria) on which an employee is appraised should reflect the larger competitive strategy of the organization. In Chapter 1, for instance, I noted the suggestion of some researchers that both the criteria and time frame of the appraisal process should vary according to whether a product innovation, quality enhancement or low-cost strategy was being pursued. This perspective has led to frequent calls for the individual performance appraisal to be closely aligned with the establishment of objectives at the level of organization, business unit, functional area, department level, etc. which are all part of a larger, coherent performance management system. Furthermore, at least one well-known study has documented the existence of differences in the appraisal systems of 'diversified' (i.e. objective, results-orientated criteria) and 'integrated' (i.e. more subjective measures) companies.[1] And secondly, the need for complementary changes in the overall HRM policy mix is frequently discussed or illustrated by reference to the case of appraisal systems. For example, some of the leading advocates of Total Quality Management (e.g. Deming) are highly critical of performance appraisals based on individual employees, while moves towards team working arrangements have frequently raised questions about whether the traditional supervisor—subordinate relationship remains an appropriate basis for appraisals.

Currently line managers are heavily involved in the process of employee appraisal, acting as appraisers and also being appraised by their own superiors. The primary purpose of employee appraisal is to improve the current on-the-job performance of the person being appraised, although a number of secondary benefits can flow from the process such as the generation of information for human resource planning, and improved communication and understanding between the individuals concerned. The long-run, development orientation of individuals, which is so prominently themed in the human resource management literature, would seem to argue strongly for separate appraisals for different purposes, although in practice this seems to occur in only a minority of cases.

The nature of employee appraisal has undergone considerable change in many advanced industrialized economies. Firstly, employee appraisal was traditionally concentrated among middle and junior managers in large private sector organizations, although in more recent times it has spread to the public sector and in some organizations has been extended to cover manual employees. Secondly, the basis on which employees are appraised has changed. Originally appraisal schemes tended · to concentrate mainly on personal traits (e.g. loyalty, initiative, etc.), an orientation which was superseded by a focus on the pattern of job performance behaviours (i.e. what an individual did, or was seen to do), while more recently the emphasis has been on job results (i.e. what an individual has achieved). The latter typically involves a joint process of setting performance objectives and then reviewing and appraising the individual on the basis of the extent to which such objectives were achieved over a given period. This type of performance appraisal system can be seen as an integral component of a larger system of management by objectives or goal-setting in an individual organization. Table 4.1 summarizes the leading points to emerge from a recent survey of performance appraisal practices in the USA; these points constitute a useful scene setting exercise for subsequent discussion.

The purpose of this chapter is to examine, in turn: some of the common problems encountered in conducting effective employee appraisals; the components or elements of a 'good' employee appraisal interviewing technique; and some proposals for improving the process of appraisal for the organization as a whole. The emphasis here is very much on the skills of the face-to-face appraisal interview, with much less attention being given to the design basis of an appraisal system; this particular concentration reflects the predominantly line management orientation of this book (and, as the first point in Table 4.1 indicates, the design of appraisal systems is overwhelmingly a staff management function). Nevertheless a few observations on the design stage seem warranted at this point. There are, for instance, some generic 'good practice' principles which are urged for the design stage of all appraisal systems, regardless of the particular format used. For example, one recent practitioner publication urges the need for a strong senior management commitment

Table 4.1 *A sketch of performance appraisal practices in the USA*

- Current performance appraisal systems, which are on average eleven years old, were designed primarily by staff management specialists, with relatively little input from line managers or employees.

- MBO is the most popular format for appraising executives, managers and professionals, whereas trait-based rating scales are more common for other categories of employees.

- The vast majority of performance appraisal comes from the immediate level superior.

- Typically seven hours per year are spent on appraising individuals at higher organizational levels, and three hours per year for employees further down the organizational hierarchy.

- Appraiser training (focusing on interview skills, provision of feedback, setting performance standards, avoiding rating errors) rarely occurs on an on-going, year-to-year basis, but tends to be disproportionately associated with the introduction of new systems of appraisal.

- Managers are rarely evaluated on how well they conduct the appraisal process.

- Fairness and justice issues are considered the most important ones in the appraisal process, although systematic data on the extent to which this is perceived to have been achieved is rarely sought.

- Typically appraisal systems provide for categorizing employees into five levels or groups of performance, although in practice three levels are overwhelmingly used.

- Indeed 60–70 per cent of the workforce is typically placed in the top two performance levels or grades, suggesting the existence of leniency bias.

Source: Adapted from Robert D. Bretz, George T. Milkovich and Walter Read, 'The Current State of Performance Appraisal Research and Practice: Concerns, Directions and Implications', *Journal of Management*, 18 (2), 1992, pp. 330–3.

to the system, extensive prior consultation with employees and unions about the design and implementation of a system, a regular monitoring (and possibly modification, adaptation and updating) of the workings of the scheme, a simple, straightforward and really comprehensible basis for appraisals; and adequate training of the individuals who act as appraisers.[2]

A recent academic publication also urges that a wide range of organizational members need to be involved in the design of an appraisal system, rather than the task being left simply to the technical experts (i.e. HRM professionals) or the politically powerful members of senior management.[3] This particular publication favours a combination of the rational, political and participative approaches to system design in order to try and ensure that the system of employee appraisal contributes to the strategic objectives of the organization, is consistent with other aspects of the organization's operation and is capable of being fully implemented; these are the potential advantages of incorporating an input from staff management, line management, employees and unions, although in practice (as Table 4.1 indicates) this rarely occurs. Secondly, as noted earlier, the particular format favoured in appraisal systems has changed quite substantially. The literature typically distinguishes three basic schools or categories of format: (1) norm-referenced formats which involve individual employees being evaluated in relation to other, similar employees (e.g. straight ranking, forced distribution); (2) behaviourally based formats which evaluate individuals, independently of others, by reference to behavioural criteria (e.g. critical incidents, behaviourally anchored rating scales); and (3) output-based measures, where the product(s) of the job is the reference point (e.g. MBO, performance standards).[4] In general the latter have gained in popularity and usage over time, although, as we shall see in a later section, there is no one best format that is clearly superior to all other formats in all organizational circumstances.

THE CONCERNS AND PROBLEMS OF APPRAISAL

It has frequently been noted that both appraisers and appraisees face the prospect of an appraisal interview with considerable apprehension. Managers, for instance, frequently worry about the appraisal process as potentially de-motivating staff or harming on-going working relationships, while employees are keen to avoid receiving any negative feedback about their performance. The nature of these inbuilt (some would say inherent) tensions and concerns are well captured in the following observations:

> Because the organization is pursuing conflicting objectives (evaluation and development), the manager must use performance appraisal in two quite contradictory ways. Similarly, individuals have conflicting objectives as they approach a performance appraisal. The most significant conflict, however, is between the individual and the organization. The individual desires to confirm a positive self-image and to obtain organizational rewards of promotion or pay. The organization wants individuals to be open to negative information about themselves so they can improve their performance. It also wants individuals to be helpful in supplying this information. The conflict is

Table 4.2   *Some common problems with performance appraisal*

---

1   *The halo effect*
The appraiser gives a favourable rating to overall job performance essentially because the person being appraised has performed well in one particular aspect of the job which the appraiser considers all-important.

2   *The pitch-fork effect*
This is the exact opposite of the halo effect, whereby the appraiser gives an unfavourable rating to overall job performance essentially because the appraisee has performed poorly in one particular aspect of the job which the appraiser considers all-important.

3   *Central tendency*
The appraiser deliberately avoids using the end points of the rating scale and rates all employees as average in virtually all aspects of job performance.

4   *The recency error*
In rating an employee's job performance over, for example, a twelve-month period, the appraiser makes disproportionate use of instances of performance which are relatively recent (i.e. close to the interview in time) to make an assessment.

5   *Length of service bias*
The assessor assumes that an experienced employee who has been rated well in the past has absorbed and responded well to any new aspects of their job, and hence does not closely monitor their performance in this regard.

6   *The loose rater*
In order to avoid conflict with a subordinate an appraiser does not discuss any weak areas of an individual's job performance.

7   *The tight rater*
An appraiser has unrealistically high expectations for all subordinates which means that no-one receives an excellent or outstanding rating.

8   *The competitive rater*
An appraiser links his/her own rating with that of their subordinates so that no-one receives a rating higher than that which they achieved.

Source: Adapted from Terry R. Lowe, 'Eight Ways to Ruin a Performance Review', *Personnel Journal*, January 1986, pp. 60–2.

over the exchange of valid information. As long as individuals see the appraisal process as having an important influence on their rewards (pay, recognition), their career (promotions and reputation), and their self-image, they will be reluctant to engage in the kind of open dialogue required for valid evaluation and personal development.[5]

The strength of these concerns, worries and tensions is obviously very considerable, and would seem to help explain the results of a widely quoted recent research study which concluded that,

> accuracy is not the primary concern of the practising executive in appraising subordinates. The main concern is how best to use the appraisal process to motivate and reward subordinates. Hence managerial discretion and effectiveness, not accuracy, are the real watchwords. Managers made it clear that they would not allow excessively accurate ratings to cause problems for themselves, and that they attempted to use the appraisal process to their own advantage. The astute manager recognizes that politics in employee appraisal will never be entirely squelched.[6]

This 'political interpretation' of the appraisal process obviously stands in marked contrast to the rhetoric of the (academic) literature which is overwhelmingly concerned with seeking an appraisal process characterized by objectivity, consistency, fairness, equity, honesty, etc. Indeed, as one recent review article argued, 'researchers and managers appear to have different conceptualizations of accuracy. What does accuracy in performance appraisal imply?'[7] To researchers accuracy involves validity and reliability, whereas, as the above quote indicates, managers are more concerned with acceptability to employees. The issue of the overlap between research and practice concerning performance appraisal is returned to later in this chapter.

In fact individuals have long recognized that the realities of organizational life have frequently led to a number of problems in the process of employee appraisals. Table 4.2 contains a listing of some of the problems most frequently mentioned.

The recognition of these sources of potential weakness in the appraisal process has led to considerable discussion of the appropriate technique(s) of performance appraisal interviewing. This is a subject to which I now turn.

APPROACHES TO APPRAISAL INTERVIEWING

Although there are no hard and fast rules it is widely argued that appraisal interviews should take place at least every twelve months, be conducted by a person's immediate superior, and typically should take 1–2 hours. However, most guidebooks emphasize that the appraisal of an employee is a continuous, on-going process, which means that feedback on their performance should not be confined or

Table 4.3   *Types of appraisal interviews*

---

1   *The tell-and-sell interview*
   The appraiser does virtually all of the talking, with the basic aims being to communicate how the employee has performed, gain their acceptance of the evaluation and have them follow the appraiser's proposals for improvement.

2   *The tell-and-listen interview*
   The interview falls essentially into two parts. Initially the appraiser does the talking and provides an appraisal which indicates the strengths and weaknesses of the employee, while in the second part the subordinate has the opportunity to respond to the evaluation. In the latter part of the interview the employee is encouraged to express any disagreement with the evaluation, with the appraiser essentially acting as a non-directive counsellor.

3   *The problem-solving interview*
   There is no evaluation of performance by the superior, with the aim being to let the subordinate interviewed express their own weaknesses and propose steps for bringing about improvement. The superior can respond to the subordinate's suggestions as to the way to bring about improvement by asking questions and possibly putting forward some suggestions of their own.

Source: Michael Beer, 'Note on Performance Appraisal', in Michael Beer and Bert Spector (eds.), *Readings in Human Resource Management*, Free Press, New York, 1985, pp. 323–5.

limited to the formal annual appraisal interview. This is because positive feedback on good performance (to be effective), for instance, needs to be given close to the time when the good performance occurred, the formal appraisal interview should only draw together in summary form what has been conveyed less formally to employees on an on-going basis and feedback from an annual interview cannot hope to compete effectively with more regular, informal sources of feedback to employees from the larger organizational setting.

Traditionally the literature has distinguished three different types of appraisal interviews which have rather different objectives and thus require different skills from the appraiser.[8] These three types are listed in Table 4.3.

According to Beer, the latter two approaches are likely to result in less defensiveness from the employee (and hence provide more valid information), the problem-solving interview is the most appropriate for the achievement of development objectives, and the skills required by the appraiser in the second half of the tell-and-listen interview and throughout the problem-solving interview are essentially the same, namely the ability to (1) listen actively (i.e. accept and try to

Table 4.4   *Recommended steps and tips in appraisal interviewing*

---

1   *Preparing for the interview*
(a)   Provide adequate notice to the employee.
(b)   Send self-assessment forms to the employee for completion.
(c)   Have notes made throughout the year of an employee's performance.
(d)   Schedule at least a one-hour interview in a setting which is informal and free of interruptions.
(e)   Establish in advance what the purpose of the interview is — i.e. what the interviewer will do with the information obtained.
(f)   Be properly briefed. Read over the relevant files, and obtain any missing information.
(g)   Identify the main issues to be addressed (e.g. past objectives agreed, successes achieved, problems encountered) and the relevant questions to ask.

2   *Just before the interview*
(a)   Ensure that phone and other interruptions are avoided.
(b)   Ensure that the room is suitable and the furniture is appropriately arranged.
(c)   Greet the appraisee and seek to put them at ease.

3   *Structure of the interview*
(a)   Explain the purpose, scope and form of the interview.
(b)   Discuss the job in terms of objectives and demands.
(c)   Encourage the employee to discuss their perceived strengths and weaknesses.
(d)   Discuss how far agreed objectives have been met.
(e)   Agree future objectives.
(f)   Discuss any development needs.
(g)   Summarize the plans agreed.
(h)   In the event of disagreement, explain the details of any appeals procedure.

4   *During the interview*
The opening
(a)   Ask (open) questions which initially draw out employee reactions and ideas (remember the appraisee should do the majority of the talking).
(b)   Start with the strong points/good performance of the employee.
(c)   Establish the sequence or order of the interview, although be prepared to be flexible.
(d)   Refrain from making hasty judgements on the basis of minimal evidence (keep any personal prejudices out of the interview).

The middle
(a)   Encourage the employee to suggest ways to continue good performance.
(b)   Encourage the employee to discuss weaknesses and ways to improve.
(c)   Keep the interview moving at an appropriate pace, balancing the need to obtain information with the planned time budget.

Table 4.4 *continued*

(d)   Take relevant notes to aid memory, although without making this too obvious by losing eye contact.

The end
(a)   Ask the appraisee to summarize the main points of the discussion and the agreed action steps.
(b)   Check agreement on and commitment to the actions.
(c)   End on a high note.

5   *Throughout the interview*
(a)   The appraiser's questioning skills are all-important. Start with open questions, use a judicious mixture of open, probes, closed and reflective questions. Tend to avoid hypothetical and multiple questions.
(b)   Exhibit active listening skills.
(c)   Ensure that any criticism is constructive in nature.

6   *After the interview*
(a)   Send a copy of the report to the employee.
(b)   Follow up any necessary action steps.
(c)   The appraiser can evaluate their own performance by usefully asking themselves certain questions, such as whether the interview produced any new knowledge for them.

---

understand the employee's attitudes and feelings), (2) make effective use of pauses, (3) reflect feelings (i.e. respond to and restate feelings in a way which indicates understanding) and (4) summarize feelings (i.e. help subordinates understand themselves). Table 4.4 provides a checklist of the sort of steps and techniques which are regarded as good practice in conducting an appraisal interview along these lines.[9]

In general it has been argued that effective appraisal interviews are characterized by participation, support, goal setting, discussing problems, limited criticism and role splitting (e.g. separate sessions for pay and development purposes).[10] Earlier I noted that employee concerns about receiving adverse feedback on their performance are a sizeable stumbling block to the process of exchanging valid information. This concern has led one recent publication to recommend that there should be at least four positive comments for each piece of criticism, and that when giving criticism particular attention should be paid to certain rules of feedback.[11] These guidelines concerning feedback are set out in Table 4.5.

These guidelines for use in a performance appraisal interview need to be seen in the larger organizational setting with its multiple sources

Table 4.5   *Feedback guidelines*

- Perceptions, reactions, and opinions should be presented as such, and not as facts.

- Feedback should refer to the relevant performance, behaviour, or outcomes, not to the individual as a person.

- Feedback should be in terms of specific, observable behaviour, not general or global.

- When feedback has to be evaluative, rather than purely descriptive, it should be in terms of established criteria, probable outcomes, or possible improvement, as opposed to making judgements such as 'good' or 'bad'.

- Feedback should avoid loaded terms, which produce emotional reactions and raised defenses.

- Feedback should be concerned with those things over which an individual can exercise some control or for which the individual can use the feedback for improvements or planning alternative actions.

- When encountering raised defenses or emotional reactions, the person giving feedback should deal with the reactions, rather than trying to convince, reason or supply additional information.

- Feedback should be given in a manner that communicates acceptance of the receiver as a worthwhile person and of that person's right to be different.

Source: Allan M. Mohrman, Susan M. Resnick-West and Edward E. Lawler, *Designing Performance Appraisal Systems*, Jossey-Bass, San Francisco, 1989, p. 153.

of feedback on the job performance of individual employees. It has been aptly noted that providing feedback with all the right qualities (e.g. constructive, specific and immediate) in an appraisal interview will not always have the desired effects, due to offsetting influences from other sources in the larger organizational setting,[12] hence the importance of not limiting constructive feedback to the occasion of the formal interview. Finally for this section, Box 4.1 contains a role play exercise for drawing together and using some of the techniques discussed here.

As well as informing and encouraging individual appraisers to adopt best practice interviewing techniques, there have been a number of other, albeit often related, ways in which organizations have sought to improve the process of employee appraisal. These include changes in the rating instrument(s) and the training of appraisers, both of which are discussed in the next section.

Box 4.1 *A role play exercise*

General Hospital – Ms Graham, a 25-year-old Nursing Graduate, has recently been appointed the 'G' Grade Sister for Ward 10 (an Acute Surgical Ward). Ms Graham is one of the new generation of nurses, and has ambitions to be a Director of Nursing Services before she is 32 years old.

She applied and successfully obtained the post in preference to Ms Ford, who had held the post of Ward Sister in the ward for three years prior to the Regrading Exercise. Ms Ford is a 30 year old who trained in the hospital and has remained in the same hospital since qualifying as a Registered General Nurse. She is reliable and loyal but perhaps a little unconfident of her own ability. She likes to be liked and she cares deeply for her patients. She is popular with all members of staff. She was slotted in as the second Sister in the Ward. Ms Graham, on the other hand, is very confident and has openly stated no one will stand in the way of her ambitions. In her last Ward she was resented as a 'know-all' and rather 'aloof'. Shortly after her appointment Ms Graham met Ms Ford and agreed that Ms Ford's objectives for the following year should be

- to ensure that the training needs of the staff would be identified and met;
- to prepare the staff for the implications of Project 2000;
- to set nursing standards for discharge of patients into community after surgery

A review meeting has been arranged to take place six months after the meeting when the objectives were agreed between Ms Graham and Ms Ford.

During this time Ms Ford has carried out a full training needs analysis and put together a programme designed to meet these needs. There have been mixed results. The College of Nursing is delighted with the practical experience its students have in this Ward. It is described as the best training area in the hospital. At qualified level the nurses are not too happy. They say they are left too often to their own devices and nothing seems to happen. They are generally forgotten about. Ms Ford rejects this and claims they just don't apply themselves to her training programme and that the continuous turn-over of staff does not allow her to formulate a proper structured programme.

Box 4.1 *continued*

Ms Ford has been placed on the Education/Service Liaison Committee to prepare for the implementation of Project 2000. It is accepted that her contribution to this Committee is very positive (the Committee meets six times a month). Her suggestion that Keep in Touch and Come Back to Nursing courses should be promoted has been accepted as a very worthwhile idea; but she does not want to be involved, claiming she has not time to do so.

Ms Ford has convened meetings of the Ward Staff to set standards relating to discharge of patients. Because of her popularity with the staff she has got their full co-operation and seems to be making progress but has not yet managed to set any standards. She is confident, however, she will do so before the end of the year.

Ms Graham is aware of Ms Ford's activities and is pleased that the College of Nursing has designated her Ward as the best training area of the hospital; but she is also aware of the disquiet among qualified staff about the quality of In-service Training. She does not accept Ms Ford's explanation that the quick turn-over of staff is to blame for the disquiet. Rather, she believes that the turn-over of staff is due to the lack of opportunity for development among qualified staff. She believes that Ms Ford is perhaps concentrating too much on learners to the detriment of qualified staff.

Ms Graham is pleased that Ms Ford has been involved with the preparation of Project 2000, but is concerned that the College may think Ms Ford unco-operative in her refusal to be involved in the Training Programme to bring nurses back to nursing. She does not accept that Ms Ford has no time: after all, her responsibility is minimal compared to Ms Graham's.

Ms Graham is satisfied at the progress which has been made in setting standards but is not confident that Ms Ford can achieve this objective before the end of the year.

Ms Graham feels that Ms Ford requires to be given a sharp reminder to get on with the programme to achieve the set objective. Failure to do so may affect Ms Graham's chances of realizing her own ambitions.

The meeting takes place.

IMPROVING THE PROCESS OF APPRAISALS

In evaluations of the effectiveness of performance appraisal systems, individual researchers have variously looked at inter-rater reliability, bias or discrimination and problems such as leniency error, halo error, etc.[13] The belief that the sorts of problems listed in Table 4.2 have stemmed from an overly subjective process has predictably produced a search for rating instruments which can minimize (if not entirely eliminate) the degree of subjectivity (particularly between individual appraisers) involved. As briefly mentioned in an earlier section, some of the better-known methods or formats include (1) the appraisal of an individual's performance by reference to the attainment of pre-set objectives; (2) the critical incidents approach, whereby the appraiser records (and provides feedback on) incidents of positive and negative behaviour over a given period; (3) the narrative report, whereby the appraiser describes an individual's work behaviour and/or per-formance in their own words, often under certain pre-set guidelines or headings; and (4) behaviourally anchored rating scales. The latter, which has been held to be a relatively objective method, typically involves the following steps:[14]

1   Meetings are held with managers and/or outside consultants to identify several key aspects or categories of performance in particular jobs.

2   The same or other sources of information are used to provide examples of good, average and poor performance for each category of performance in an individual job.

3   A number of such categories or 'anchors' is generated (frequently 6–9 per job) and each is given a value from, for instance, 1 to 7.

4   Appraisers use this format to evaluate the expected behaviour of individual employees holding the job(s) concerned.

The original, underlying job analysis is obviously critical in this approach and many proponents of it argue that employees and their superiors should be actively involved in the process to ensure relatively realistic performance expectations. However, it has been argued that:

> The lengthy job analyses and complex scale construction require a major investment of a company's time and money. A scale designed for use in one department may not apply in another. In fact, separate scales may be necessary for each job category within the same department, since the requirements for good performance may differ markedly. Comparative studies have found that the BARS method, because of its behavioural specificity, results in greater reliability than

do traditional rating scales, and that it may reduce leniency, halo effects and central tending error. But the improvements may be too slight to justify the time and money required. In addition, while BARS scales are suitable for jobs such as production or clerical work, they are harder to devise for managerial positions in which performance cannot easily be reduced to specific kinds of observable behaviour. In such jobs, complex judgement, not easily reduced to a 6-point scale, may be more important than measurable behaviour.[15]

There are in fact certain potential limitations and weaknesses which are specific to virtually all of the individual measuring instruments or formats which have been used in performance appraisal. Indeed despite considerable experimentation and the changing popularity of individual measuring instruments over the course of time, it now appears that 'the literature on formats has shown no marked superiority of one over another. Perhaps most telling is that . . . an extensive review of different formats could find no superiorities for one over the others in terms of psychometric qualities.'[16] As a result, researchers' recommendations concerning an appropriate measuring instrument are frequently limited to an essentially contingency-based one, namely that individual organizations should choose the instrument that suits their particular needs (following a full diagnosis of these) rather than basing their choice on the current popularity of a particular instrument.[17]

In recent years, particularly in the USA, the search for ways to improve the effectiveness of the process of employee appraisal has taken rather a different direction, namely that of training the individuals responsible for carrying out appraisals. A recent review article identified three types of training programmes, as shown in Table 4.6.[18]

Table 4.7 contains an illustration of a training programme designed to try and ensure that appraisers have a reasonably common frame of reference.

A review of a number of studies of the impact of such training programmes reported a number of positive effects,[19] although the external validity of these findings is currently limited by the fact that these studies largely involved student trainees in laboratory or classroom settings. However if, as seems likely, such training programmes become more common in organizational settings, a corresponding volume of research activity is likely to centre around them.

Table 4.6   *Appraisal training programmes*

---

1   *Rater error training*
The aim here is to reduce rating errors by exposing raters to examples of common errors such as leniency, halo, central tendency, etc. As they become familiar with these sources of errors, they are encouraged to avoid them.

2   *Performance dimension training*
The aim here is to familiarize raters with the dimensions along which performance is appraised. This is done by providing descriptions of job qualifications, reviewing existing rating scales or having them participate in the development of such scales.

3   *Performance standards training*
The aim here is to try and get the raters to share common perceptions of performance standards. This is done by presenting samples of job performance to those undergoing the training, together with the ratings assigned to the performance by trained experts.

Source: Adapted from David E. Smith, 'Training Programs for Performance Appraisal: A Review', in Tim O. Peterson (ed.), *Human Resource Management: Readings and Cases*, Houghton Mifflin, Boston, 1990, p. 334.

Table 4.7   *A frame of reference training programme for appraisers*

---

1   Appraisers are given a job description and instructed to identify appropriate criteria for evaluating the job.

2   When agreement is reached, appraisers view a tape of an employee performing a job.

3   Independently, they evaluate the videotaped employee's performance, using the organization's appraisal system.

4   The ratings are compared to each other and to those of job experts.

5   With a trainer as a facilitator, the appraisers present the rationales for their ratings and challenge the rationales of other appraisers.

6   The trainer then helps appraisers to reach consensus regarding the value of specific job behaviours and overall performance.

7   A new videotape is shown, followed by independent ratings.

8   The process continues until consensus is achieved.

Source: Randall S. Schuler and Vandra L. Huber, *Personnel and Human Resource Management*, West Publishing, St Paul, Minn., 4th edition, 1990, p. 219.

DEVELOPMENTS IN APPRAISAL

As indicated earlier in the chapter, performance appraisal has begun to spread from its traditional base among private sector white collar and managerial grades of employees. One direction in which it has begun to move is towards manual groups of employees, often as part of some change towards performance-related pay arrangements. A recent study of appraisal schemes for manual workers in seven case study organizations in Britain,[20] for instance, reported that the performance factors in these schemes were those set out in Table 4.8.

As well as the linkage with performance-related pay arrangements in some existing organizations, such appraisal arrangements for manual employees appear to be particularly associated with new plants where there are relatively few individual job classifications,

Table 4.8   *Performance factors in manual worker appraisal schemes*

*1   Job knowledge/abilities (ability to perform in all aspects of own job)

2   Adaptability/flexibility (ability to cope with change; multi-skilling for craftsmen)

3   Productivity (individual work output)

*4   Quality of work (attention to detail; consistent quality)

*5   Attitude to work (commitment; motivation; enthusiasm)

*6   Interaction with others (communication skills; team working)

7   Originality/initiative (problem-solving)

8   Perception (ability to interpret job requirements)

9   Judgement/use of resources (setting of priorities; ability to plan and organize work)

*10   Attendance/time-keeping (number of and reasons for absences; punctuality)

11   Safety awareness (awareness of health and safety standards)

12   Need for supervision (reliability; degree of independence)

13   Supervisory ability, where appropriate (leadership; ability to train and develop staff)

14   Performance against set targets (the extent to which previously set targets have been met)

*   Most commonly used

Source: IDS Study No. 442, *Appraising Manual Workers' Performance*, September 1989, p. 3.

there are team work arrangements, and responsibility for quality control is built into the job descriptions of production employees. A second, admittedly very limited, line of development in performance appraisal is that of 'reverse-appraisal' in which employees are given the opportunity to report on the performance of their manager. This approach has been initiated in a small number of well-known firms in the USA, such as the Chrysler Corporation.[21] At this stage, however, there is too little experience and research to make any judgement about the impact of arrangement along these lines. Finally, increased concern has been expressed about the limited overlap between research and organizational practice in the performance appraisal area.[22] The essence of this concern is that the issues which currently preoccupy researchers (e.g. cognitive processing of information) and their methodology (i.e. laboratory settings with student subjects) are not closely aligned with organizational realities. These concerns were, at least to some extent, reflected in a recent review article which concluded as follows:

> The conclusion we draw from this and earlier reviews of appraisal research is that our knowledge of the rating process has expanded greatly in recent years but remains fragmented. This fragmentation appears to be caused by fundamental differences between the measurement aspects of appraisal research and the organizational purposes of performance appraisal. From a measurement perspective, the necessity to isolate specific effects has resulted in single-issue studies conducted in laboratory settings. Moreover, most of this research addresses the consistency, not necessarily the relevance, of the measurement. The effects of prior expectations, prior knowledge of performance, and memory decay have been studied separately from the alternative uses of appraisals (administrative or developmental), the characteristics of raters/ratees, or the types of scales and formats employed. Furthermore, certain appraisal issues have received considerable attention but others have been virtually ignored. Moreover, research is only beginning to address how context affects employee perceptions of appraisal, their reactions to appraisal outcomes and how appraisal purpose (administrative versus developmental) moderates these relationships.[23]

The failure to embed appraisal research in context is particularly worrying. Obviously the extent of actual change in appraisal systems can easily be exaggerated (see Table 4.1), but the changing environmental context confronting organizations is currently leading to at least a partial rethinking of many appraisal practices and it is to be hoped that research becomes increasingly attuned to any resulting changes in organizational practice in the appraisal area.

APPENDIX: EMPLOYEE COUNSELLING

APPROACHES TO COUNSELLING

The term 'employee counselling' hardly figures at all in the strategic HRM literature. Nevertheless in the preceding discussion of employee appraisal it was observed that 'best practice' appraisal interviewing skills, particularly for developmental purposes, involve essentially an employee counselling orientation. Moreover it is apparent, at least implicitly, that interpersonal skills of a counselling, coaching or influencing nature are essential in many of the most substantive areas of human resource management that will confront line managers. This is most obviously the case in the area of career planning and development, particularly as organizations have increasingly adopted mentoring programmes (see Chapter 6). Furthermore, the counselling role itself has spread beyond its traditional basis of dealing with individual employee problems/difficulties (e.g. high absence) into a number of areas and issues raised by changing organizational circumstances. For example, as organizations have laid off employees in response to business pressures, line managers have, frequently with some outside specialist assistance, found themselves involved in redundancy counselling exercises.

Accordingly I review a number of aspects of the techniques and skills of employee counselling on the grounds that the process and interpersonal skills of counselling are important in their own right and may contribute to improvements in a number of related areas of human resource management.

There are a number of different schools of counselling. For example, one review has identified five main schools of thought: psychoanalytic approaches, client-centred approaches, behavioural approaches, cognitive approaches and affective approaches.[24] In workplace settings the client-centred approach has been increasingly favoured. This is a non-directive approach, particularly associated with the work of Carl Rogers,[25] that starts from the position of an employee who is experiencing some problem, with the basic aim being to help them recognize, analyse and resolve the problem or resolve the situation (i.e. learn to live with the problem). Table 4A.1 shows some conditions which have been identified as essential for achieving success with this approach.[26]

In essence the non-directive, or client-centred, approach involves relatively little input from the counsellor in the sense of proposing or advocating a solution to the problem. Rather the counsellor seeks to

Table 4A.1   *Prerequisites for non-directive counselling*

`1   *Empathy*

- This involves the counsellor attempting to see and understand the situation as perceived by the person being counselled.

- For this to occur the counsellor must avoid making any prior judgements or assumptions.

- This notion is quite different from sympathy.

2   *Congruence*

- This involves the counsellor recognizing their own feelings concerning the issue and sharing them with the person being counselled.

- This does not necessarily mean that the counsellor has to agree with everything the person being counselled says.

3   *Non-possessive warmth*

- The counsellor must convey a genuine sense of interest in and concern for the person being counselled.

Source: Adapted from Roger Bennett, *Managing People*, Kogan Page, London, 1989, pp.162–7.

facilitate the recognition and analysis of the problem by the person being counselled, with the latter being the one who must come up with a solution which is suitable for themselves. This approach is frequently contrasted with a more directive, or task-centred one, in which the counsellor adopts a more pro-active stance by proposing a number of possible solutions. In Table 4A.2 these differing approaches are illustrated by reference to dealing with an employee who is frequently absent.

There still remain differing opinions as to how much direction a counsellor should seek to impose in the interview process. For example, some individuals favour a contingency approach in which the amount of direction should vary according to the circumstances of each particular case. There is also the possibility, not to say desirability, of varying the amount of direction according to the particular stage of the interviewing process. Indeed it has become increasingly common to view and discuss a counselling interview as a sequential process involving a number of different phases or stages. Table 4A.3 indicates one such view of the counselling interview.

Table 4A.2 *Directive and non-directive approaches to employee absence*

Directive approach	Non-directive approach
1 Get all the *facts* about the person's absence (avoid hearsay, rumour and opinion).	1 Describe the absenteeism problem in detail.
2 Determine that negative disciplinary action has been taken consistently against other employees who have committed similar infractions.	2 Indicate why it concerns you.
	3 Ask for employee's reasons and listen openly to the explanation.
3 Ensure that the employee knew it was an infraction.	4 Indicate the situation must be changed and ask for ideas for solving the problem.
4 Talk to employee in private.	5 Discuss each idea and offer your help.
5 Confine the discussion to the facts of the infraction only, keeping out 'personalities' and not implying the person is 'bad'.	6 Agree on specific action to be taken and set a specific follow-up date.
6 Keep calm.	
7 Give the worker the chance to express his views.	
8 Get the worker to agree to the facts of absence.	
9 Fit the punishment (reprimand, suspension) to the facts in a consistent manner.	
10 Don't harbour a grudge – consider the incident closed.	
11 Be as friendly as possible.	
12 Document the action taken.	
13 Follow up to check on improvement.	

Table 4A.3   *The three phases of counselling*

Phase	Counsellor tasks	Client tasks	Techniques and skills (Counsellor)
I	Understanding	Defining the problem	Suspending judgement, active listening skills, accuracy, understanding and acceptance
II	Challenging	Redefining the problem	Empathy, understanding and communication of understanding, probing, challenging
III	Resourcing	Managing the problem	Co-acting, giving feedback, advising and recommending

Source: Michael Reddy, *The Manager's Guide to Counselling at Work*, British Psychological Society and Methuen, London, 1987.

THE COUNSELLING INTERVIEW

Before a counselling interview with an employee with a current performance problem a number of background considerations need to be addressed. Such considerations will typically involve gathering all the relevant factual information on the nature of the performance problem and considering any other parties or individuals who may be relevant to the process.[27] This being done, one has to choose an appropriate time and place for the interview in which the counsellor should, according to some commentators, always follow two 'golden rules': make it easy for the person being counselled to do what you want; and, secondly, handle the problem, not the person.[28] In essence this translates into a strategy for a counselling interview which should proceed as follows:[29]

- Agree standards.
- Agree that there has been a gap.
- Agree the size of the gap.
- Agree who has responsibility for reducing the gap.
- Agree on actions to reduce the gap.
- Agree measures and time for reducing the gap.
- Set time for follow-up meeting.

The leading skills required of a manager to ensure the successful carrying through of such an interview strategy are those of asking

Table 4A.4   *A checklist of individual counselling skills*

---

1   The ability to establish rapport by building on an existing relationship.

2   Questioning skills, such as the early use of open questions, to get them talking freely.

3   Active listening skills:
(a)   Concentrate and look interested.
(b)   Actively look for the main points of the problem.
(c)   Seek to identify any unspoken meanings, feelings, etc. that may lie behind what is said.
(d)   Note any contradictions, but don't confront these at the time.
(e)   Tolerate silences.
(f)   Avoid making early interpretations of what is said.

4   The ability to proceed at the pace of the person being counselled.

5   The ability to summarize and clarify the main points of the problem in a non-critical way.

6   The ability to foster the insight of the person being counselled: help frame the questions which the person concerned needs to ask and answer.

7   The ability to separate process and content: knowing when the person being counselled would welcome an input from the counsellor.

8   The skills of problem-solving:
(a)   The ability to widen the perspective of the person being counselled in the search for solutions.
(b)   The ability to help the person being counselled identify, focus and discuss the advantages and disadvantages of different possible courses of action.
(c)   The ability to encourage and support the person being counselled when they make and implement decisions to deal with the problem.

Source: Adapted from Gerald Egan, *The Skilled Helper*, Wadsworth, Belmont, Calif., 1975.

questions, testing understanding and summarizing. Table 4A.4 provides a further checklist of these particular skills.

A counselling interview, like an appraisal interview, places a premium on interpersonal skills centred around the process of communication. It has in fact been suggested that 'a surprisingly large proportion of communication (perhaps 70 per cent) between people takes place in the form of body language; yet this area rarely receives as much attention as its importance might lead one to expect.'[30] Unfortunately the complexities and uncertainties of body language are many and varied which makes any attempt at interpretation and understanding far from straightforward. Nevertheless any manager

Table 4A.5   *Non-verbal cues and possible underlying processes*

Non-verbal cues	Possible processes
Furrowed forehead, knitted brows	Thinking, rehearsing in an internal dialogue; giving self a bad time
Tapping foot and/or drumming fingers	Impatience; irritation; anger; agitation
Avoiding eye contact	Discomfort; anxiety; suspicion; confusion
Intense eye contact	Anger; concern; sexual attraction
Rapid, light breathing	Anxiety; fear; distress
Irregular breathing	Approaching an important issue; forcing self; controlling feelings
Deep, slow breathing	Supporting strong feelings – often precedes catharsis
Physical stroking of face, arms and neck	Comforting self or holding back from stroking others or holding back the need for comforting
Scratching, pinching, gouging, severe pressing	Punishing self, reflecting self-criticism or holding back from provoking or punishing someone else
Controlled, low, quiet voice	Suppressing energy/interest; excitement
Fast, high voice	Excitement; tension; fear
Tightness/rigidity in jaw, neck, shoulder	Holding back anger, sadness
Clenching fists, tightness in arms	Holding back anger, sadness
Body leaning forward in chair	Interested; concerned; about to 'happen'
Body leaning backward in chair, sprawling	Detached; uninvolved; unconcerned
Arms tightly folded; legs tightly crossed	Defending; putting up barriers; resistance
Lounging extravagantly in the chair	Detachment; cynicism; discounting
Hand covering mouth	Hiding; playing games; uncertain
Finger jabbing	Critical; putting down; fencing with

Source: Keri Phillips and Tony Fraser, *The Management of Interpersonal Skills Training*, Gower, Aldershot, 1982, p. 74.

Table 4A.6 *A self-evaluation checklist for a counselling interview*

---

1 Did I put the employee at ease?

2 How did I cope with anxiety or hostility?

3 Did I listen effectively and encourage the employee to talk?

4 Did I see the problem from the employee's point of view?

5 Did I try to understand the employee's silences?

6 Did I go at the employee's own speed?

7 Did I provide relevant factual information at the appropriate time?

8 Did I clarify confused ideas?

9 Did I give the interview a pattern or framework?

10 Did I discuss with the employee what the meeting was intended to achieve and how it would be carried out?

11 Did I impose insights or did I encourage them?

12 Did I avoid unnecessary emotional involvement and treat the problem in a detached, objective way?

13 Did I give advice that I was qualified to give?

14 Did I not pry unnecessarily into the private life of the employee, his family or friends?

Source: *Cromer's Guide to Interviews*, Cromer Publications, New Malden, 1985, reproduced in *Managing People*, The Open University Business School, Milton Keynes, 1986, pp. 16–17.

involved in a counselling interview needs to be sensitive to the signals of their own body language and that of the individual being interviewed. In view of this fact, Table 4A.5 lists some of the better-known 'cues' of body language with some suggestions concerning the possible underlying processes.

It is generally held that the quality of counselling (as well as appraisal interviews) can be improved by interpersonal skills training. At the same time experience is also likely to facilitate an improvement in the process over time if the individual conducting such interviews remains sensitive to the task of evaluating and seeking to learn and improve on their own past performance. To this end it is frequently urged that managers acting as counsellors should review their interviewing techniques and performance according to certain criteria. Table 4A.6 provides one such checklist. Finally, Box 4A.1 contains two role play exercises designed to illustrate the use of the techniques discussed in this section.

Box 4A.1   *Two role play exercises*

Exercise 1

Historically, company X has employed relatively few engineers. Those engineers who did work for the company were located in a separate division, called A. A was essentially a service-type organization for the rest of the company.

However, company X has recently acquired another company which has substantially increased the number of engineers who now work for it. The population of engineers is now split between division A and division B.

Ideally the senior management of company X would like all their engineers 'under one roof', preferably in division A. This they feel would provide the engineers with an enhanced sense of identity and broader based career opportunities. To this end, they have already indicated that in the future newly recruited engineers will exclusively be based in division A.

However, they face a problem with their existing population of engineers. The board are unwilling to instruct or order all existing engineers to move to division A, as this would be inconsistent with the sort of organization culture they are seeking to develop. The current engineers have therefore been given a choice; they just opt for A or B by a certain date. The line managers to whom the engineers are responsible are to provide a series of counselling interviews to all engineers to help inform the decision they will take.

The 'grapevine' has already indicated the existence of some strong feelings on the part of engineers regarding the desirability of being located in A or B. To some of the engineers A is undesirable because its service-type orientation may mean relatively short assignments outside Britain that will be a disruption to their home life. However, if they elect to stay in B (where no new engineers will be recruited) will their longer-term career prospects in the company be damaged?

At the counselling sessions, senior management anticipate three different responses from engineers: (1) I will happily move to A; (2) I will never move to A; (3) I am confused and uncertain. As a line manager involved in these counselling sessions, how would you approach this problem, given that senior management ideally wants all engineers in A?

Box 4A.1 *continued*

Exercise 2

A newly graduated PhD takes up a research appointment at another university. He is well-trained (holding three degrees from well- known universities), has already published a journal article from his PhD research, received good references and interviewed relatively well. The research appointment is for two years, with the individual concerned being the senior research fellow responsible for planning and co-ordinating the activities of two junior research fellows on the externally funded project. The senior research fellow reports to the head of department who is also the grant holder for the project.

After some six months, the department head begins to have some worries concerning the extent of progress with the research. The senior research fellow spends long hours in the office, but no overall plan or design for the project has been prepared. Furthermore some company contacts provided by the department head for possible case study purposes have not been actively pursued. At periodic meetings of the research team the senior research fellow claims still to be reviewing the existing literature with a view to providing a solid basis for the development of the project. However, one of the junior research fellows, who has befriended the senior researcher, indicates to the department head that the senior fellow has just separated from his wife and has on one or two occasions been seen drinking heavily in local pubs. Furthermore the other junior research fellow comes to the department head to express his concern that the project is going nowhere; he feels there is no leadership to the project, he is learning or gaining nothing from it and is beginning to think seriously of applying for a research post elsewhere. Subsequently, the senior research fellow turns up at a departmental meeting clearly the worse for drink, and has to be persuaded to leave.

CONCERNS ABOUT COUNSELLING

There remain some long-standing concerns about counselling in the workplace. For instance, there is the problem of evaluating its success given the difficulties of establishing what are the appropriate criteria and to what extent they are measurable; indeed the subject matter of this appendix is most obviously differentiated from the discussion elsewhere in the book by its essential lack of any reference to the results and findings of empirical research. Secondly, there is concern at the practical level about possible role conflicts for managers involved in counselling, particularly with regard to the receipt and handling of confidential information.

And finally, something of a gap has opened up between actual organizational practice and the starting premise of the employee counselling literature. The latter is overwhelmingly concerned with individuals who have a variety of problems that are impeding their current on-the-job performance, whereas in many organizations the practice of counselling has begun to spread to issues and activities that have very little to do with the problems of individual employees. For instance, financial and career counselling are increasingly prominent features of outplacement programmes in situations of plant closures and large-scale employee lay-offs and redundancies. Although such counselling is frequently conducted by outside specialist consultants, line managers may nevertheless find themselves (see example 1 in Box 4A.1) involved in non- (individual employee) problem-based counselling situations where the appropriate techniques may not be entirely those contained in the available literature.

REFERENCES

1   Cited in Charles Fombrun, Noel M. Tichy and Mary Anne Devanna, *Strategic Human Resource Management*, Wiley, New York, 1984, p. 47.
2   ACAS Advisory Booklet No. 11, *Employee Appraisal*, pp. 8–11.
3   Allan M. Mohrman, Susan M. Resnick-West and Edward E. Lawler, *Designing Performance Appraisal Systems*, Jossey-Bass, San Francisco, 1989.
4   Randall S. Schuler and Vandra L. Huber, *Personnel and Human Resource Management*, Wiley, New York, 1984, p. 47.
5   Michael Beer, 'Note on Performance Appraisal', in Michael Beer and Bert Spector (eds.), *Readings in Human Resource Management*, Free Press, New York, 1985, p. 316.
6   Clinton O. Longenecker, Henry P. Sims and Dennis A. Gioia, 'Behind the Mask: The Politics of Employee Appraisal', *Academy of Management Executive*, 1 (3), August 1987, p. 191.
7   Robert D. Bretz, George T. Milkovich and Walter Read, 'The Current State of Performance Appraisal Research and Practice: Concerns, Directions and Implications', *Journal of Management*, 18 (2), 1992, p. 334.
8   Norman R. F. Maier, 'Three Types of Appraisal Interviews', *Personnel*, March–April 1958.
9   See, for example, Jane Allan, *How to Solve Your People Problems*, Kogan Page, London, 1989, Chapter 5.

10 K. N. Wexley, 'Appraisal Interview', in R. Berk (ed.), *Performance Assessment: Methods and Applications*, Johns Hopkins University Press, Baltimore, 1986.

11 Mohrman et al., *Designing Performance Appraisal Systems*, p. 154.

12 Donald B. Fedor, 'The Many Faces of Feedback in the Performance Appraisal Process', in Gerald R. Ferris, Kendrith M. Rowland and M. Ronald Buckley (eds.), *Human Resource Management: Perspectives and Issues*, Allyn and Bacon, Boston, Second edition, 1990, pp. 196–201.

13 Michael J. Kavanagh, 'Evaluating Performance', in Kendrith M. Rowland and Gerald R. Ferris (eds.), *Personnel Management*, Allyn and Bacon, Boston, 1982, pp. 202–3.

14 This is essentially based on ACAS Advisory Booklet No. 11, *Employee Appraisal*, p. 16.

15 Berkeley Rice, 'Performance Review: The Job Nobody Likes', in Gerald R. Ferris, Kendrith M. Rowland and M. Ronald Buckley (eds.), *Human Resource Management: Perspectives and Issues*, Allyn and Bacon, Boston, Second edition, 1990, p. 184.

16 Kavanagh, 'Evaluating Performance', p. 208. The reference here is to F. J. Landy and J. L. Farr, 'Performance Rating', *Psychological Bulletin*, 87, 1980, pp. 72–107.

17 Kavanagh, 'Evaluating Performance', p. 208.

18 David E. Smith, 'Training Programs for Performance Appraisal: A Review', in Tim O. Peterson (ed.), *Human Resource Management: Readings and Cases*, Houghton Mifflin, Boston, 1990, p. 334.

19 Smith, 'Training Programs', pp. 342–4.

20 IDS Study No. 442, *Appraising Manual Workers' Performance*, September 1989.

21 J. E. Santora, 'Rating the Boss at Chrysler', *Personnel Journal*, 71 (5), May 1992, pp. 38–45.

22 Bretz et al., 'Current State of Performance Appraisal Research and Practice', pp. 321–2.

23 Ibid., pp. 329–30.

24 B. Hopson, 'Counselling in Work Situations', in Peter B. Warr (ed.), *Psychology at Work*, Penguin, Harmondsworth, 1978, pp. 311–13.

25 C. Rogers, *On Becoming a Person*, Houghton Mifflin, Boston, 1961.

26 Roger Bennett, *Managing People*, Kogan Page, London, 1989, pp. 162–7.

27 Valerie Stewart and Andrew Stewart, *Managing the Poor Performer*, Gower, Aldershot, 1988, pp. 93–100.

28 Ibid., p. 102.

29 Ibid., p. 105.

30 Keri Phillips and Tony Fraser, *The Management of Interpersonal Skills Training*, Gower, Aldershot, 1982, p. 67.

5

REWARD AND COMPENSATION SYSTEMS

INTRODUCTION

In the judgement of many individuals the nature of reward and compensation systems is central to the notion and discussions of strategic human resource management. This is because the nature of such systems can, at least in principle, so strongly shape, reinforce and complement many of the leading individual themes so prominent in the strategic HRM literature. For instance, in Chapter 2 the discussion of the notion of corporate culture made some limited reference to the potential role of reward systems in either reinforcing or changing the nature of organizational culture. This proposition has been taken a stage further in a recent book by Lawler which argues that the reward system of any organization needs to embody certain core principles (concerning matters such as pay for performance, market comparisons, internal comparisons, benefits, process issues and due process), principles which should reflect both the competitive strategy and the core values of the organization.[1] Secondly, the importance of establishing a multi-skilled and flexible workforce is frequently stressed in the HRM literature. And to this end, reward and compensation systems are seen to be particularly important in view of their potential for encouraging certain aspects of functional flexibility such as multi-skilling (via pay for knowledge schemes) and team working (via group performance payments), while the very notion of financial flexibility pivots on the idea of contingent compensation systems in which individuals share in the rewards of overall organizational performance. Finally, the discussion in Chapter 2 outlined Walton's view of the major HRM demands involved in seeking to move from a 'workforce control' to a 'workforce commitment' approach. These demands included compensation policies involving individual pay being linked to skill attainment, gain-sharing and profit-sharing schemes and minimum status differentials in order to de-emphasize the hierarchy of organizational arrangements and practices.

This prior discussion provides the obvious lead-in to this chapter where I discuss, in turn, performance-related pay, profit-sharing, gain-sharing and pay for knowledge schemes and single status arrangements. However, before considering these individual subjects in turn the next section discusses two larger matters, concerning reward and compensation systems, namely some of the strategic issues involved in designing them, and their conceptual or theoretical underpinnings.

A LARGER PERSPECTIVE ON COMPENSATION AND REWARD SYSTEMS

According to leading compensation theorists there should ideally be a two-way relationship between reward systems and strategic planning, which requires an organization to consider the essence of its compensation philosophy.[2] The need for such consideration in order to establish such a linkage follows from the potentially powerful impact of compensation systems on organizational performance via a number of routes, such as attracting and retaining labour, motivating employees and reinforcing organization culture, etc. Accordingly Table 5.1 lists some of the leading issues and questions that need to be considered.

The point stressed by Lawler is that there are no universal, or one set of best practice, answers to these questions. The answers are contingent upon the operating circumstances and objectives of individual organizations, although all organizations should ideally examine and explore the various implications raised by this set of questions.

Secondly, as a prime purpose of all compensation–reward systems is to enhance the motivation of individual employees, and hence their current on-the-job performance, some consideration needs to be given to the differing theories of employee motivation. Over time, attempts to understand employee motivation have moved from needs-based theories (e.g. Maslow) to theories viewing behaviour as caused by some cognitive process. The leading cognitive based theories are in fact expectancy theory, goal-setting theory and equity theory.[3] In essence expectancy theory argues that employees will be motivated to perform a certain type of behaviour if (1) they believe it is possible to perform at the expected level of behaviour, (2) this behavioural performance will be rewarded, and (3) the rewards on offer are ones which they value. Goal-setting theory argues that an organization can strongly influence on-the-job behaviour by influencing

Table 5.1   *Strategic issues in the design of compensation systems*

---

1   *The basis for rewards*
The issue is whether pay is to be job-based or skills or competence-based.

2   *Pay for performance*
Questions here include the extent of performance-based pay, the particular aspects of performance and whether it is based on individual or group performance.

3   *Market position*
The issue here is how their reward system compares to that of other organizations.

4   *Internal–external pay comparison-orientated*
The issue here is the relative emphasis given to the attainment of internal or external equity.

5   *Centralized–decentralized reward strategy*
The issue here is the extent to which one seeks to standardize reward systems throughout the organization.

6   *Degree of hierarchy*
The question here concerns whether an organization seeks a relatively hierarchical or egalitarian reward system.

7   *Reward mix*
The issue here is the balance between pay and benefits.

8   *Process issues*
(a)   Communication policy   The question is how relatively open or closed communication policy concerning reward systems should be adopted.
(b)   Decision-making practices   The question here concerns the extent or range of individuals involved in the relevant processes of decision-making.

9   *Reward system congruence*
The need is to ensure that the various design features of reward systems are internally consistent and consistent with the nature of larger organizational strategy.

Source: Adapted from Edward E. Lawler III, 'The Strategic Design of Reward Systems', in Charles Fombrun, Noel M. Tichy and Mary Anne Devanna, *Strategic Human Resource Management*, Wiley, New York, 1984, pp. 131–46.

employees' goals, with more challenging goals and employee participation in the goal-setting process being especially likely to result in relatively high performance. Finally, equity theory contends that employees compare their inputs (e.g. abilities, effort, experience, etc.) with their outcomes (e.g. pay), which constitutes their ratio of exchange. Individuals then compare their ratio of exchange with those of other relevant individuals, which forms the basis of their perceptions of equity or inequity. For example, a situation of perceived inequity arises where individuals believe that unequal ratios of exchange exist between themselves and comparable individuals, with the result that they may seek to alter their inputs, outputs or reference points.

Each of these theories has its advocates and supporters, although all are subject to some conceptual uncertainties or question marks and in all cases some of the empirical evidence is not fully supportive.[4] Furthermore there exist alternative theories which stress the key importance of environmental contingencies, whereas these three are overwhelmingly driven by some internal psychological process. It is important for managers to be aware of the debates, controversy, disagreement and uncertainty surrounding motivation theory because different compensation and reward systems in individual organizations tended to be grounded, if only implicitly, in different views of employee motivation. For instance, performance-related pay schemes generally tend to be based on notions of expectancy theory, a body of theory which, as noted above, is not fully subscribed to by all academic researchers.

Finally it is useful to consider some of the more recent general changes in compensation and reward systems that academics feel are or should be taking place in individual organizations. Kanter, for example, points to a variety of economic, social and organizational pressures which are gradually shifting the basis for pay from that of status to that of contribution.[5] This change is indicated by the increased attention being given to merit pay, gain-sharing plans, pay for knowledge schemes and comparable worth issues. However, Newman and Milkovich go further to argue that new compensation arrangements should increasingly address not just the issue of distributive justice, but also the issue of procedural justice.[6] In their view compensation systems need to be (and are indeed slowly beginning to be) concerned with establishing consistent, accurate, ethical, representative, etc. ground rules for determining the size of employee rewards. This concern with procedural justice has arisen as the result of increased product market competition limiting the ability of individual organizations to go on providing ever larger increases in wages.

Box 5.1   *Moving to performance-related pay*

In 1986 an employee attitude survey in the organization concerned revealed considerable dissatisfaction with regard to employee appraisals, the identification of training needs, succession planning and career development. These findings led to the establishment of an internal task force which produced a number of recommendations for change in these areas. These recommendations formed an important part of the background to the 1988 pay negotiations in which agreement was reached on the principle of developing a new integrated grading structure covering all manual, craft, clerical and technical level jobs. Such a structure would replace the 72 rates of pay and would simplify the 250+ job titles which then existed within these groups.

The new integrated grading and pay structure (from 1990) involves individual salaries being a function of job placement and grading, and individual contribution. The former were determined by evaluation using Hay criteria.* Every grade has a normal maximum pay band which most job holders can attain within five years given acceptable performance. For some jobs a minimum rate is determined by collective bargaining arrangements. As to individual contribution, the previous system of merit reviews has been replaced by performance reviews which emphasize the achievement of mutually agreed goals. For lower level jobs (i.e. below project manager or section manager) more emphasis is placed on incremental pay increases (based on experience and length of service) relative to individual performance, whereas for higher level jobs the emphasis is reversed.

*   Hay is a management consultancy particularly noted for its points rating system for job-evaluation-based payment schemes.

PERFORMANCE-RELATED PAY

An integral element of the general movement from 'status to contribution' based payment systems (noted above) has been the increased introduction and adoption of various forms of performance-related pay. One illustration of such a movement is set out in Box 5.1.

This being said, it is important to recognize that performance-

Table 5.2 *Ten questions to answer before implementing a performance-based pay system*

---

1 Is pay valued by employees?

2 What is the objective(s) of the performance-based pay system?

3 Are the values of the organization conducive to a performance-based pay system?

4 What steps will be taken to ensure that employees and management are committed to the system?

5 Can performance be accurately measured? If not, what type of an appraisal system will be used?

6 How frequently will performance be measured or evaluated?

7 What level of aggregation (individual, group or organization) will be used to ˙distribute rewards?

8 How will pay be tied to performance (e.g. merit increase, bonus, commission, incentive)?

9 Does the organization have sufficient financial resources to make performance-based pay meaningful?

10 What steps will be taken to control and monitor the system?

Source: Randall S. Schuler and Vandra L. Huber, *Personnel and Human Resource Management*, West Publishing, St Paul, Minn., 4th edition, 1990, p. 308.

related pay is a very heterogeneous set of measures, some of which have been around for a relatively long time. Under this broad heading one can include individual piecework, payment by results, merit pay, group bonuses, payments linked to overall organizational performance and numerous variants of each of these. In recent times the spread of performance-related pay arrangements into the public sector has been particularly noticeable in a number of countries. For example, in Britain some 400,000 (out of a total of 585,000) civil servants in 1989 had some part of their pay determined by performance appraisal.[7] The spread of such arrangements has certainly not been without its difficulties and controversies. For example, the operation of performance-related pay arrangements in the Inland Revenue Service in Britain has been criticized for involving confused targets and allowing inadequate time for satisfactory performance appraisals, with a workforce survey suggesting that only a small minority believed that the scheme had enhanced their job motivation and performance (*Financial Times*, 27 September 1991).

This sort of controversy about performance-related pay is not unique to the British public sector. Indeed Lawler has argued:

> Having a true merit pay or promotion system is often easier said than done, however. Indeed, it has been observed that many organizations would be better off if they did not try to relate pay and promotion to performance and relied on other bases for motivating performance. The logic of this statement stems from the difficulty of specifying what kind of performance is desired and then determining whether, in fact, it has been demonstrated. There is ample evidence that a poorly designed and administered reward system can do more harm than good.[8]

In view of the difficulties of effectively and successfully operating a performance-related pay system, it has been suggested that any organization contemplating such a system should consider the list of questions set out in Table 5.2 (p. 107).

In general one can distinguish between performance-related pay schemes at the individual, group and organization-wide levels. According to Lawler such schemes can be variously evaluated according to: (1) effectiveness in creating the perception that pay is tied to performance; (2) negative side effects (e.g. social ostracism of good performers, defensive behaviour, false data about performance); (3) encouragement of employee co-operation; and (4) acceptance by employees.[9] In general his review leads to the following conclusions:

1   Individual-based schemes perform better than group and organization-wide ones in creating the perception that pay is tied to performance. In the latter cases important influences on an individual's behaviour and performance are exogenous to the control of individuals.

2   Individual schemes based on objective measures of performance produce the strongest perceived connection between pay and performance.

3   Individual bonus and incentive plans at the non-management level are the most likely to produce negative side effects, particularly in situations of relatively low trust and where performance is subjectively based.

4   Group and organization-wide schemes are generally rated higher than individual-based schemes in generating employee co-operation.

5   Employee acceptance of all performance-based schemes is only relatively moderate, with the least acceptance being for individual-based schemes because of the perceived difficulties of administering them fairly and encouraging competitive relationships between employees.

There are numerous articles, based on research in various countries, which stress the relatively wide gap which frequently exists between the ideal of a pay for performance system and the reality of its workings.[10] This gap is often attributed to the problems of expectancy theory (the underlying conceptual basis of performance-related pay schemes), the inadequacy of the process of performance appraisal (see Chapter 4) and the economic and budgetary realities of organizational life. Resource constraints may limit the ability to fund adequate merit-based increases over an extended period; some commentators, for instance, have suggested that only a 10–15 per cent merit-based increase is likely to have much impact on employee motivation.[11] A number of these concerns are reflected in one practitioners' guide to performance-related pay, or appraisal-related pay (ARP) as they choose to call it, where it was observed that:

> If not suitably designed and introduced sensibly into an environment where trust is high and there is a readiness to adapt to the change, employee relations may suffer. ARP may not only fail to motivate but may in fact demotivate. Employees may soon become discouraged if they are not aware of the levels of performance they need to attain or where ARP awards are not applied consistently across the eligible participants. There may be doubts about the credibility of the scheme where financial constraints, for example by the use of budgets or 'quotas', unnecessarily restrict the extent or amount of ARP awards. A carefully developed scheme should minimize the scope for complaints about subjectivity in assessment and divisiveness in operation. In particular, the ARP scheme should be designed to avoid any tendency to mark higher each year to retain employees during periods of labour shortage. Any beneficial link between performance and reward may be lost with pay costs rising but without a corresponding rise in corporate or individual performance.[12]

As the above suggests, there are a number of potential problems involved in the operation of performance-related pay arrangements and certainly there is no guaranteed formula for the successful introduction and operation of such a scheme. However, Table 5.3 does contain a number of necessary, if not sufficient, conditions for the effective operation of such arrangements.

Table 5.3 *Key requirements for performance based pay*

1 *Trust in management*

2 *Absence of performance constraints*
Variables exogenous to the control of individual employees because of interdependent jobs or external circumstances are the concern here.

3 *Trained supervisors and managers*
Training is needed in the skills of the performance appraisal process.

4 *Good measurement systems*
The information systems which underlie the process of performance appraisal need to contain objective information on the specific requirements and outcomes of individual jobs.

5 *Ability to pay*
The merit component of the salary increase budget must be sufficient to motivate performance and fund the increases.

6 *Valid job evaluation and externally competitive pay levels*
Merit pay increases must be integrated into a larger set of reward arrangements concerned with internal and external equity.

7 *Distinction between cost of living, seniority and merit*
Evidence needs to be provided as to the relative proportions contributed by each of these sources to an overall wage increase.

8 *Open pay policy*
Employees must clearly understand the workings of the arrangements.

9 *Flexible reward schedule*
The importance of the timing of a merit increase (as well as its amount) may argue for different merit dates for different groups of employees.

10 *Consistency with the prevailing culture*

Source: Frederick S. Hills, Robert M. Madigan, K. Dow Scott and Steven E. Markham, 'Tracking the Merit of Merit Pay', in Gerald R. Ferris, Kendrith M. Rowland and M. Ronald Buckley (eds.), *Human Resource Management: Perspectives and Issues*, Allyn and Bacon, Boston, 2nd edition, 1990, pp. 248–9.

A similar recent list in Britain also urged that the effective operation of performance-related pay arrangements requires strong management commitment, a top down introduction process, the maintenance of a competitive base salary structure, a valid job evaluation system, a well designed, accurate and trusted appraisal system, a comprehensive and effective communication strategy, a speed of introduction that fits the organizational culture, regular and systematic training for managers in performance review and feedback, and an on-going monitoring and evaluation process (*Financial Times*, 20 July 1992). Other commentators have also stressed the importance of prior consultation and discussion with employees and their representatives in order to ensure that the arrangements are understood and accepted by those covered under the arrangements.[13] The potential importance of this latter consideration follows from the earlier observation that payment systems increasingly need to incorporate the key elements of procedural justice. Finally it is important to emphasize that a poorly designed and poorly implemented performance-related pay scheme may not only fail to deliver the benefits that management expected or hoped for, but may actually be a source of new problems.[14]

PROFIT-SHARING, EMPLOYEE SHAREHOLDING AND GAIN-SHARING SCHEMES

Various forms of profit-sharing and share ownership schemes have become increasingly popular in a number of advanced industrialized economies in recent years. For example, a number of surveys in Britain, the United States and Canada in the mid-1980s revealed that around a quarter to a third of the establishments surveyed had some form of profit-sharing scheme.[15] (It needs to be recognized that not all employees in the organizations concerned will be covered by the arrangements.) Furthermore, such growth appears to have continued in more recent years. For instance, a recent survey in Britain reported that:

> there can be little doubt that there was a very substantial growth in profit-sharing arrangements between 1984 and 1990. The proportion of establishments in the industrial and commercial sector of the economy that had either cash-based or share-based profit-sharing rose from 18 to 43 per cent. Both manufacturing and services were affected, although services showed the faster rate of increase ... The growth of profit-sharing arrangements was strongly confirmed by our panel data. A third of establishments that were not covered by a scheme in 1984 were covered by one in 1990. Those adopting schemes outnumbered those abandoning them by a ratio of nearly six to one.[16]

A number of economists have argued that the increased adoption and diffusion of such schemes will produce important macro-level benefits for the economy concerned, notably an improved trade-off relationship between the level of unemployment and inflation.[17] For this reason, governments in a number of countries have sought to encourage the increased adoption of such schemes through the provision of tax-based incentives.[18] There are basically two comments to make about this process of encouraging the adoption of profit-sharing schemes. The first is the view of a number of industrial relations researchers to the effect that a more comprehensive spread of such schemes would require certain complementary changes in management practices: such changes include an increased sharing (with employees and their representatives) of financial and business planning information, and ensuring that senior management pay and bonus levels do not move in an inconsistent manner with the 'pay-outs' from the profit-sharing scheme for the rest of the workforce.[19] Secondly, it needs to be recognized that arrangements encouraged by tax concessions do not always operate in the way envisaged, or hoped for, by the policy-makers. For example, in Britain profit-related pay arrangements have been encouraged by tax concessions, but one review of their operation suggests that linking pay to profits has not (as the government hoped) replaced a significant part of basic pay;[20] instead it has become a bonus paid on top of basic pay.

There has been considerable discussion of, and research concerning, the impact of profit-sharing schemes. The alleged advantages (to management) of such schemes include enhanced productivity, reduced turnover rates, improved employee commitment to and identification with the organization, etc. One recent review of evidence from a range of countries sought to assess the impact of such schemes on a variety of organization-level indicators such as profitability, productivity, industrial relations, employee involvement, organizational identity, and employee satisfaction and commitment. The general conclusion reached was as follows:

> This survey of international arguments and data on the impact of profit-sharing and employee shareholding schemes indicates that there is a wide range of possible consequences. Overall, a note of caution is apposite. The effects of schemes appear to be broadly positive but they do typically fall short of the claims of the most ardent enthusiasts for financial participation. However, from a general manager's perspective, it should be stressed that competitiveness, in particular, is often the consequence of a series of small-scale improvements which have a significant cumulative effect. Viewed in this light, the development of profit-sharing and share ownership schemes is likely to prove valuable so long as expectations of benefits are realistic and schemes are seen as only a part of a broad range of measures designed to improve company performance itself.[21]

In view of the continuing growth of profit-sharing schemes it is not surprising that research on the subject continues. For instance, economists continue to use survey evidence to investigate the questions of whether, firstly, profit-sharing increases productivity and, secondly, any resulting increase in productivity is sufficient to pay for itself.[22] The answer to the first question seems to be yes, but the second question still remains essentially unanswered. Other economists have also investigated, and found limited support for, the notion that profit-sharing increases the level of employment stability in individual organizations.[23] In contrast, other researchers have utilized case studies to examine whether employee attitudes towards their organizations have changed significantly as a result of the introduction and operation of employee share ownership schemes.[24] Perhaps the one important area of emerging consensus among these varied researchers is that ' . . . worker participation apparently helps make alternative compensation plans like profit-sharing . . . work better – and also has beneficial effects of its own'.[25] This finding seems to point to the importance of the need for an internally coherent HRM policy mix.

A gain-sharing plan, or what some commentators have labelled a cost-reduction plan is best known in the North American context. For instance, surveys in the USA and Canada in the mid-1980s reported gain-sharing plans in some 13 per cent and 10 per cent of surveyed establishments respectively.[26] Moreover, a recent survey of Fortune 1000 companies identifies such plans as one of the projected areas for growth in terms of employee involvement arrangements.[27] The best-known gain-sharing plans in operation in North America are the Scanlon plan, the Rucker plan and IMPROSHARE, although some organizations have developed their own particular variants of such schemes.[28] The Scanlon and Rucker plans are distinguished from profit-sharing schemes because they are not simply economic incentive plans: rather they embody a strong emphasis on employee involvement (which is viewed as reflecting the overall philosophy of management) and (as such) are held to be an organization development intervention, rather than simply an incentive plan. Under Scanlon plan arrangements, for example, production committees at the department level develop suggestions to improve productivity and quality which are then passed to a screening committee, consisting of management and employee representatives, which is responsible for their review and implementation. The central concern of the plan is with improving the ratio between labour costs and the

Table 5.4   *Conditions favouring gain-sharing plans*

Organizational characteristic	Favourable condition
Size	Small unit, usually less than 500 employees
Age	Old enough so that learning curve has flattened and standards can be set based on performance history
Financial measures	Simple, with a good history
Market for output	Good, can absorb additional production
Product costs	Controllable by employees
Organizational climate	Open, high level of trust
Style of management	Participative
Union status	No union, or one that is favourable to a co-operative effort
Overtime history	Limited or no use of overtime in past
Seasonal nature of business	Relatively stable across time
Interdependence of jobs on the work floor	High to moderate interdependence
Capital investment plans	Little investment planned
Product stability	Few product changes
Comptroller (chief financial officer)	Trusted, able to explain financial measures
Communication policy	Open, willing to share financial results
Plan manager	Trusted, committed to plan, able to articulate goals and ideals of plan
Management	Technically competent, supportive of participative management style, good communications skills, able to deal with suggestions and new ideas
Corporate position (if part of larger organization)	Favourable to plan
Workforce	Technically knowledgeable, interested in participation and higher pay, financially knowledgeable and/or interested

Table 5.4 *continued*

Organizational characteristic	Favourable condition
Plant support services	Maintenance and engineering groups competent, willing and able to respond to increased demands

Source: Edward E. Lawler III, *Pay and Organization Development*, Addison-Wesley, Reading, Mass., 1981, p. 144.

sales value of production, with gains paid out for improvements in this regard. The potential strength of such a scheme has been held to be its recognition of the fact that 'effective use of participatory management requires a congruence between the pay system of an organization and its style of management'.[29]

However, gain-sharing schemes are not considered appropriate for adoption in all types of organizations, and Table 5.4 lists some of the alleged leading prerequisites for the introduction and operation of such schemes. Although an individual organization will rarely have all such prerequisites currently in place, Lawler argues that the majority of them are necessary for the successful operation of such a scheme, with union opposition and inadequate financial measures being particularly strong signals not to embark down the gain-sharing route.[30]

It is generally conceded that the introduction and operation of gain-sharing arrangements are not quick, smooth and straightforward. It has, for instance, been suggested by one commentator that as many as one in three gain-sharing schemes in the USA have failed due to the absence of the necessary prerequisites, poor implementation or complex administration;[31] problems with such arrangements have frequently arisen as a result of bonus payments not coming up to expectations, inconsistent treatment of different groups within the workforce, overall operating losses being recorded, etc. Nevertheless the positive results of gain-sharing schemes in a number of settings has led to the view that they can be a particularly useful first step in the direction of establishing a larger high (employee) involvement management system.[32]

PAY FOR KNOWLEDGE SCHEMES

Arguably the most recent innovation in the compensation area is pay for knowledge or skill-based pay systems. The essence of these schemes is that individual employees can progressively increase the level of their pay through attaining (and using) an increased number of skills. These arrangements have their origins in the North American context, although even there the extent of their diffusion to date is relatively limited; survey evidence for the mid-1980s indicates that only some 5 per cent and 8 per cent of surveyed establishments had such schemes in the USA and Canada.[33] Nevertheless some recent survey evidence in the USA reported that 'knowledge or skill-based pay plans are projected for increased use by 50 per cent of the companies. This finding fits with the expected increase in the utilization of self-managing work teams, since they often go together. Even with this increase, however, they are not likely to cover a high percentage of the total workforce.[34] As suggested here, the introduction of pay for knowledge schemes has frequently been associated with work design changes that involve team working, reduced job classifications and work rules and the integration of quality control responsibility into jobs on the shopfloor. Although pay for knowledge schemes have been introduced into some established organizations the best-known schemes are in new plants or greenfield sites.[35]

Various sets of guidelines have been provided for managers contemplating the introduction of knowledge-based pay schemes. For example, one set of implementation principles stresses that: (1) an organization must have an overall HRM philosophy which is consistent with and supportive of such arrangements; (2) such a scheme needs to be embedded in a larger set of HRM policies and practices (e.g. extensive job rotation); (3) it should accompany other organizational changes (e.g. introduction of new technology); (4) it should be supplemented by gain-sharing arrangements; and (5) union support in the design and implementation process is all-important.[36]

There is, as yet, relatively little in the way of systematic empirical evidence concerning the operation of such schemes. However, a number of commentators have highlighted various considerations, not to say potential problems, that need to be closely watched in the operation of such schemes. For instance, individual workers must fully understand the details of the scheme, must not be allowed to develop unrealistic expectations about the pace of skill acquisition and the consequent rewards, and must be able to make regular use of the newly acquired skills on the job.[37] In one organization with a pay for knowledge scheme (the acquisition of four skill modules increased annual salary by 2.5 per cent) which I have observed, two particular problems were apparent. First, the absence of a skills audit prior to the introduction of the scheme meant that not all of the acquired skills were regularly used on the job and, secondly, a performance-related pay scheme for team leaders resulted in some leaders being very reluctant to release members for the purposes of training; the latter generated considerable inter-team equity concerns about the operation of the scheme. It is also possible that not all employees will want to be involved in such schemes, which points to the natural advantage that a new plant or greenfield site has in operating such arrangements; employees whose motivation and values accord well with pay for knowledge schemes can be targeted via the selection process. Finally, Box 5.2 indicates the differing approach to and experience with pay for knowledge schemes in two organizations.

Box 5.2   *Two pay for knowledge schemes*

Scheme 1

The organization concerned is a foreign-owned subsidiary which was established as a greenfield site and has been in operation for some three years. There are currently some 152 employees on site. The integrated pay structure for all employees below the managerial grades consists of three elements: a basic salary, a shift allowance and a pay for knowledge component. Currently all employees below managerial level are divided into two grades, A and B. A grades have a basic salary of £9,000, B grades a basic salary of £11,000, with both having a common shift allowance of £2,244. The pay for knowledge component involves an offering of some 20 skill modules, with the attainment of 1 module adding an extra £300 to salary. In the last 12–18 months the organization has specified that an individual can only have a maximum of 7 skill modules at any point. This 'capping procedure' was introduced largely to try and ensure a manageable volume of training and retraining activity. Currently the distribution of skill modules for the 127 A and B employees is as follows: no modules (5 employees), one (21), two (16), three (31), four (19), five (13), six (11), and seven (11).

The pace at which skill modules have been acquired has not been

Box 5.2 *continued*

as fast or straightforward as was originally envisaged. This has been due to a number of 'disruptive factors'. The operational performance needs of the organization in the first two years have consistently taken a higher priority over the implementation of the skill modules training. Moreover, the training and personnel function has not been in a position to argue the case constantly for skill modules training due to the turnover of personnel staff (four different personnel managers since the organization was established). There has also been some concern about an adequate supply of trainers for ensuring a comprehensive and consistent training programme, while the relatively small numbers of administrative staff have posed coverage problems for ensuring skill module acquisition in the administrative side; administration staff have typically acquired only two modules compared to the 3–4 figure for production staff.

At present a review is being conducted of various aspects of the human resource management package in the organization. And as part of this review some thought is being given to the future of the pay for knowledge scheme. For example, do employees favour more priority being given to raising basic salary relative to the pay for knowledge component? And is the pay for knowledge component of value only as a limited life initiative?

Scheme 2

The organization concerned has faced a variety of product market pressures from the mid-1980s. These include general over-capacity in the industry and the emergence of new sources of competition, particularly from Japan. Employee numbers on the site have fallen from a peak figure of around 3,000 in the late 1970s to the current figure of some 800 employees. Against this background a new product line, involving a computer-integrated manufacturing process, was scheduled for possible introduction. For this new product line to be successful a competitive strategy emphasizing the themes of cost, quality and delivery was deemed to be essential. Prominent among these themes was the specific target of achieving a 30 per cent reduction in labour costs over a 30-month period (1984–6). As a consequence, a package of measures including JIT (just in time) and TQM (total quality management) was introduced. Some elements of the existing payment system (as a bonus scheme based on batch production) were viewed as inconsistent with the needs of JIT, while at the same time it was considered important to have a compensation

Box 5.2 *continued*

and reward system which supported the cost reduction effort, encouraged team working, was consistent with JIT, reduced demarcation blockages and facilitated further harmonization moves.

The substantially revised compensation and reward system involved a single, integrated pay structure for all unionized employees, broader job descriptions (100 reduced to 30 on the shopfloor) to encourage and facilitate flexible working, a reduced number of pay bands (sixteen down to five) for all employees and an element of pay progression based on skill attainment. The latter involved six module payments in each of the five pay bands, with no automatic transfer from one band to the next. All employees (shopfloor and administration) were restricted to attaining one module per year, which was originally viewed as likely to involve some ten days of training. However, after one year it was agreed that flexibility regarding the length of training was necessary, with the length of time involved varying according to the individual and subject area. Modules on the shopfloor covered subjects such as cost, JIT, team building, set-up reduction techniques, etc. The shopfloor teams were largely given responsibility for identifying their particular training needs within the parameters of achieving a set of larger business objectives.

The new payment system has been associated with the absence of grading disputes, while the skill attainment element has encouraged training and flexible working particularly on the new product line. At the same time, however, it was found that the skill-based element generated 'a lot of bureaucracy' (writing modules, completing the training, etc.), particularly given existing resource constraints (only three trainers to act as catalysts). Indeed it was conceded that the resource demands of the scheme had been substantially underestimated. As individual employees reached (via the skill attainment process) the top of their pay bands over four to five years, this particular element of the system has largely ceased to operate from the late 1980s. In effect it has been used as a limited-life trigger of change within a larger package of measures designed to encourage flexible working, training and workforce commitment. More recent developments include the move towards a Kaizen (continuous improvement) type process of problem-solving.

HARMONIZING TERMS AND CONDITIONS OF EMPLOYMENT

It has long been apparent in virtually all advanced industrialized economies that white collar or non-manual employees enjoy substantially better terms and conditions of employment than blue collar or manual employees in the same organization. Such differences in fringe benefits, job security, promotion prospects, length of the working week, etc. have been traced to the (management) belief that non-manual or white collar employees identify relatively closely with their employing organization, and hence should be appropriately rewarded for this relatively high level of organizational loyalty.[38] However, as we saw earlier (Table 2.3), the academic HRM literature which urges a movement from a workforce control to workforce commitment strategy places a great deal of emphasis on removing inequitable sources of status differentiation within the workforce as a whole. This theme has been echoed in a number of public policy and practitioner-orientated publications in advanced industrialized economies for some considerable time.[39]

The general desire for more flexible working arrangements, together with the specific influence of Japanese management practices, has apparently stimulated considerable moves along these lines in more recent years. Such moves frequently involve different names in different countries. For instance, in the United States the term 'all-salaried workforce' is frequently used, with 11 per cent of surveyed establishments in the mid-1980s claiming to have such arrangements, but with a further 31 per cent claiming to be likely to move in that direction over the next five years.[40] In Britain the term 'single status' is frequently used to describe this process of eliminating unjustifiable manual/non-manual distinctions in the terms and conditions of employment. However, one practitioner has interestingly contended that:

> in my view the term 'single status' is a misnomer. It is simply not possible for everyone to have the same status in an organization – the plant manager has a different status to the supervisor or to the line worker simply because of the positions held. Nothing will change that, for status is a state of mind – your perception of your position in relation to another. What we can do, however, is to eliminate many of the differences in the way we treat people and end up with the same or similar employment packages. Thus the term 'common terms and conditions of employment' is more accurate.[41]

In fact one commentator suggests a three-way classification of the various approaches which organizations have adopted in attempts to improve the terms and conditions of manual employees relative to those of the non-manual workforce.[42] Firstly, there are 'staff status policies' in which some or all of the conditions of non-manual workers are spread to a proportion of the manual workforce. Secondly, there is the 'harmonization approach', which is the process of moving towards the equalization of some or all employment conditions, although this process frequently involves equating the terms and conditions of manuals only with those of the non-managerial group of non-manual employees. Finally, the most comprehensive in terms of coverage are 'single status policies' under which all general terms and conditions are common to all employees. The latter are frequently held to be disproportionately associated with new plants or greenfield sites. Table 5.5 contains examples of practices and moves along these lines.

Although the more comprehensive harmonization packages are in place in greenfield sites and new plants, it is apparent that staged or phased moves in this direction are increasingly characterizing older, established organizations. For instance, in one plant I have observed, a single canteen or eating area was operated from its establishment in the mid-1960s. Since then it has harmonized all significant fringe benefits (in the 1970s) and most recently has tackled the residual areas, such as providing salaried contracts for all workers, introducing common hours of work and eliminating a lay-off clause in the contract of shopfloor employees. More generally, a survey of some 83 organizations in Britain in the late 1980s revealed the following basic picture:[43]

1   Harmonization was most evident in relation to holiday and leave entitlement, redundancy pay, occupational pensions, canteen/ restaurant facilities, product discounts and allowances, car parking and loans.

2   Harmonization was least advanced as regards pay systems, grading structures, hours of work and methods of recording attendance.

3   Approximately 50 per cent of the organizations had made most of their harmonization moves in the last five years.

4   Management usually initiated the moves, although the process typically involved union–management negotiations.

5   Harmonization was generally introduced as part of the normal pay review process, although it was frequently coupled with other changes.

Table 5.5   *Examples of harmonizing terms and conditions*

Organization*	Formal components	Additional comments
1 A US-owned subsidiary	Same pension scheme, same holiday entitle-ment, same sickness pay scheme; all monthly paid; employee share purchase scheme for all; same handwritten time sheets (in and out) for all; single canteens; only three reserved spaces in car park (for logistics reasons: individuals with meetings all over the site)	Use of first name terms; overtime paid up to first level management (beyond this level, access to company car scheme)
2 A Japanese-owned subsidiary	Same pension scheme, same holiday entitlement, same sick pay scheme; single canteen; no reserved spaces in car park; similar clothing at work; all employees can purchase one company product per year; same plastic identification badges to facilitate checking in and out	All staff and technicians are monthly paid, although 90 per cent of shop floor are weekly paid; all shopfloor, supervisors and junior management are paid overtime (a grading allowance to compensate beyond this level); private health insurance coverage for middle managers and above, but currently a union claim for all to be covered
3 A Japanese-owned subsidiary	Same pensions, holiday entitlement, sickness pay entitlement; all monthly paid; single canteen; all wear the same uniform at work; no reserved car park spaces; all clock in and out (except managing director); profit-sharing scheme for all	All but managerial grades receive overtime payment (private medical insurance and company car for managerial grades)

Table 5.5 *continued*

Organization	Formal components	Additional comments
4 An Italian-owned subsidiary	Single canteen; no clocking in and out; all monthly paid; no reserved spaces in car park; same sickness, pension and holiday entitlements	Shopfloor work 37.5 hour week and management grades a 40 hour week (no overtime payment for the latter)
5 A recently privatized organization which has moved from industry-wide to individual company level bargaining	A proposed phased programme of moving towards single status: a single negotiating/consultative body (July 1991); 37 hour week for all (April 1991); monthly pay for all (September 1991); common conditions, policies and procedures (December 1991)	These individual moves and changes are embedded in a larger programme of organizational change involving a review/revision of the pay structure, increased flexibility–productivity enhancement changes and measures to enhance job security
6 A British-owned organization	Since 1988, pension scheme and sickness pay scheme arrangements harmonized, all employees' pay directly deposited in bank accounts; number of canteen or eating areas reduced from seven to two (with one kitchen). Movement to new location in 1992 accelerated the process, with all employees monthly paid, single canteen, no reserved spaces in the car park, all employees clocking in and out, and fully harmonized fringe benefit package	The moves in this direction have been related to moves in the total quality management direction, the latter being part of a larger organizational change programme emphasizing a task (rather than role) culture, decentralized decision-making, employee involvement, etc.

* Organizations 1–4 have been single status from their inception.

6 A majority of the organizations phased in the moves over a period.

.7 Nearly two-thirds of the organizations expected further harmonization moves in the 1990s, largely as a result of pressures to reduce costs and improve the recruitment/retention of labour.

How have harmonization moves worked out in practice? It is difficult to provide any conclusive answers to this question because of the relative absence of systematic research studies. One can, however, point to a considerable range of both a priori and impressionistic views. The more pessimistic views are likely to emphasize the fact that harmonization moves in a single organization are unlikely to offset completely the historical and larger societal forces and influences that have produced the substantial status differences (i.e. a state of mind) between blue collar and white collar employees, and that formal status moves may not always be matched by changes in informal practices and arrangements. A second group of commentators have tended to argue that the gains of harmonization are likely to be essentially intangible, with measurement difficulties particularly resulting from the fact that the process is likely to involve other significant changes in the HRM area. The nature of some of these accompanying changes may in fact pose some problems for the larger union–management relationship. For instance, in Britain in recent years a number of well-publicized cases of union de-recognition have involved the substitution of harmonized terms and conditions of employment (*Financial Times*, 5/6 October 1991), a development which must have raised some uncertainty among unions about the desirability of the harmonization process. At the same time, however, (management) participants involved in certain individual organizations which have made such moves do report a resulting increase in workforce morale and commitment which has facilitated the introduction and operation of team and flexible working arrangements.[44] Finally, Box 5.3 contains an illustrative example of a greenfield site where the operation of a single status policy has not been without its implementation difficulties.

The example in Box 5.3 should not be viewed as an argument against the introduction and operation of single status arrangements. Rather it illustrates the possibility that the operation of such arrangements may not be entirely free of some difficulties: a perspective that is notably lacking in the published literature on the subject. Perhaps the biggest operational lesson to draw from this particular experience is that management should spend sufficient time at the outset spelling out just what single status does and does not mean.

Box 5.3   *Single status at a new plant*

In this new plant, single status arrangements have operated from the outset. The formal components of these arrangements consist of: (1) all employees being paid on a monthly salaried basis; (2) a common fringe benefits package in which all employees have the same holidays (five weeks plus the statutory days), sickness pay provisions (13–26 weeks on full pay based on length of service) and pension scheme arrangements (a 5 per cent contributory scheme based on 1/60th of final earnings); (3) no time check or clocking-on arrangements; (4) a single canteen for all employees; and (5) a common car park, with no reserved spaces for any groups of employees.

These arrangements were originally introduced for a number of reasons and with a number of expected or hoped-for benefits in mind. Primarily they were viewed as a natural *quid pro quo* for the relatively highly skilled, trained and motivated workforce that was being selected and developed for the plant. The hope was that a purely instrumental orientation on the part of the shopfloor employees could be avoided, with such individuals exhibiting the sort of attitudes and commitment associated more with staff employees. Single status arrangements were also deemed to be administratively convenient and highly consistent with, and complementary to, the sort of organizational culture that was being sought at the plant.

However, some two years after production had begun in the plant, a comprehensive workforce attitude survey revealed a number of complaints about the 'failings' of the single status arrangements in practice, a finding that was highly consistent with a number of the other results of the survey. In reflecting on these findings, the personnel director suggested that these complaints may well have stemmed from some initial misunderstandings and exaggerated expectations about what single status arrangements can and did mean in practice. He also suggested the likelihood of different groups of workers having different complaints and grievances. The office staff (or at least some of them), for example, seemed to feel that the shopfloor employees were getting the best of both worlds. The shopfloor had the same fringe benefits as the office staff, but at the same time, unlike them, were paid for overtime working. At the same time the shopfloor employees seemed to resent the fact that, although paid for overtime, they had no choice as to whether they

Box 5.3 *continued*

could work overtime or not. Furthermore, the shopfloor employees (or at least some of them) seemed to feel that single status meant that all employees' 'votes' in organizational decision-making would be of equal value, with a democratic decision-making process reflecting the views of the majority of all employees. As a result they were aggrieved at certain strictly enforced process rules in the workplace (e.g. no smoking in all areas; no radios in all areas) which they felt were imposed on them by senior management without consultation in a way that was inconsistent with the spirit of single status working arrangements. Moreover, the nature of the production process in the plant meant that (night) shift workers were denied the benefit of access to the single status canteen.

With the aid of hindsight, the personnel director felt that senior management should have spelt out much more explicitly to the workforce just what single status arrangements did and did not involve in practice.

REFERENCES

1   Edward E. Lawler, *Strategic Pay*, Jossey-Bass, San Francisco, 1990, Chapter 3.
2   Edward E. Lawler III, 'The Strategic Design of Reward Systems', in Charles Fombrun, Noel M. Tichy and Mary Anne Devanna, *Strategic Human Resource Management*, Wiley, New York, 1984, pp. 129–30.
3   Terence R. Mitchell, 'Motivational Strategies', in Kendrith M. Rowland and Gerald R. Ferris (eds.), *Personnel Management*, Allyn and Bacon, Boston, 1982, pp. 283–9.
4   See John B. Miner, *Theories of Organizational Behaviour*, Dryden Press, Hinsdale, Illinois, 1980, Chapters 5–7.
5   Rosabeth Moss Kanter, 'From Status to Contribution: Some Organizational Implications of the Changing Basis for Pay', in Fred K. Foulkes (ed.), *Human Resources Management: Readings*, Prentice Hall, Englewood Cliffs, New Jersey, 1989, pp. 169–92.
6   Jerry M. Newman and George T. Milkovich, 'Procedural Justice Challenges in Compensation: Eliminating the Fairness Gap', in *Proceedings of the Industrial Relations Research Association*, Madison, Wisconsin, Spring 1990, pp. 575–9.
7   P. B. Beaumont, *Public Sector Industrial Relations*, Routledge, London, 1991, pp. 147–8.
8   Lawler, 'Strategic Design of Reward Systems', pp. 132–3.

9   Ibid., pp. 135–6.
10 Arie Halachani and Marc Holzer, 'Merit Pay, Performance Targeting and Productivity', *Review of Public Personnel Administration*, 7 (2), Spring 1987, pp. 80–91.
11 Kanter, 'From Status to Contribution', p. 172.
12 ACAS Advisory Booklet No. 14, *Appraisal Related Pay*, p. 5.
13 Ibid., p. 7.
14 See John F. Geary, 'Pay, Control and Commitment: Linking Appraisal and Reward', *Human Resource Management Journal*, 2 (4), Summer 1992, pp. 36–54.
15 See, for example, Neil Millward and Mark Stevens, *British Workplace Industrial Relations, 1980–1984*, Gower, Aldershot, 1986, p. 259; Eugene P. Buccini, 'Performance-Based Pay Systems in Health Care', in Amarsit S. Sethiand and Randall S. Schuler (eds.), *Human Resource Management in the Health Care Sector*, Quorum, New York, 1989, p. 133; Thomas A. Kochan, 'Looking to the Year 2000: Challenges for Industrial Relations and Human Resource Management', Mimeographed paper, Sloan School of Management, MIT, 1988, p. 9.
16 Neil Millward, Mark Stevens, David Smart and W. R. Hawes, *Workplace Industrial Relations in Transition*, Dartmouth, Aldershot, 1992, p. 264.
17 M. L. Weitzman, 'Some Macroeconomic Implications of Alternative Compensation Systems', *Economic Journal*, 93, 1943, pp. 763–83.
18 See Tom Schuller, 'Financial Participation' in John Storey (ed.), *New Perspectives on Human Resource Management*, Routledge, London, 1989, pp. 130–1.
19 Kochan, 'Looking to the Year 2000', pp. 10–11.
20 IDS Study No. 471, *Profit-Related Pay*, December 1990.
21 Michael Poole and Glenville Jenkins, 'The Impact of Profit-Sharing and Employee Shareholding Schemes', *Journal of General Management*, 16 (3), Spring 1991, p. 67.
22 Alan S. Binder (ed.), *Paying for Productivity*, Brookings, Washington, 1990.
23 James Chelius and Robert S. Smith, 'Profit Sharing and Employment Stability', *Industrial and Labor Relations Review*, 43 (3), February 1990, pp. 256–73.
24 Stephen Dunn, Ray Richardson and Philip Dewe, 'The Impact of Employee Share Ownership on Worker Attitudes: A Longitudinal Case', *Human Resource Management Journal*, 1 (3), Spring 1991, pp. 1–17.
25 Binder, *Paying for Productivity*, p. 13.
26 Buccini, 'Performance-Based Pay Systems', p. 133; Kochan, 'Looking to the Year 2000', pp. 10–11.
27 Edward E. Lawler, Susan Albers Mohrman and Gerald E. Ledford, *Employee Involvement and Total Quality Management*, Jossey-Bass, San Francisco, 1992.

28　Kanter, 'From Status to Contribution', pp. 184–5.
29　Edward E. Lawler III, *Pay and Organization Development*, Addison-Wesley, Reading, Mass., 1981, p. 147.
30　Ibid., pp. 145–6.
31　Cited by Kanter, 'From Status to Contribution', p. 188.
32　Edward E. Lawler, *High Involvement Management*, Jossey-Bass, San Francisco, 1980, Chapter 9.
33　Buccini, 'Performance-Based Pay Systems', p. 133; Kochan, 'Looking to the Year 2000', pp. 10–11.
34　Lawler et al., *Employee Involvement*, pp. 117–18.
35　Lawler, *Strategic Pay*, pp. 174–5.
36　Henry Tosi and Lisa Tosi, 'What Managers Need to Know About Knowledge Based Pay', *Organizational Dynamics*, 14 (3), 1986, pp. 61–2.
37　Ibid., p. 63.
38　Robert Price, 'The Decline and Fall of the Status Divide?', in Keith Sisson (ed.), *Personnel Management in Britain*, Basil Blackwell, Oxford, 1989, pp. 276–8.
39　See, for example, ACAS Advisory Booklet No. 16, *Effective Organisations: The People Factor*, 1991, p. 16.
40　Buccini, 'Performance-Based Pay Systems', p. 133.
41　Peter Wickens, *The Road to Nissan*, Macmillan, London, 1987, p. 7.
42　Alan Arthurs, 'Towards Single Status?', *Journal of General Management*, 11 (1), Autumn 1985, p. 19.
43　*Industrial Relations Review and Report*, No. 445, 1989.
44　T. Pegge, 'Hitachi Two Years On', *Personnel Management*, October 1986, pp. 42–7.

6

CAREER MANAGEMENT AND DEVELOPMENT

INTRODUCTION

Historically, training and development in many organizations have had the relatively short-term aim of enhancing current on-the-job performance, with the important exception of succession planning arrangements for the potential senior managers of the future. More recently, however, changes in the produce market environment, the introduction of new technology and changes in organizational characteristics have all had the effect of raising the profile of training and development in both the HRM literature and practice. In fact, many of the leading HRM issues that organizations are currently grappling with are essentially training and development ones: witness, for example, attempts to inject interpersonal and problem-solving skills into shopfloor training programmes to facilitate cross-functional and team working there, steps to build international experience into the career development programmes of managers, and initiatives to develop a system of lateral or horizontal career moves that attempt to change the traditional view that career success and progress must always involve an upwards move.

Over and above the circumstances of individual organizations, training and development have also become very prominent in attempts to develop national employment and HRM policies and programmes. For instance, a number of governments in recent years have introduced legislation, regulations, incentives, etc. to try and influence the level of training and development in organizations. Such initiatives reflect the increasingly widespread view that the absence of an adequate level of training and development will hinder the competitive performance of the national system as a whole. And even the more successful national economic systems of recent years may still have some important training and development issues to confront in the years ahead. For instance, it has been observed that:

Japan's strength (its powerful cohesive internal culture) is also its weakness. Japanese firms have demonstrated a first class ability to manage foreign workers (often they get more productivity out of foreign workers than foreign managers can), but to the extent that the economic game of the twenty-first century requires firms to integrate managers and professionals from different cultures and nationalities into a homogeneous team, Japan has a problem. Japanese history, traditions, culture and language make it very difficult to integrate foreign managers and professionals as equals. If winning requires absolutely first-rate foreign managers, Japanese firms will have a problem. To hire the very best foreign managers, these foreigners must have a chance to get to the top, but such a chance cannot be provided in the closed Japanese corporate culture.[1]

In short, the training record of Japanese organizations for blue collar workers is well known and respected, but as these organizations become increasingly involved in operations outside Japan, one of their chief tasks will be to develop effective long-run career development programmes for non-Japanese white collar people.

The human resource management literature places a great deal of emphasis on the importance of having relatively well-developed internal labour market arrangements in the matters of promotion, training and development, so as to ensure a relatively long-term perspective on 'matching' individual and organizational needs concerning employee career development. This theme is pursued here through an examination of career development from the point of view of both individual employees and individual organizations, with the all-important process being that of matching individual and organizational needs at any one point in time and over the course of time. Following a general discussion along these lines I then briefly refer to some career-related issues that are likely to be of considerable importance in the current operating circumstances of many organizations. Finally I discuss the role of career mentoring and the attempts of an increasing number of organizations to develop 'international managers'. These two subject areas, which are discussed in some detail, are useful examples of both particular (current) organizational concerns and one of the leading themes in the HRM literature, namely the importance of adopting a long-term, strategic orientation to human resource development. Moreover, given the line management orientation of this book it seemed entirely appropriate that the discussion of career management should essentially centre on line management positions.

INDIVIDUAL CAREER STAGES

Existing discussions of careers as individual attributes (something individual employees experience and pursue) invariably revolve around the notion of career stages. As Milkovich and Anderson have commented:

> Researchers have attempted to identify the major developmental tasks that employees face during their work lives and to organize these into career stages. As might be expected, several theoretical alternatives have emerged, with certain consistencies and inconsistencies among them. At one level of abstraction, the sequencing of stages is consistent across researchers, resembling biological growth and decay cycles – trial and growth, exploration, establishment, maintenance, decline, and withdrawal. Differences between perspectives include the number of distinct stages an individual may pass through, the overlapping tasks and issues faced in each stage, the role of transition periods between stages, and the degree to which career stages are seen as age-linked.[2]

One of the most widely quoted studies along these lines is that of Dalton, Thompson and Price.[3] This was a study of scientists, engineers, accountants and professors in a number of organizations, which essentially concluded that 'high performers' early in their career performed very different functions from high performers at both the mid and late career stages. The result was the formulation of the four-stage career model set out in Table 6.1.

In Stage I, individuals join an organization, learn to perform certain tasks competently and discover which elements of the job are critical and require the highest priority. They identify and work closely with a mentor to learn and appreciate the 'politics' of the organization. Their major psychological task is to accept a dependent role, when they were expecting or hoping for independence. In Stage II they develop their own ideas and judgement, have their own project or area of responsibility, build up their professional skills, increase their visibility in the organization, and rely less on a mentor relationship and more on peer group relationships. Stage III sees them exerting more responsibility for influencing, guiding, directing and developing the work and skills of others. They operate more as mentors, idea generators or managers and develop their self-confidence as regards producing results and helping others. The final stage involves assuming responsibility for directing the organization, or a substantial

Table 6.1   *Activities, roles and psychological issues in four career stages*

	I	II	III	IV
Central activity	Helping, learning, following directions	Independent contributor	Training, interface	Shaping the direction of the organization
Primary relationship	Apprentice-ship	Colleague	Mentor	Sponsor
Major psycho-logical issues	Dependence	Indepen-dence	Assuming responsibility for others	Exercising power

Source: G. W. Dalton, P. H. Thompson and R. L. Price, 'The Four Stages of Professional Careers: A New Look at Performance by Professionals', *Organizational Dynamics*, Summer 1977, p. 23.

proportion of it, in which they negotiate and interface with key parts of the environment, develop new initiatives, direct resources and are heavily involved in the external representation of the organization. This approach raises the question of whether all individuals wish to, and indeed should, seek to move right through from Stage I to Stage IV. This is a particularly important question for discipline-based professionals (e.g. engineers) who may not want to be drawn too far into management and hence lose touch with their basic disciplinary role and training.

In practice there has been very little systematic empirical research on the determinants and consequences of individual career stages, with most research on careers (from the perspective of individual employees) concentrating on the attitudinal and behavioural outcomes of career experience. That is, various measures of career experience (e.g. level reached in the hierarchy, number of promotions, etc.) are examined to see if significant relationships exist with regard to job satisfaction, organizational commitment, performance and turnover.[4] The literature on career management from the point of view of the individual employee in fact tends to be overly dominated by self-examination and self-help manuals which, in essence, view planning one's own career as similar to any other planning process. That is, one needs to develop a self-inventory, establish personal occupational objectives, obtain occupational and organizational information, design actions to achieve objectives and evaluate progress.[5] These self-help guidebooks invariably make the rather questionable assumption that all individuals have a relatively common set of aspirations and values.

More generally, the extent of well-informed knowledge about individual career management is, to say the least, rather limited. For example, the notion of career stages seems to have considerable intuitive appeal in accounting for individual employees' attitudes and behaviours, but 'the theoretical frameworks of career stages and their associated characteristics and tasks need to be more fully developed; operational definitions and hypotheses need to be complete enough to allow an understanding of a process that spans entire work lives'.[6] The relatively sizeable body of literature on career outcomes certainly suggests that career experiences are important influences on employees' attitudes and behaviours, but the ability to generalize from such studies is somewhat limited because of differences in the ways careers have been measured and because of inadequate controls for a range of other possible sources of influence.[7]

In addition to the considerable deficiencies in empirical research already noted, it is important to recognize that there are some criticisms and limitations of the stages approach to individual career development. Firstly, the studies which have formulated this type of approach are overwhelmingly based on male, professional employees. As such, they take relatively little account of contemporary demographic developments such as the increased presence of women employees and dual career families. Secondly, the approach very much embodies the view that career advancement involves moving up the organizational hierarchy. However, given changing organizational circumstances (such as reduced middle management layers) such movement may not be possible for all individuals who desire it, so that organizations are increasingly having to grapple with the question of whether career advancement can involve (and be seen to involve) horizontal or lateral moves, rather than simply hierarchical ones. Furthermore, even if hierarchical moves were reasonably feasible for a substantial number, they may not be desirable for all of them and for the organization as a whole. For example, in one organization I have worked with closely it is currently felt that too many of their engineers have moved beyond Stage II into Stages III and IV, with the result that they have lost good engineering talent and only gained poor quality managers. This was an important reason for their recent introduction of a dual career ladder system, an issue discussed in a later section.

THE ORGANIZATIONAL PERSPECTIVE ON CAREERS

In principle the notion of a career structure within an individual organization can be viewed as involving (1) a patterned sequence of positions related in work content, and (2) an ordered movement of individuals among these positions.[8] The former characteristic can be sub-divided into the length of the sequence (i.e. the number of positions involved in a sequence) and the ceiling of the sequence (i.e. the highest position reached in a sequence), while the latter attribute involves the rate of movement of individuals between jobs in a sequence and the direction of that movement.

This being said, it is important to recognize that in practice, as many commentators have suggested, the patterns of mobility within individual organizations are much more random, with a relative absence of explicitly designed career paths.[9] Admittedly many organizations have long engaged in some form of succession planning for senior management positions, but beyond this it has frequently been essentially short-term, *ad hoc* decisions that have been held to shape the sequencing of job positions and the movement of individuals. There is very little systematic empirical research on the impact of career systems, *ceteris paribus*, on levels of organizational performance.

THE MATCHING PROCESS

The strong prescriptive approach of so much of the strategic HRM literature is well evidenced by the emphasis attached to matching individual and organizational career development needs. This literature has been heavily influenced by the career stages perspective set out earlier (Table 6.1), and typically involves a model with the following three components: (1) *individual needs*, which covers the key developmental tasks faced by employees at various stages of their work lives; (2) *organizational needs*, as identified by human resource planning activities such as planning for staffing, growth and replacement; and (3) the *matching process*, involving techniques such as job analysis, recruiting, and training.[10] More recently, a Management Development Matrix has been proposed as a way of both understanding the career progress of individuals and guiding organizational efforts to assist this progress.[11] In essence it links the four career stages of Table 6.1 with four types of career intervention applicable at all four stages. The career interventions are as follows:

1 *Dominant job elements.* The 'make or break' tasks that will partially determine a person's success in/impact on their organization.

2 *People relationships.* The key individuals a person interacts with to accomplish their job assignment.

3 *Organizational adjustments.* The accommodations an individual makes from the initial role of apprentice to the final role of spokesman.

4 *Management development activities.* A range of supportive programmes for educating and developing a manager.

Table 6.2 indicates the nature of this matching process of career stages (individual perspective) and career interventions (organizational perspective).

In practice most organizations appear to have largely viewed the matching process in terms of management development activities, that is, in terms of off-the-job management education and skills training. Among the leading questions typically asked about such programmes of education and training for managers are whether they are consistent with the future needs of the organization, and whether they are based on sound theoretical principles of *adult* learning.[12] The importance of the former is continually stressed in the strategic HRM literature, although, as I have observed in earlier chapters, the difficulties of forward planning in a rapidly changing environment and the lack of a widespread (across organizations) two-way linkage between competitive strategy/planning and HRM planning are among the reasons why many individuals view such programmes as having been driven by more immediate performance needs. As regards the second question, it has been suggested that adults and children learn in very different ways, and that such differences should be reflected in the content and teaching methods of management education and training programmes. Specifically, the content and presentation of management training programmes should draw and build on the experience of managers, be problem-centred and have some immediate applicability in the workplace. However, as I note in the subsequent discussion of mentoring, there is increased recognition of the fact that most management development actually occurs on the job. As well as formal mentoring programmes the importance of on-the-job experiences in career development suggests that there may be certain organizational influences besides formal development programmes that can have an important influence (for good or bad) on the longer-term development potential of individual employees. For

Table 6.2   *Management development matrix*

Stages	Dominant job elements	People relationships	Organizational adjustments	Management development activities
Apprenticeship	Apply and enhance technical expertise Build performance record Look at business enterprise and work with formal organization Test creative ideas	Establish mentor, supervisory, and peer relationships	Accept job tasks, but reach out for challenges Tolerate low visibility while building influence Get confirmation from supervisor	Orientation and skill building programs Task force participation Assume responsibility of completing a major assignment
Craftsmanship	Choose technical specialty and establish visibility Solve job-related problems and assume more managerial responsibility	Maintain peer relationships in other offices Accept responsibility for others' work Become less dependent on supervisor	Anticipate transitional problems Evaluate what is needed in the technical area Get feedback on performance	Career assessment and planning Identification of managerial skills

Table 6.2 *continued*

Stages	Dominant job elements	People relationships	Organizational adjustments	Management development activities
Mentorship	Assume leadership role in organizational unit and make business decisions Relate objectives to company objectives Contribute to policy statements	Become a mentor Extend interpersonal relationships to include external constituencies Provide feedback to subordinates	Mediate organization's and individuals' demands Balance giving freedom to and controlling subordinates	Acquire managerial skills of planning, organizing, and leading Acquire 'people' skills of career appraisal, coaching, and counseling
Spokesmanship	Lead business management team Implement corporate objects Perpetuate business enterprise through strategic planning	Frequent contact with other executives and also 'grassroots' Increased visibility to large community	Make more complex decisions Manage demands of multiple constituencies Balance career with outside demands	University-sponsored executive programs Executive sabbaticals and individual counseling Manage organizational change

Source: David W. Lacey, Robert J. Lee and Lawrence J. Wallace, 'Training and Development', in Kendrith M. Rowland and Gerald R. Ferris (eds.), *Personnel Management*, Allyn and Bacon, Boston, 1982, p. 319.

Table 6.3   *Some general organizational influences in early career development*

---

1   *The first assignment*
A challenging and demanding first assignment is important.

2   *The supervisor*
Supervisors should be trained and rewarded for developing new employees.

3   *Performance reviews*
Constructive, corrective feedback will reduce role ambiguity for new employees.

4   *Career planning and goal setting*
Meetings with supervisors and staff specialists can seek to match the individual's career goals with the opportunities and expectations of the organization.

5   *The peer group*
A peer group is a powerful instrument of socialization which can aid or hinder a newcomer's sense of identification with the organization.

6   *Family changes*
The newcomer may be simultaneously experiencing change in other aspects of their life.

Source: Douglas T. Hall and Francine S. Hall, 'Career Development: How Organizations Put their Fingerprints on People', in Lee Dyer (ed.), *Careers in Organizations: Individual Planning and Organizational Development*, New York State School of Industrial and Labor Relations, Cornell University, 1976, p. 10.

example, it has been argued that early career challenge is related to later career success, a relationship which can be strengthened by organizations taking note of the influences listed in Table 6.3.

A BRIEF NOTE ON SOME EMERGING CAREER ISSUES

A number of nationally representative employee attitude surveys in various countries have revealed that dissatisfaction frequently centres around concern about the perceived absence of promotion opportunities.[13] This fact combined with certain features of contemporary organizational life (e.g. downsizing, flatter organizational hierarchies and the 'baby boom' generation limiting future promotion opportunities for newcomers) means, as mentioned earlier, that a substantial and varied number of career-related issues are currently high on the agenda of both HRM practitioners and researchers. It is not possible to do full justice to the complete range of such issues in the confines of a single chapter. However, in this section I briefly highlight some of those which will increasingly confront a variety of organizations now and in the future, and then in the remainder of the chapter discuss two issues in rather more detail.

The first issue considered here is that of establishing a 'dual ladder' system of career advancement, which basically involves two parallel career hierarchies for management and technical personnel respectively. This is not a new issue for many organizations, although it has become of increased significance for some organizations in recent times as a result of some of the changes noted above. The rationale for such an organizational arrangement lies in a point made earlier in the chapter, namely that not all technical personnel (e.g. engineers, scientists) seek to (or indeed should) move through and into the latter stages of individual career development which increasingly involve managerial responsibilities. The basic aims in establishing such a dual career hierarchy are (1) to attract, retain and motivate high-quality technical and other professional personnel, (2) to provide individual opportunities to follow more optimal career paths, and (3) to focus strong technical skills on important projects with minimum distraction caused by administrative details and managerial responsibilities.[14]

In principle individuals are offered a choice in such a system of advancing up the managerial hierarchy (and obtaining increased organizational power and influence) or advancing up the technical hierarchy (and obtaining increased autonomy), with equal levels of compensation and status attaching to equivalent positions in the two hierarchies. Some research in the USA, however, has revealed considerable divergence between the theory and practice of dual career hierarchies.[15] In reality it appears that individuals in the technical hierarchy lack the organizational influence of their counterparts on the managerial ladder, and that the technical ladder often becomes the 'dumping ground' for failed managers. These findings have led to the suggestion that the management of technical specialists, such as scientists and engineers, should increasingly emphasize the role of significant and challenging projects.[16] This is a theme returned to in Chapter 8's discussion of team working arrangements.

A second set of career-related issues increasingly confronting organizations has stemmed from the increased workforce participation rates of women in advanced industrialized economies over recent decades. At first this change stimulated concern about possible discrimination at the initial recruitment and selection stage. More recently concerns have been expressed about the possible existence of a 'glass ceiling' which limits the progress of women up the managerial ladder. For instance, a recent report in Britain indicated that, although women made up nearly 80 per cent of the workforce in the National Health Service, they were seriously under-represented in senior management positions, accounting for only 17 per cent of unit general managers and 4 per cent of district and regional general managers (*Financial Times*, 2 August 1991). Such findings have shown up the need for more research on women in managerial positions,[17] while some organizations, particularly in the USA, have initiated mentor-based development programmes to try and assist progress in this regard. The increased participation of women in the workforce has also meant that organizations are more often having to confront the fact of dual career families. Employees are often reluctant to undertake career moves that involve geographical relocation because of disruption to the working career of their spouse or partner. As a consequence it is not surprising to find that relocation packages increasingly involve some form of job-finding assistance for the spouse or partner.

This set of issues is now entering a third stage, and raising the larger issue of relationships between work and home life. Kanter has used the phrase, the 'myth of separate worlds', to describe the process whereby organizations have traditionally acted as if employees only had the world of work and no home world.[18] Organizations are gradually coming to realize that such an orientation is neither valid nor desirable; at one leading US university with which I have had some association, the president recently established a taskforce concerned with work/home life boundaries on the grounds that the pace of work for many senior faculty members had adverse consequences for their home life which, in turn, fed back into their work performance. One recent review paper, for instance, has argued that organizations need to help employees define the boundaries between home and work, that these boundaries should be increasingly flexible, that the value of transition time between home and work should be recognized, and that the family should be more consciously integrated into career and human resource management considerations.[19] This paper contains a number of interesting, not to say potentially controversial, proposals. For example, the authors argue against working at home and the provision of child care facilities at work on the grounds that a greater separation, rather than integration, of the home and work domains is desirable. They also discuss various other means of producing a more balanced, complementary relationship between work and home life, which should be of interest to both HRM practitioners and researchers. Other individuals have gone further in arguing that *ad hoc* additions to employee benefits (e.g. flexi-time, job sharing, personal leave) are not sufficient to address the full range of work/family issues; rather there is a need to question more comprehensively the traditional assumptions that underlie career development practices in individual organizations.[20]

The final issue to be mentioned here is managing 'plateaued' employees, individuals who have reached a career point beyond which further promotion in the hierarchy is unlikely. This group has been sub-divided into two basic groups: 'solid citizens', whose current on-the-job performance is adequate, but whose further promotion is unlikely, and 'dead wood', who are currently performing below expectations and for whom further promotion is unlikely.[21] The latter sub-group is of the most obvious concern to organizations in the increasingly competitive environment which they have to confront. There has been a limited amount of research which indicates sizeable differences between the job histories, attitudes and career stages of plateaued and non-plateaued managers, with some linkages being made with the business strategies pursued by the organizations concerned.[22] There are also suggestions that the appropriate organizational strategies for 'solid citizens' might include job changes or career counselling, whereas for the 'dead wood' it tends to be the dismissal, demotion or early retirement options which are most often discussed. There is, however, a very real need for more research to examine the success of the various means adopted for dealing with plateaued employees, as well as more basic research on the reasons for career plateauing. This is because of increasing suggestions that the likelihood of serious career plateauing will affect many more members of the baby boom generation in the next ten years or so.[23] Accordingly it has been argued that organizations will increasingly need to find ways of substituting 'psychological success' for the finite (and shrinking) amount of promotional success. To this end a variety of recommendations have been put forward, which typically involve the development of more differentiated and self-directed career paths pivoting on lateral (rather than vertical) mobility.

CAREER MENTORING PROGRAMMES

Formal mentoring programmes in individual organizations, particularly in the USA, have grown in number in recent times. There are a number of reasons for this fact. First, some mentoring programmes have been initiated to try and help eradicate some of the more subtle influences that have limited the passage of women into the higher reaches of management. Secondly, there has been increasing organizational concern about, not to say criticism of (culminating in the so-called 'management competences' debate), the content, relevance and transferability of the skills and knowledge of external training and management development programmes. As a consequence there has been renewed interest in utilizing on-the-job experience as an important influence in the management development process. Related to this view has been the belief that the relatively informal mentoring process which is widely recognized to have been so important in the early career (Stage I) of many 'high performers' can be built upon and expanded through a formal programme; some individuals have, however, questioned whether such formal, 'imposed' programmes can fully replicate the strength and depth of mentor–protégé relationships that are naturally and informally established. Box 6.1 shows some of the factors that led to the establishment of such a programme in one organization.

There are numerous lists of the alleged advantages of a mentoring programme to both the mentor and the individual being mentored. For the mentor the benefits listed typically include satisfaction from developing others, peer recognition, exposure to new ideas and enhanced personal and professional reputation, while the protégé is viewed as likely to gain from career advice, improved self-confidence and greater understanding of both the formal and informal operations of the organization. For the organization as a whole it is frequently alleged that a formal mentoring programme can assist the management succession process, aid internal communication and reduce turnover among individuals with high potential for senior management positions in the future. It has also been suggested that mentoring can be an important process for transmitting some of the leading values and beliefs of the culture of individual organizations;[24] there may, however, be a potential problem here if the organization needs some form of cultural change. The decision to introduce a formal mentoring programme obviously raises a number of important questions about the appropriate design and features of the programme, in particular the issue of who should act as mentors. Table 6.4 lists one view of the appropriate and inappropriate characteristics of mentors.

Such a listing should be viewed in the light of some research findings concerning the characteristics of managers willing to act as mentors for others. It has been reported that such managers are those

Box 6.1 *Mentoring and career development: an example*

For this example I return to the engineering organization featured in Box 2.3. In the historically paternalistic culture described there, any mentoring occurred solely on an informal basis. The introduction of formal mentoring came about in the late 1980s as an integral component of the larger training and career development programme which was a prominent part of the general programme of cultural change in the company (see Box 2.3).

As we saw, training expenditure increased, but laid much more emphasis on managerial, as opposed to technical training. Second, the workforce was reduced from some 2,200 in 1988 to a projected 1,000 in 1992. Two more specific stimulants for the mentoring programme were (1) the general belief that too many 'good', professional engineers had moved into the managerial ranks in order to obtain promotion and (2) the findings of a workforce attitude survey (carried out prior to the introduction of a TQM programme) which revealed considerable concern about the lack of a long-term career development programme.

An internal project team of some six individuals visited a number of 'blue chip' companies to examine their approaches to career development. The result of the team's deliberations and findings was the introduction of a dual career ladder system, one for management and the other for technical specialists. And firmly embedded in this dual career system was a formal mentoring programme.

This mentoring programme has basically two elements. First, all new graduate entrants from university (the organization takes on between two and six new graduates each year) in the last three or four years are paired with a mentor. This is a longer-term, essentially open-ended arrangement which is expected to last at least five years. The graduates meet with their mentor every two or three months for the first year or so, and then on something like a six-month basis in subsequent years. The second component of the mentoring programme involves individuals (non-graduates) who have been with the organization for three to five years and have been identified as having considerable longer-term development potential. As part of the succession planning process such individuals are put through an assessment centre exercise (typically one to two exercises occur each year involving groups of ten employees). The organization stresses to these individuals that it is their responsibility to manage their own

Box 6.1 *continued*

careers, but a mentor is provided for each of them; it is, however, up to the individual to arrange meetings with their mentor. Currently an attempt is being made to spread the mentoring principles of the assessment centre exercise more widely, albeit informally, throughout the organization via, for example, the process of performance appraisals.

From the late 1980s, anywhere between twelve and twenty individuals in any one year have acted as mentors. These are invariably members of senior management or technical specialists with a high reputation in their discipline. Mentors are selected on the basis of their influence and authority within the organization, and their interpersonal skills. The organization has also provided training workshops on how to act as a mentor. Although the primary onus is always on self-development, the mentors help individuals map out their career plans through the identification of individual job assignments, relevant training courses and the means of improving individual aspects of their on-the-job performance. The immediate superior of the person being mentored is frequently involved in three-party meetings in order to try and ensure reasonably clear lines of communication and responsibility. Although there has been some concern expressed that the assessment-centre-based programme may lead to a loss of 'key workers' (through a broadening of career horizons) this has not occurred, at least to date, on any worrying scale.

who are well educated, are satisfied with their own career progress and performance, attach considerable importance to the notion of career planning and have themselves benefited from being involved with a mentor.[25] How have monitoring programmes worked out in practice? The answer seems to be a rather mixed, and variable, performance, with positive outcomes for both parties tending to be associated with a process of relatively frequent interaction, in which high levels of trust, informality and openness with information are apparent;[26] the mentor involved in such successful relationships exhibits 'both a people and professional' orientation. It is, however, important to note that: (1) the alleged benefits of mentoring programmes for the organization as a whole have rarely been examined; (2) mentoring programmes may fit the competitive strategy of some organizations better than others; and (3) there may

Table 6.4 *The characteristics of a mentor*

A good mentor:

1 Already has a good record for developing other people.

2 Has a genuine interest in seeing younger people advance and can relate to their problems.

3 Has a wide range of skills to pass on.

4 Has a good understanding of the organization, how it works and where it is going.

5 Combines patience with good interpersonal skills and an ability to work in an unstructured programme.

6 Has sufficient time.

7 Can command the respect of the protégé.

8 Has a network of contacts and influence.

In contrast, a mentor should *not* be someone who is

1 Heavily engaged in company politics.

2 A recently appointed job holder.

3 Involved in low-profile work,

4 'Obviously on the way down in the company'.

5 A manager of a high labour turnover department with low morale.

Source: Adapted from David Clutterbuck, *Everyone Needs Mentor*, Institute of Personnel Management, London, 2nd edition, 1991.

be some negative, unintended consequences of a formal mentoring programme, such as adverse effects on individuals who are not sponsored and a 'reproduction' of essentially similar types among senior managers.[27]

LOOKING FOR THE INTERNATIONAL MANAGER

The increasingly integrated and competitive world economy has meant that individual organizations have an enhanced number and range of dealings with other organizations in different countries. As a result, organizations are more and more seeking to ensure that the career paths of their managers, particularly those of the potentially high performers, contain some element of international experience. In

---

Box 6.2   *The development of international management teams*

These teams are based in one of ten product divisions of a large British corporation. The division concerned currently accounts for one-third of the corporation's total turnover and employs some 27,000 people, which is approximately 50 per cent of total employment in the corporation. Currently the division has manufacturing operations in some 35–40 countries.

The division has a long history of manufacturing operations based in countries outside the UK. Indeed as early as the late nineteenth century, manufacturing operations were based in six or seven different countries with sizeable numbers of British workers (across the full range of skills and positions in the division) being temporarily transferred abroad to help train local workers and start up the operations. For more than fifty years all foreign subsidiaries were run by teams of four or five senior managers who were almost exclusively British expatriates. Such individuals were recruited from a relatively small select group of British universities. The division has always made it clear that international experience is essential for anyone seeking to enter the ranks of senior management. This fact is well illustrated by the career history of the present chairman of the division, who in his twenty years in the division has held positions in Venezuela, Peru, Indonesia, the Far East and Brazil.

Some five years ago the division took the decision to build up a group of internationally mobile managers which was not exclusively British. This decision reflected the concern that they were losing some good local managerial talent in a number of foreign subsidiaries because the senior positions were reserved for British expatriates. At the same time they felt, in the context of the increased globalization of the market place, that it was desirable to avoid management teams that were very largely 'home grown' and 'inward looking'.

As a result they are now building up an internationally mobile group of managers who are recruited directly from universities in a number of countries, as well as in Britain. Their average age is early to mid-twenties. They sign a contract indicating a willingness to work anywhere in the world and are viewed as high potential performers on the basis of an initial management assessment centre exercise. The qualities sought include academic excellence, intellectual strength, the ability to live with and manage change, mobility, flexibility, the ability to become fluent in foreign languages and a sensitivity to the

Box 6.2 *continued*

nuances of working in different cultures. Typically seven or eight (at most ten) are recruited each year and they initially undergo a period of some 27 months training; three months in Britain (where they are trained as a team to help cement interpersonal relations) and then job training in their particular functional areas in two different countries. Before being sent abroad for the first time they undertake an intensive two-week language course. Following their 27 months of training, their first substantive assignment will be a two-year one in a country in which they were not trained and then thereafter they will typically work in different countries for two to four years on each occasion. As the managers move up the organization (i.e. management role through committee or team member and then into general management) these overseas assignments are interspersed with involvement in a number of external training programmes based in business schools in Britain and elsewhere.

The 1990 intake consisted of one individual from Turkey, one from India, two from Germany and three from Britain. In the same year a new subsidiary in Argentina had a senior management team consisting of five individuals drawn originally from Britain, Italy, Argentina and Spain. Currently some 110 of the total number of 300 senior managers in the division are members of this internationally mobile group. There has been very little loss of people from this group due to cultural adjustment problems, etc., because international assignments are the essence of their career path from when they first join the division.

the Philips company, for example, the traditional job rotation approach to management development has been recently broadened so that Philips managers work on assignment in international joint venture operations in which the company is involved.[28] The aim here is to bring about a senior management team with a genuine international orientation through the process of exposing them to a variety of organizational and national cultures. Box 6.2 outlines a rather different organizational approach to the development of a set of international managers.

Organizational managers are increasingly talking of the need to 'manage cultural diversity' in a more integrated, global economy with a particular premium being placed on minimizing interpersonal conflict and communication difficulties in order to try and ensure organizational effectiveness. Such a view raises the question of what are the ideal characteristics and features of an effective manager in such a setting? One recent report based on company responses concluded that 'the significant thing about their replies is that, in contrast to the relatively lower priority assigned to hard or functional skills, four of the six top characteristics identified are soft skills, emphasizing the human skills involved in managing people from other countries and the manager's ability to handle unfamiliar situations' (*Financial Times*, 9 April 1991). The six leading characteristics identified in this particular report were strategic awareness, adaptability in new situations, sensitivity to different cultures, ability to work in international teams, language skills and understanding international marketing.

It needs to be recognized, however, that there is no single type of 'international manager'. One recent article[29] has, for instance, distinguished between:

- the home-based manager, with a central focus on international markets and on overseas individuals;
- the multi-cultural team member, who works on a series of international projects;
- the internationally mobile manager, who undertakes frequent, short visits to numerous overseas locations but who remains loyal to the parent culture;
- the traditional expatriate, who carries the parent company culture, but spends lengthy assignments in a limited number of host countries representing the parent company; and
- the transnational manager, who moves across borders on behalf of the corporation and is relatively detached from any single company HQ.

Even these categories are capable of further division. For instance, the traditional expatriate category may consist of 'high potential' employees sent on assignment to widen their perspective as part of a longer-term career development programme, individuals who are simply available and willing to fill an available post, and technical experts. Most of the existing research literature is concerned with the expatriate category of individuals.

A recent review of the issue of 'intercultural competence' in relation to expatriate assignments identified a number of separate themes and strands in this literature.[30] Firstly, there has been considerable emphasis on the adjustment process involved in such assignments, with commentators talking of crisis (or culture shock), recovery and adjustment stages. Secondly, there has been the personality and attitudes approach in which traits such as empathy, tolerance and flexibility are emphasized as important selection considerations. Further studies have emphasized the importance of knowledge about other cultures, while yet others emphasize the importance of displaying appropriate communicative behaviour. Finally, others have identified the role of spouse and family considerations as being of particular importance in shaping the success or failure of expatriate assignments.

A number of these considerations and influences will overlap to a considerable extent, although there still remains considerable debate as to the relative importance to attach to some of these factors in making selection decisions for expatriate assignments. The importance and difficulties of such decisions are in fact revealed by the relatively high 'failure' rates (i.e. poor performance leading to early recall home or dismissal) of expatriate assignments, although there appears to be some inter-country variation in this regard.[31] (In general, individuals from US companies appear to perform less well in this regard than individuals from companies in Japan, Europe and Scandinavia. Failure rates in US companies are frequently put at 20 per cent or more.) Among the leading reasons for 'expatriate failures' are poor selection criteria (i.e. too much emphasis on technical criteria), inadequate preparation and support and family difficulties. Box 6.3 reports on one expatriate assignment which appears to have worked out (for the individual concerned) rather better than many.

The failure of many expatriate assignments led practitioners and researchers to concentrate initially on the identification of problems at the selection decision stage. The general belief here was that organizations had tended to over-emphasize technical abilities relative to other attributes necessary for effective performance in a different culture. The result was an increased emphasis on trying to identify individuals with the appropriate 'inter-cultural competence' skills and characteristics discussed earlier. A second phase of development has involved the increased use of training programmes to assist expatriates on assignment; the cultural sensitivity training programme at Farnham Castle in Britain is frequently mentioned in this regard.[32] There have been numerous suggestions regarding the appropriate content of such programmes, with considerable emphasis being placed on involving the spouse or family members, although some individuals have raised questions about the appropriate timing of such training.[33] More recently, organizations and researchers have

Box 6.3   *Expatriate assignment*

This 39-year-old production manager is a Finn who has been on assignment for 28 months in a subsidiary in Britain. He has worked for the parent company for eight years and this was his first assignment outside Finland. However, he already spoke English before the assignment and has a long history (stretching back into his childhood) of moving house and changing area of living (largely within Finland, although including a period in Sweden) which, in his view, has tended to make him a relatively flexible and adaptive individual. The parent company also has a long history of foreign involvement, with subsidiaries, joint ventures and projects existing outside Finland. Indeed it has a board-level individual specifically responsible for foreign projects, who has acted as something of a 'mentor' for the production manager. The production manager was able to draw on his mentor's knowledge before going on assignment and has been 'looked after' by him back at head office. The mentor is due to retire shortly and the production manager has been promoted into his post when he returns to Finland.

   The production manager took part in a series of cross-cultural training sessions provided by two British teachers in Finland before he went on assignment. These were spread over something like twelve months when many British individuals newly recruited to the subsidiary were over for counterpart training in the Finnish parent company. The cross-cultural training sessions were also available for the spouses of Finns like him going on assignment to the British subsidiary. He felt the training was useful, although not sufficiently workplace-based in focus. Indeed, he found the information provided by his mentor, other experienced managers (in foreign assignments) in the Finnish parent company and the interactions with British employees over for training in Finland more useful as preparation for his own assignment.

   He commented on a number of the differences he found as a Finn working in a British organization over the 28 months of the assignment. These included the fact that things happen more slowly in British organizations, there is less of a team working tradition among managers in Britain, there is much more written, as opposed to verbal, communication among managers ('too many memos'), and actions are not always followed up as quickly or closely as in Finland. Nevertheless, the assignment has worked out well for him. He has

Box 6.3 *continued*

been promoted and his wife and children have enjoyed living in Britain, so much so that he wonders if his wife may have something of a 're-entry' problem to Finland. However, he did stress that much of the satisfaction with the assignment may have been more the result of good luck than careful organizational planning. For instance, he only began thinking about his move back to the parent company in the last eight months of his assignment in Britain. He felt that he was fortunate in obtaining a promoted position back in Finland because his mentor was due to retire and a number of managers he was friendly with back home had also been promoted. He cited another company in Finland which gives an assurance to employees before they go on assignment that they will be promoted on their return if they perform well there. He had no such guarantee and felt as a consequence he had been thinking much more about his future than his job in Britain for the last eight months. In addition, his wife's enjoyment of the time in Britain was again due more to fortunate circumstances than to careful planning. She had made friends in the local area largely through the managing director's wife, who was also a Finn, and as a result of her children in the local school bringing her into contact with other wives and parents. In general he felt that the human resource management function of the subsidiary had not done enough to ensure that expatriates like him were not subject to spouse and family pressures due to a failure to integrate into the local community.

begun to consider questions concerning the re-entry of individuals to the home organization following an assignment abroad.[34] This repatriation phase appears to be relatively more successful as a result of a variety of HRM initiatives undertaken prior to, during and after the assignment abroad. As a summary of these various approaches to trying to produce more effective expatriate assignments, Table 6.5 sets out a list of proposed initiatives under the headings of selection, preparation, support and repatriation.

The topic of international managers is picked up again and pursued in subsequent chapters where reference is made to the subjects of international management teams (Chapter 8) and international HRM, specifically international joint venture operations (Chapter 9).

Table 6.5   *Steps to facilitate the success of expatriate assignments*

---

1   *Selection*

The domestic employment record of potential expatriates should be examined to see:

- how well they have responded and adapted to change;
- how they have handled opinions, attitudes and behaviour that is different from their own;
- how self-confident and self-reliant they are;
- how well they deal with stress;
- whether they are at ease with meeting and learning from new people.

2   *Preparation*

- Comprehensive and detailed information is provided by the company about the compensation package (and its implications) involved in the assignment.
- A training orientation programme concerning the country's culture and customs is provided by the company.
- A site visit for employee and family is arranged beforehand as a familiarization step.
- The organization makes clear to the employee its expectations and performance criteria in relation to the assignment.
- Some language training is provided.
- Time off from the current home-based work is provided to help ease the transition to the foreign site.

3   *Overseas support*

- Regular channels of communication are established between HQ and the expatriates on assignment.
- Attention is given to organizing social activities for expatriates.
- Language instruction continues in the early stages of the assignment.
- Mentors are provided for the expatriates both at the home and foreign sites.

4   *Repatriation*

- The organization begins to initiate steps to reposition the person on expatriate assignment at least six months before the assignment is completed.
- The re-entry position should reflect and utilize the skills, perspectives and experience gained from the assignment.

Source: Gary R. Oddou, 'Managing Your Expatriates: What the Successful Firms Do', *Human Resource Planning*, 14 (4), 1992, pp. 301–8.

REFERENCES

1 Lester Thorow, *Head to Head*, William Morrow, New York, 1992, p. 248.

2 George T. Milkovich and John C. Anderson, 'Career Planning and Development Systems', in Kendrith M. Rowland and Gerald R. Ferris (eds.), *Personnel Management*, Allyn and Bacon, Boston, 1982, p. 367.

3 G. W. Dalton, P. H. Thompson and R. L. Price, 'The Four Stages of Professional Careers: A New Look at Performance by Professionals', *Organizational Dynamics*, 6, 1977, pp. 19–42.

4 See, for example, Douglas T. Hall and Francine S. Hall, 'Career Development: How Organizations Put their Fingerprints on People', in Lee Dyer (ed.), *Careers in Organizations: Individual Planning and Organizational Development*, New York State School of Industrial and Labor Relations, Cornell University, 1976, p. 8.

5 Milkovich and Anderson, 'Career Planning', p. 374.

6 Ibid., p. 375.

7 Ibid., p. 377.

8 Ibid., p. 378.

9 Ibid., p. 378.

10 Edgar G. Schein, *Career Dynamics: Matching Individual and Organizational Needs*, Addison-Wesley, Reading, Mass., 1978.

11 David W. Lacey, Robert J. Lee and Lawrence J. Wallace, 'Training and Development', in Kendrith M. Rowland and Gerald R. Ferris (eds.), *Personnel Management*, Allyn and Bacon, Boston, 1982, p. 318.

12 Thomas A. Kochan and Thomas A. Barocci, *Human Resource Management and Industrial Relations: Text, Readings and Cases*, Little, Brown, Boston, 1985, p. 193.

13 See, for example, J. E. Thurman, 'Job Satisfaction: An International Overview', *International Labour Review*, 117 (3), November–December 1977, pp. 252–5.

14 Kochan and Barocci, *Human Resource Management*, p. 192.

15 Thomas J. Allen and Ralph Katz, 'Managing Engineers and Scientists: Some New Perspectives', in Paul Evans, Yves Doz and André Laurent (eds.), *Human Resource Management in International Firms: Change, Globalization, Innovation*, Macmillan, London, 1989, p. 193.

16 Ibid., pp. 194–6.

17 See, for example, Richard Scase and Robert Goffre, 'Women in Management: Towards a Research Agenda', *International Journal of Human Resource Management*, 1 (1), June 1990, pp. 107–26.

18 R. M. Kanter, *Work and Family in the United States: A Critical Review and Agenda for Research and Policy*, Russell Sage, New York, 1977.

19 Douglas T. Hall and Judith Richter, 'Balancing Work Life and Home Life: What Can Organizations Do to Help?', *Academy of Management Executive*, 11 (3), 1988, pp. 213–23.

20   Lotte Bailyn, 'Changing the Conditions of Work: Responding to Increasing Work Force Diversity and New Family Patterns', in Thomas A. Kochan and Michael Useem (eds.), *Transforming Organizations*, Oxford University Press, New York, 1992, pp. 188–201.

21   T. P. Ference, J. A. Stoner and E. K. Warren, 'Managing the Career Plateau', *Academy of Management Review*, 2, 1977, pp. 602–12.

22   John W. Slocum, William L. Cron, Richard W. Hansen and Sallie Rawlings, 'Business Strategy and the Management of Plateaued Employees', *Academy of Management Journal*, 28 (1), March 1985, pp. 133–54.

23   Douglas Hall and Judith Richter, 'Career Gridlock: Baby Boomers Hit the Wall', *Academy of Management Executive*, 4 (3), August 1990, pp. 7–22.

24   James A. Wilson and Nancy S. Elman, 'Organizational Benefits of Mentoring', *Academy of Management Executive*, 4 (4), November 1990, pp. 88–94.

25   G. Roche, 'Much Ado about Mentors', *Harvard Business Review*, 57 (1), 1979, pp. 14–24.

26   K. E. Kram, *Mentoring at Work: Developmental Relationships in Organizational Life*, Scott Foresman, Glenview, Illinois, 1985.

27   Ference et al., 'Managing the Career Plateau'.

28   George Van Houten, 'The Implications of Globalism: New Management Realities at Philips', in Paul Evans, Yves Doz and André Laurent (eds.), *Human Resource Management in International Firms: Change, Globalization, Innovation*, Macmillan, London, p. 110.

29   John Storey, 'Making European Managers: An Overview', *Human Resource Management Journal*, 3 (1), Autumn 1992 pp. 3–4.

30   Martine Gertsen, 'Intercultural Competence and Expatriates', *International Journal of Human Resource Management*, 1 (3), December 1990, pp. 341–62.

31   Rosalie L. Tung, 'Expatriate Assignments: Enhancing Success and Minimizing Failure', in Tim O. Peterson (ed.), *Human Resource Management: Readings and Cases*, Houghton Mifflin, Boston, 1990, pp. 610–23.

32   John Hutton, *The World of the International Manager*, Philip Allan, Oxford, 1988, pp. 114–19.

33   Ingemar Torbiörn, *Living Abroad: Personal Adjustment and Personnel Policy in the Overseas Setting*, Wiley, Chichester, 1982, p. 175.

34   Rosalie L. Tung, 'Career Issues in International Assignments', *Academy of Management Executive*, 2 (3), August 1988, pp. 241–4.

7

EMPLOYEE–MANAGEMENT
COMMUNICATIONS

INTRODUCTION

In advanced industrialized countries where collective bargaining was traditionally the centrepiece of the human resource management system, management communication with employees was essentially indirect, with information to employees reaching them (essentially as union members) via the union. This occurred through the medium of employee representatives on both joint negotiating and joint consultative committees; admittedly these indirect flows of information were often supplemented with notice board postings and company newsletters. In such systems it was in fact the 'household name' non-union firms which were characterized by the most comprehensive communication arrangements targeted at individual employees.[1] Such firms, for instance, frequently conducted employee opinion surveys in order to identify (and remedy) any sources of possible job dissatisfaction that could trigger a demand for union representation among their employees.

The HRM literature strongly emphasizes the importance of extensive internal communication arrangements as an integral component of a comprehensive human resource management policy mix; this literature views the subject area of employee–management communication as important in its own right and as an integral element of proposed changes in other areas of the HRM policy mix (witness, for instance, the importance attached to prior consultation/ discussion in relation to performance appraisal and performance-related pay). And certainly in recent years a number of companies in various countries have expanded both the number and nature of mechanisms for communicating more directly with individual employees. Accordingly in this chapter I review the evidence concerning the alleged growth of new communications arrangements, using Britain as an example, and then discuss in some detail two particular communication mechanisms, namely team briefing arrangements and employee opinion or attitude surveys. These two mechanisms are chosen for discussion because they illustrate the desirability of a set of communications arrangements which facilitate the passage of information both up (i.e. attitude surveys) and down (i.e. team briefing) the organizational hierarchy.

THE GROWTH OF COMMUNICATION ARRANGEMENTS IN BRITAIN

The 1984 workplace industrial relations survey provided a number of useful pointers in this area.[2] Firstly, the authors reported that overall 'systematic use of the management chain' and regular meetings between management and employees were the leading channels of communication, although there was considerable inter-sectoral variation in this regard. Secondly, terms and conditions of employment and major changes in working methods were, according to management respondents, the leading subjects of such communication, although employee representatives reported considerably less communication concerning changes in working methods. And finally the information on recent employee involvement initiatives suggested an increase in two-way communications, whereas structural innovations (such as the presence of a joint consultative committee) remained essentially stable in the early years of the 1980s. This suggested growth in two-way communications arrangements tends to be confirmed by examinations of individual organization employee-involvement statements issued under Section 1 of the Employment Act 1982.[3]

One review article, which drew together the results of a number of surveys specifically concerned with communications arrangements, reported that written employee reports and oral team briefings were the increasingly favoured methods of employee communication.[4] For example, the proportion of companies using employee reports increased from 22 per cent in the mid-1970s to 62 per cent in 1981, while the proportion using team briefing arrangements increased from 51 per cent in 1975 to 58 per cent in 1981. Finally, a survey of communication methods at corporate, divisional and establishment levels indicated that a substantial number of respondents used multiple methods of employee communication.[5]

The use of a multi-method or package approach to employee communications reflects a number of considerations. These include the varied aims or reasons for communicating with employees, such as the desire to 'educate them in the economic realities of the business' or to try and build a closer employee—organization identification and commitment process, and the fact that different methods of communication have individual strengths and weaknesses. For example, the belief that face-to-face, verbal communication with immediate supervisors concerning 'local matters' is particularly favoured by individual employees has clearly influenced the increased importance attached to team briefing arrangements. Table 7.1 sets out an example of the multiple methods approach to employee communication.

Two obvious questions arise concerning the increased organizational attempts to communicate directly with employees. First, what, if any, evidence exists concerning its degree of success, and, secondly, how have the trade unions responded to such initiatives? It is obviously difficult to provide tangible, objective evidence of any 'bottom line' pay-off to communication initiatives. Nevertheless one or two findings can be usefully noted here. Firstly, most organizations rarely formally evaluate their processes of employee communication, tending to rely largely on informal employee feedback. And in general, such feedback has suggested that: (1) employees value information that is directly relevant to their immediate local working needs and concerns and (2) the information provided is generally regarded as credible, although there is some variation here according to the characteristics of the employees and the subject matter of the information;[6] younger, male, skilled manual workers tend to be the most sceptical about the credibility of information, with information concerning financial performance producing an above-average degree of scepticism. Management frequently looks to communications programmes as a way of enhancing 'employee morale', and certainly both the 1980 and 1984 workplace industrial relations surveys have suggested a positive relationship between the reported industrial relations climate of an establishment and the extent of information provision to employees, particularly concerning major changes in work practices, investment plans and the financial position of the organization.[7] However, there has been little systematic research designed to identify the relevant lines of causation involved here and to control simultaneously for the effect of other possible factors.

As to the second question, the unions in British Telecom (UK) have expressed the concern that the increased emphasis on direct employee communication (see Table 7.1) may result in reduced union–

Table 7.1   *The employee communications package at British Telecom (UK)*

---

1   *Attitude surveys*
    Two major ones were conducted in 1986 and 1988, with a smaller one occurring between these two.
    The results provide a range of communications targets and objectives for line managers to achieve which are to be assessed in the light of the results of subsequent surveys.

2   *Team briefings/meetings*
    The 1986 attitude survey revealed that some 60 per cent of respondents felt this to be the most effective form of communication.
    Voluntary team briefings occur on a monthly basis, with more than three quarters of managers and employees in districts being regularly involved in them.

3   *The 'Speak-Up Campaign'*
    Initiated in 1987, employees can seek a phone or written reply to questions concerning company matters.

4   *The 'Open-Line Facility'*
    This variant of the above is a recorded telephone message (updated daily) covering national and local developments in the company.

5   *'Walking the Job'*
    Local managers are encouraged to be more visible and accessible to their staff.

6   *Video*
    Videos are increasingly used to explain and promote particular initiatives or developments.

7   *Publications*
    More than 70 regular publications (largely produced in-house) are aimed at various groups of staff.

8   *Training*
    The training unit (more than 2,000 employees) provides in-house courses to improve the communications skills of managers (e.g. appraisal, counselling, effective meetings) and support related developments, such as the total quality programme.

9   *Direct mail*
    This has involved circulation of the company newspaper and a short report on company performance.

Source: Adapted from *Industrial Relations Review and Report No. 449*, 10 October 1989, pp. 11–14.

management consultation, while a newspaper article (*Financial Times*, 11 February 1991) indicated that some union officers feel that developments such as team briefing pose a threat to 'collectivist' notions in the workplace unless the unions are fully involved. However, there is clearly considerable variation in individual union attitudes and responses at individual workplaces:

> Responses to the introduction of communication programmes have varied. From initial 'veto' responses of attempting to implement boycotts, there has been an increasing tendency for trade unions to respond in like manner by improving communication to their members. In general, trade union response has been highly contingent upon the nature of the existing relationship with the employer, the extent to which they have been involved in the new systems, and on the attitudes of key individuals such as convenors.[8]

It has been further suggested that (1) there is little evidence that communication packages have been designed, or successful, as a union substitution device on any sizeable scale and (2) such packages appear to have influenced more obviously the conduct rather than the outcomes of collective bargaining.

However, these attempts to develop more of a cohesive, package approach to communications in individual organizations, with in particular an emphasis on having both top down and bottom up measures, are arguably the most positive developments in the communications area. The less positive aspects are that communications arrangements tend to be evaluated (if at all) in a very loose, informal manner and that some individual approaches to communication have been rather 'over-sold' in recent years. Against this general background I now turn to discuss in more detail the nature of team briefing as an employee communication device.

TEAM BRIEFING

The essence of team briefing is typically a 'top down' communication approach in which information flows or cascades down the management hierarchy through a series of linked meetings, involving a superior verbally communicating information to, and answering questions from, a group of employees for whom they are responsible. The information conveyed covers, in the main, their immediate work area and situation, although information concerning certain higher-

Table 7.2   *Principles for preparing and presenting a team brief*

Preparing

1   The majority of the brief (i.e. 70 per cent) should be of local, specific interest and concern to the particular group being briefed.

2   The brief should involve a mixture of information covering longer-term, on-going items and issues, and shorter-term, more immediate issues.

3   The items to be included in a brief should be gathered and built up over the full period of time between individual briefs.

4   To the locally based information should be added any items from the 'core' brief which are intended for the organization as a whole.

5   The items in a brief should typically cover four broad subject areas:
(a)   progress (e.g. measures of performance, budget, targets);
(b)   policy (e.g. procedural changes);
(c)   personnel (e.g. appointments, leavers, promotions);
(d)   points for action (e.g. housekeeping items).

6   For the *first* brief:
(a)   try and anticipate any questions you may be asked;
(b)   choose items carefully to avoid conveying any impression that this will be a mechanism always associated with 'bad news';
(c)   start with items which you feel most knowledgeable about and comfortable with;
(d)   ask the team for any suggestions concerning the sort of items they would hope to see covered in the future;
(e)   explain the basic 'ground rules' (e.g. it is not a session for airing grievances).

Presenting

1   Have briefing notes but avoid reading them out verbatim.

2   Welcome the team.

3   Note any absentees and brief them when they return to work.

4   Indicate the time involved (e.g. 30 minutes) and the structure of the brief: (a) what you will cover; (b) cover it; (c) summarize major points of it.

5   Encourage note-taking.

6   Encourage questions:
(a)   after individual items or a block of items;
(b)   confined to the subject of the brief;
(c)   essentially questions of clarification and elaboration.

7   Maintain eye contact as much as possible, particularly if using visual aids.

8   Certain material can be prepared as hand-outs.

9   Use your own words.

Table 7.2   *continued*

---

10   Illustrate points with examples which the team can relate to.

11   Periodically check understanding, particularly in absence of questions.

12   If you cannot answer a relevant question, say so. Indicate you will seek the information and get back to the individual concerned as quickly as possible (e.g. within three days).

13   Keep to time schedule.

14   End on a positive note.

15   Summarize main points.

16   Thank for attendance.

17   Indicate time and place of next brief.

Source: Based on material from the Industrial Society.

level developments will also be presented as a result of its coverage in the 'core brief' (which goes to all briefing groups). Typically, briefing occurs on a monthly basis, with the size of briefing groups varying between four and fifteen individuals.

The team briefing approach in Britain is very much associated with the advocacy and work of the Industrial Society, which has claimed to have helped introduce such arrangements into over 500 organizations. Accordingly, Table 7.2 sets out some of the leading principles advocated by the Industrial Society for the preparation and presentation of team briefs.

The alleged benefits of the team briefing approach have been listed as follows:[9]

1   It reinforces management by emphasizing the role of the individual manager as a leader, a reliable source of information and as the individual who is accountable for the performance of their staff.

2   It increases employee commitment to the immediate task and the larger organization itself by informing and explaining to employees matters concerning their performance, achievements and objectives.

3   It prevents misunderstandings by providing accurate and up-to-date information from a key source.

Box 7.1   *Team briefing: guidance notes for briefers*

1   *Headlines*

Major items of interest to be covered in the brief (cf. 'News at Ten').

2   *Overall state of business*

Derived from MD's brief, includes general comments on economic situation, markets, corporate developments.

Questions

3   *The other businesses in outline*

Covering previous month's business performance and derived from individual business directors' briefings. Special items of interest including marketing promotions or new product should be expanded on – possibly by having specialist at brief. *Heavy reliance on visual aids.*

Questions

4   *Your business in detail*

Detailed look at business performance covering:
- Health and safety
- Business indicators (sales, profits, turnover)
- Production matters (methods, equipment, manning etc.)
- New products and marketing etc.
- Organization changes (transfer, promotions, retirals)
  (Some of these issues briefed by company/dept specialists)

Questions

5   *Personnel issues*

Derived from Personnel – job news in other departments, changes in senior management, industrial relations issues, new procedures, update of negotiations, welfare issues. 'Topic of the Month'. Preferably delivered by a Personnel Specialist.

Questions

6   *General*

Any 'one-off' items, visits, news of employee success in sport, charity, etc.

Box 7.1 *continued*

Final questions

Where handouts are thought suitable they should be distributed at the end of the briefings for taking away, rather than during it.

4 It helps employees to accept the need for change by setting out the reasons for the necessity of change.

5 It helps to control the informal 'grapevine' by ensuring that the information which management wish to convey actually reaches the employees.

6 It improves upward communication by permitting and indeed encouraging constructive feedback, suggestions and responses from employees.

It has to be said that many HRM researchers would view this as a very (overly?) ambitious set of objectives (particularly as regards the likelihood of successfully confronting the 'grapevine'), which may have tended to inflate management's expectations concerning the impact and performance of such arrangements.

Box 7.1 sets out the guidance notes that one personnel manager in a manufacturing plant has prepared for the individuals acting as team briefers.

The increasing popularity and use of the approach outlined in Table 7.2 is well illustrated by Box 7.2. This is an extract from a bigger company document produced in mid-1990 concerning organizational change in one large private sector organization.

Unfortunately, there has been relatively little systematic empirical research concerning the nature and effectiveness of team briefing arrangements. One recent case-study-based research exercise, however, found little evidence to support any view that team briefing had substantially enhanced individual employees' sense of organizational commitment.[10] Moreover, one employee communications consultancy organization has conducted a survey which suggests that the principles of team briefing tend to be rather loosely implemented in practice (*Financial Times*, 19 July 1991). Specifically, they highlighted the fact that the message of the core brief is frequently distorted as it passes down successive levels in the management hierarchy. In addition, a study of the operation of team briefing in a manufacturing plant, retail organization and NHS district has highlighted a number

---

Box 7.2   *Introducing team briefing*

Six guiding principles for the communication processes were established, referring to both written and oral communications, formal and informal channels:

- Information should be shared.

- Communications should be honest, clear, timely and relevant.

- Face-to-face communication by line management is the preferred means of communicating.

- A primary responsibility of every line manager is two-way communication.

- The content of decisions should be explained and answers given in a timely manner.

- Competitive sensitivity and personal privacy should be respected.

Team briefs are to be held at least once a month (after four months, regularity of team briefs will be reviewed). These will be the main vehicle for communications within [the organization]. Until the team briefs are up and running the [internal] Bulletin will communicate the kind of information which will form the basis of the team briefs once they are operating.

Team briefs should provide information on business progress, policy changes, staff changes and postings, and the local implications of corporate decisions. More importantly they provide a means by which employees can ask questions and express opinions.

Team briefs are based on a model created by the UK Industrial Society. In [the organization] they operate as follows, with the entire process taking less than 72 hours. Senior executives at each major site meet with their direct subordinates. Some of the topics will cover the deliberations of the previous GMG meeting. A question and answer session forms part of each meeting; lengthy written handouts should not. Questions should be answered (or at least acknowledged) within 48 hours. Members of these team briefs then hold meetings with their subordinates and so on until the whole of [the organization] has been covered. Each team brief should ensure that the implications and context of all decisions taken is explained. Notes on staff feedback should be made and passed back up the line.

The size of each group, where possible, should be limited to

Box 7.2 *continued*

> between eight and ten people. For employees in remote locations, videos and written summaries will replace team briefs. Extraordinary team briefs may be called from time to time.
>
> Training material will be available, and training in communications skills incorporated into management training programmes. Line managers will be assessed on their communications skills.
>
> Surveys of employee attitudes will back up the communications process.

of practical problems in the operation of such arrangements.[11] These problems included the irregularity of briefing sessions, employee absences, the continuing strength of the grapevine as an alternative (and more favoured) source of information and the difficulty of ensuring relevant material that will be of interest and concern to employees. Various individual company-based reports of the workings of team briefing arrangements also report a number and variety of difficulties, such as inadequate training of briefers, union opposition to involvement and highly variable levels of employee attendance.[12] Nevertheless the majority of management (only) respondents apparently view their team briefing arrangements as reasonably effective.[13]

My own experience with a number of organizations that operate team briefing arrangements suggests very much a mixed picture, with the nature of the arrangements, and their resulting effectiveness, being highly variable. For instance there appear to be basically three models of team briefing operated by management. The first (and least satisfactory) is the management monologue whereby managers and supervisors simply tell employees what is going on – i.e. it is very much a one-way process of communication. The second is where management permits questions from the employees being briefed, but these are strictly limited to questions of clarification and further detail of the points raised by management (the aim here being to ensure that team briefing does not become a grievance session). The third approach is where management seeks a 'constructive input' from employees by asking for their comments, suggestions and reactions to some of the items raised in the brief. Furthermore the workings and perceived performance of team briefing appears to be highly contingent upon the circumstances of individual workplaces, as I have continually encountered views from management ranging from 'team briefing has been a great success' to 'it has been full of problems and

Box 7.3   *Contrasting cases of team briefing*

Organization A is a 400-bed psychiatric hospital which is being run down and is scheduled for closure in the mid-1990s. Team briefing was introduced some five years ago, following very much the model of the Industrial Society; indeed the Industrial Society was instrumental in the original training and establishment arrangements. It is compulsory to attend briefing sessions which occur on a monthly basis and typically involve groups of ten employees. Team briefing is very much viewed as a management tool, with the two-way aspect of the process being restricted to employees asking questions only of detail and clarification. The basic aim has been to ensure that 85 per cent of all employees receive a face-to-face briefing within a three-day period. This aim has been consistently achieved over the five-year period of operation. Relatively minor problems have been encountered such as sessions initially taking too long, but the overall success of the programme is not questioned. This judgement reflects the fact that the basic objective (above) has been consistently achieved, team briefing has been diffused to the rest of the health district, some positive innovations in the basic arrangements 'have ironed out certain early problems (e.g. monitoring of briefers to ensure consistency and accuracy of message and improve individual presentation styles) and there have been positive spillover effects to other aspects of communication (e.g. helped to revive the moribund joint consultative committee) and management within the hospital.

Organization B is a manufacturing plant with some 400 employees, where team briefing has been in operation for nearly two years. The briefing occurs on a monthly basis and involves sessions after normal working hours (which the company pays for) that tend to last 30–40 minutes. In some areas of the plant there is nearly 100 per cent attendance at these sessions, whereas in other areas the figure is as low as 30 per cent. Furthermore, the union representatives on the joint consultative committee have continually voiced criticisms of its operation, suggesting that its content is often of limited interest and relevance to employees (e.g. industry sales trends), is poorly presented (e.g. too much use of graphs and tabled information) and some briefers do not adequately follow up and respond to employee questions. Management is also concerned about the current workings of team briefing. Some feel that it is conveying too much bad news

Box 7.3 *continued*

which is depressing employee morale, whereas others point to instances of incorrect and inconsistent interpretations of material provided by individual briefers. Some managers feel that the arrangements should be temporarily suspended and then relaunched after the aims of team briefing are more clearly formulated, the briefers are put through an interpersonal skills training programme and the market situation facing the company shows some considerable improvement.

difficulties to the extent that we are thinking of revamping it or even abandoning it'. These highly variable stories are illustrated by Box 7.3. In organization A, team briefing has been judged (at least by management) to be a great success, whereas in organization B the arrangements are experiencing very considerable operational difficulties; indeed organization B is currently devising a new training programme for its briefers to enhance both their confidence and presentation skills. An important task for future research is to determine which of these two cases is the more typical of the experience with team briefing in the system at large, and to identify the organizational contingencies which aid or hinder the operation of such arrangements.

Finally, I recently conducted an 'audit' of a pilot experiment with team briefing in one part of a large public sector organization. The pilot experiment lasted six months and discussions with both briefers and those being briefed led to a number of recommendations. Among those I would highlight as larger, potential lessons are these:

1   Because the core brief went to everyone, it has an 'implied importance' which made for some difficulty in ensuring a 70–30 split in favour of local level material (see Table 7.2). Indeed employees consistently urged that the brief needed to be more locally specific in nature – i.e. cover matters of direct interest and relevance to their own individual department.

2   Some 85 per cent of all employees in the pilot scheme area were briefed on a monthly basis for the six-month period. However, management were concerned that so few questions were asked by employees in the sessions. According to employees the lack of questions resulted from the fact that the briefing tended to cover items and issues where decisions had already been made by management so there was little point in raising questions.

3   Related to the above point, the organization concerned was undergoing considerable change and employees wanted more coverage in the briefs of issues concerned with the future direction of the organization.

4   The organization concerned has a newsletter and some briefers felt that the content of the newsletter and briefs overlapped too much, with the appearance of the newsletter before the briefing sessions tending to downplay the importance of the latter.

5   The information conveyed in the briefs and the answers to questions were overwhelmingly viewed by employees as credible and honest. However, some concern was expressed that certain key items of information (particularly concerning future organizational directions) were being held back from the briefing sessions.

The latter observation is particularly important. Team briefing is a device for improving employee–management communications, although its success will be strongly influenced by the extent and quality of communications between the different levels of management. Obviously there are certain items of information that senior management will always want to (and indeed need to) treat as 'confidential ones'. This being said, serious thought needs to be given to the notion of reducing the extent of such 'limited circulation' items. Nothing will undermine the operation of team briefing more effectively than the non-appearance of an item of priority concern (to employees) in a brief, although it has been picked up and reported elsewhere (e.g. the local newspaper) and thus has pushed the grapevine into operation. Such a message or lesson would appear to transcend the particular circumstances of the organization discussed here.

EMPLOYEE ATTITUDE SURVEYS

As indicated earlier, historically the use of employee attitude surveys has been disproportionately associated with certain well-known non-union firms, particularly in the United States;[14] attitude surveys (and feedback) have also been a prominent intervention technique utilized by many organization development and change practitioners from the 1970s (often in non-union organizations). Although one would not want to exaggerate the extent of the change, the 1980s and 1990s have certainly seen more organizations, particularly in the unionized

Table 7.3 *Issues in the organization and administration of an employee attitude survey*

Organization

1   Who assumes responsibility?
    Typically this is the personnel management department, although a strong senior management commitment to the exercise is necessary to ensure the co-operation of line managers.

2   Who will carry out the survey?
    The options here are:

(a)   in-house, which is relatively cheap, although they may lack expertise and employees may feel that there is less guarantee of anonymity in the responses and that the results may not be acted upon by management;

(b)   commercial agencies which may have the necessary experience and can help management put the results in some sort of context (i.e. comparison with results in other companies), although they are relatively expensive;

(c)   university researchers, who may be a useful half-way house between (a) and (b). Their potential strengths are experience and being less expensive than commercial agencies, although they may wish to publish some of the results.

3   Who will participate?
    The aim here is to achieve a relatively high response rate from a cross-section of the workforce which will provide a valid basis for generalization to the workforce as a whole. This could involve:

(a)   seeking responses from the population or full workforce; or

(b)   seeking responses from a sample of the workforce which is representative of the workforce as a whole according to factors such as gender, age, length of service, etc.

Techniques

1   There are certain key or core sets of questions that inevitably figure in such surveys, although a pilot test is useful to help identify any organization-specific issues that should be included in the final instrument.

2   The length of the questionnaire needs to balance out the need for a reasonably comprehensive coverage of issues and items with that of maintaining workforce willingness to complete all questions.

3   Simple 'Yes/No' answers are less popular than scaled categories of response (strongly disagree through to strongly agree), with an even number of response options tending to minimize the opportunity to respond always in the middle ground.

4   Although they may pose some coding difficulties, it is useful to provide the opportunity at the end of the questionnaire for employees to add extra observations and comments of their own.

Table 7.3 *continued*

---

5   The communication and administration of the questionnaire should both emphasize and guarantee the anonymity of answers and responses. This means that both the feasibility and desirability of 'chasing up' non-respondents is and should be limited.

6   The 'disaggregation' of the full set of responses should not reach too fine a level of detail to maintain the anonymity of individual respondents in, for example, small departments.

7   Pilot tests are useful to ensure all important issues are covered, individual questions are understood and the length of time required for completion can be assessed.

8   Publicity of the survey by various means contributes to the final response rate and signals the importance attached to the exercise.

9   All the questionnaires should be administered and completed over a relatively short space of time, such as two working weeks.

Source: Adapted from IDS Study No. 462, *Employee Attitude Surveys*, July 1990.

sector, making use of regular or one-off employee attitude surveys to investigate individual topics (e.g. communications arrangements) or else a more broad-ranging set of questions and issues; the 1990 Workplace Industrial Relations Survey indicates that the use of surveys/ballots increased from 12 to 17 per cent of all establishments in the period 1984–90, although this method was much less used than other communications devices.[15] Table 7.3 lists some of the key issues that any organization contemplating an employee attitude survey needs to consider.

It is also important to take heed of the following:

> It is vital that the objectives of a proposed survey are made very clear from the outset, as there is a real danger of raising expectations which the company is not prepared to fulfil. If you are not definite about the issues on which you are prepared to take action, it is counter-productive to include them. Inclusion of a specific issue implies that management is planning to do something about it.[16]

Obviously no two surveys are exactly alike in terms of the basic pattern of results and findings obtained. Nevertheless on the basis of the employee attitude surveys I have conducted in a variety of organizations in recent years, the following observations are worthy of some note: (1) some of the results in individual surveys simply

---

Box 7.4   *Selected findings from two employee attitude surveys*

Organization A was a long-established public sector body with nearly 1,000 employees. A 10 per cent random sample of the workforce in 1989 revealed that 42 per cent expressed some degree of overall job dissatisfaction, 61 per cent expressed some degree of dissatisfaction with employee–management communications, 69 per cent expressed strong dissatisfaction with the level of consultation and information concerning job changes, 90 per cent claimed that they were rarely, if ever, praised by supervisors for a good day's work, and 20 per cent expressed strong dissatisfaction with their level of pay.

Organization B was a manufacturing plant which had some 400 employees and had been in operation for about two years. A 78 per cent response rate from the workforce as a whole in 1990 revealed that 33 per cent expressed some degree of dissatisfaction with supervisor–employee relations, 68 per cent felt that the company did not listen to and respond to the concerns and views of employees, 53 per cent were critical of the system of internal communications, and 52 per cent felt that the level and quality of employee–management co-operation was poor.

---

confirmed what management felt to be the case; (2) some of the results in individual surveys were really quite different to what management had expected; and (3) in both new plants and established organizations undergoing substantial recent change, the process-related issues and items of consultation, communication, etc. have most frequently been at the centre of employees' dissatisfaction. These observations are illustrated by Box 7.4. In organization A, managers either felt there would be relatively little dissatisfaction (because of the absence of any increase in turn-over rates) or it would be solely wage-centred (as a result of constraints in the public sector), whereas in organization B the personnel director who commissioned the survey largely did so because of his belief that there was increased friction between employees and supervisors. As the selected findings in the box indicate, the two attitude surveys produced rather different results to what was expected by management.

When the results of an employee attitude survey are fed back to management, almost inevitably two questions are raised: How do

Box 7.5   *Following up a workforce attitude survey: a class exercise*

In this organization a workforce attitude survey was conducted in 1990. The responses obtained revealed considerable workforce dissatisfaction with certain aspects of internal communications, promotion opportunities, and meals in the workplace for employees working on shifts. There was also concern expressed that the single status arrangements were not working consistently across the organization as a whole, with the management being viewed as having failed to keep certain promises to the workforce and not always responding well to the expressed concerns of the workforce about certain matters.

These findings were presented to and discussed at a meeting of the joint consultative committee which, with the agreement of the board, established a special sub-committee to review the findings and present a set of proposals for possible change to the board. The board did, however, make clear that, although it would respond to all of the proposals from the sub-committee, there was no question of giving a guarantee to implement all of the recommended changes automatically.

The sub-committee consisted of four employee representatives from both the administrative and production sides of the workforce, together with a representative of line management and the personnel manager, who chaired the sub-committee. The sub-committee had seven meetings in the period May–November 1991. Their deliberations concentrated on the issues and areas of dissatisfaction noted above, with a number of proposals for change being transmitted to the branch via the personnel manager who chaired the sub-committee.

As a result of these proposals to the board the company has made a number of changes. These include (1) changes in the timing and manner of presentation of team briefing sessions, (2) attempts to improve promotion opportunities through first advertising internally all existing vacancies and increasing the pace of cross-functional training for production employees, (3) allowing radios to be played at work stations on the night shift (only), (4) increasing the variety of food available for workers on shifts, and (5) issuing a board-level statement as to what the single status policy in the organization does (and does not) mean in practice. Although pleased with these individual

Box 7.5 *continued*

> changes, the employee representatives on the sub-committee have experienced some frustration at the fact that some of their other recommendations and proposals have been referred to other bodies for further discussion and deliberation, or have been refused by the board on the grounds that 'it is not company policy'.
>
> Q1 Was the employee attitude survey useful from the management and employee points of view?
>
> Q2 How are employees likely to respond to management's proposal to repeat the survey in two years' time?

these results compare with those in other organizations? And what active steps should be taken to help improve the position? On the first matter, it is obviously desirable if one can compare the results of two or more surveys in the same organization over the course of time or if some comparison can be made with the results from a survey in a very similar organization (i.e. a matched pairs type of approach). However, one is rarely in the situation in which this can be done, with the result that one has frequently to assess the results in something of a vacuum, judging largely on the basis of intuitive feel. Nevertheless an outsider can help to provide something of a context in which to place the results by indicating, for example, that: (1) the pattern of results is sensitive to the precise wording of individual questions, (2) such results reflect the level of employee expectations, as well as the more objective circumstances of the workplace, (3) the levels of expressed job dissatisfaction vary systematically according to certain workforce characteristics (e.g. women and older workers typically express relatively high levels of satisfaction), and (4) expressed dissatisfaction will not automatically translate into employee turn-over, as the latter is a function of not only the incentive to quit but also the ability to quit.[17]

As to the second question, it has been commented that 'while managers, by and large, eagerly look forward to the results of a survey – and find the initial presentation of the data "extremely interesting" – the enthusiasm and interest seem almost to disappear within a few weeks. Getting anybody to *do* anything about survey findings becomes a Herculean task.'[18] This observation has led to the suggestion that the degree to which any survey results produce any subsequent change will be largely a function of the extent to which senior management are prepared to stimulate change through rewards or penalties.

In fact all too often the report of an employee attitude survey simply gathers dust on managers' shelves or else a consultant is called in to help make any changes which management deem to be necessary, and then these are reported to the workforce after the event. Only in a minority of cases are members of the workforce brought into the process of discussing the survey's findings, considering some options and then putting forward some recommendations for change. And even in this minority of cases one is rarely likely to see a whole set of substantive changes following an employee attitude survey; perhaps the notable exception here is if the survey has been about a single issue such as communications arrangements (recall here the earlier British Telecom example). Box 7.5 sets out the details of the follow-up stage to an employee attitude survey, with some accompanying questions for discussion purposes.

REFERENCES

1   P. B. Beaumont, *The Decline of Trade Union Organization*, Croom Helm, London, 1987, pp. 117–23.
2   Neil Millward and Mark Stevens, *British Workplace Industrial Relations, 1980–1984*, Gower, Aldershot, 1986, pp. 151–67.
3   *Industrial Relations Review and Report No. 396*, 14 July 1987, pp. 2–7.
4   Barbara Townley, 'Employee Communication Programmes', in Keith Sisson (ed.), *Personnel Management in Britain*, Basil Blackwell, Oxford, 1989, pp. 330–2.
5   Paul Marginson, P. K. Edwards, Roderick Martin, John Purcell and Keith Sisson, *Beyond the Workplace*, Basil Blackwell, Oxford, 1988, p. 106.
6   Townley, 'Employee Communication Programmes', pp. 345–9.
7   Millward and Stevens, *British Workplace Industrial Relations*, pp. 159–60.
8   Townley, 'Employee Communication Programmes', pp. 347–8.
9   J. Grummitt, *Team Briefing*, Industrial Society, London, 1983, pp. 4–7.
10 Mick Marchington, John Goodman, Adrian Wilkinson and Peter Ackers, *New Developments in Employee Involvement*, Employment Department Research Series No. 2, May 1992.
11 M. Marchington, P. Parker and A. Prestwich, 'Problems with Team Briefing in Practice', *Employee Relations*, 11 (4), 1989, pp. 21–30.
12 For a summary see ibid., pp. 22–3.
13 CBI, *Employee Involvement – Shaping the Future*, Study by KPMG Peat Marwick Management Consultants, London, 1990.
14 Sanford M. Jacoby, 'Employee Attitude Surveys in Historical

Perspective', in Fred K. Foulkes (ed.), *Human Resource Management: Readings*, Prentice Hall, Englewood Cliffs, New Jersey, 1989, pp. 272–85.

15   Neil Millward, Mark Stevens, David Smart and W. R. Hawes, *Workplace Industrial Relations in Transition*, Dartmouth, Aldershot, 1992, p. 167.

16   Personnel Management Factsheet No. 21, *Attitude Surveys*, September 1989.

17   P. B. Beaumont, 'Job Satisfaction: An Empirical Overview', *Quality of Working Life Journal*, 1 (5), 1984, pp. 17–29.

18   David Sirota, 'Why Managers Don't Use Attitude Survey Results', in Saul W. Gellerman, *Behavioural Science in Management*, Penguin, Harmondsworth, 1974, pp. 86–7.

8

EMPLOYEE PARTICIPATION, SMALL GROUP ACTIVITIES AND TEAM WORKING

INTRODUCTION

The well-known Harvard Business School approach to strategic HRM urges the need for all the various stakeholders (shareholders, employees, unions, suppliers, customers, local communities, etc.) to be taken into account in organizational governance arrangements, with 'employee influence' being one of the leading policy areas involved in their attempt to develop a pro-active, strategic and broad-based HRM orientation in individual organizations. In relation to the latter area it has been observed that:

> The issue of employee influence is not a simple or static matter. Society's views of what employees are entitled to in terms of influence differ across national boundaries and change over time. The expectations of employees also shift. Finally, managers' own values and their judgements about what constitutes effective management involve shifting standards about how much the enterprise should accommodate employees' interests, and especially how much influence is desirable. Judgements concerning employee influence involve either implicit or explicit trade-offs between the interests of shareholders (and of top management as the representatives of those shareholders) and those of employees. Managers are not always aware, however, that such trade-offs are taking place, or even that different stakeholders in the enterprise may hold differing views of how those trade-offs should be made.[1]

In keeping with the observation about the non-static nature of employee influence, it is important to note that in the 1970s reference to 'employee participation' or 'employee involvement' in many countries invariably involved discussions of worker or trade union representation on company boards of directors. The 1980s and 1990s have, however, seen the content of these terms changed quite considerably, with much more emphasis now being placed on financial participation, two-way communication arrangements and small group problem-solving activities. I have already discussed some of these arrangements in previous chapters (e.g. profit-sharing in Chapter 5 and communication in Chapter 7) so that here I concentrate on small group problem-solving activities by considering firstly quality circles and then various possible lines of development or evolution beyond such circles, such as total quality management (TQM) and team working arrangements for manual and non-manual employees.

QUALITY CIRCLES

In response to the perceived success of Japanese HRM practices, management in a number of advanced industrialized economies initiated the introduction of quality circle programmes in the early to mid-1980s. For example, some 500 organizations were reported to have quality circles in Britain in the mid-1980s, [2] and nearly 45 per cent of the hundred largest firms in West Germany (as it then was) had such programmes in the mid-1980s,[3] while a survey in the USA in the early 1980s reported that some 44 per cent of the organizations surveyed had some degree of quality circle activity.[4]

The essence of a quality circle has been defined as follows:

A quality circle is a group of employees that meets regularly to solve problems affecting its work area. Generally, 6 to 12 volunteers from the same work area make up the circle. The members receive training in problem-solving, statistical quality control, and group process. Quality circles generally recommend solutions for quality and productivity problems which management then may implement. A facilitator, usually a specially trained member of management, helps train circle members and ensures that things run smoothly. Typical objectives of QC programs include quality improvement, productivity enhancement, and employee involvement. Circles generally meet four hours a month in company time. Members may get recognition but rarely receive financial rewards.[5]

There are numerous sources of advice for management contemplating the establishment of a quality circle programme, with a number of continually recurring themes. Table 8.1 lists some of the leading suggestions.

Table 8.1   *Issues in establishing quality circles*

---

1   A steering committee(s) to oversee the programme should include representatives of staff management, line management and employees. A senior management presence is essential for organizational credibility/commitment purposes.

2   The appointment of a facilitator to be responsible for the day-to-day administration of the programme is a critical one. Such an individual is usually a member of middle management, with their commitment, input and skills being frequently a major determinant of the success (or not) of the programme.

3   All circle members need to be trained in a variety of matters including the organizational rationale for the programme, problem-solving techniques, presentation and interpersonal skills.

4   A pilot programme involving a limited number of circles in a limited number of work areas can constitute a useful 'learning by doing' exercise. The choice of work areas in which to conduct the pilot test is all-important, with a balance needing to be struck between the ability to generalize any lessons to the rest of the organization and producing sufficient 'good' early results to overcome any organizational resistance.

5   A decision has to be made as to whether circle leaders are always supervisors. The need is to strike a balance between the supervisors dominating the circles, and the supervisors feeling threatened by their operation and hence likely to work to undermine their effectiveness.

6   Circles usually meet in paid work time, although there is some variation between organizations in the frequency and length of individual meetings.

7   The question of what is and what is *not* the appropriate subject matter of circle discussions needs to be considered. In unionized organizations one of the most difficult decisions concerns the desirability and feasibility of separating the substantive areas of circle discussions from the coverage of collective bargaining.

8   Circle members need to receive regular feedback on the extent to which their recommendations have been implemented by management.

Source: Based on Ron Collard and Barrie Dale, 'Quality Circles', in Keith Sisson (ed.), *Personnel Management in Britain*, Basil Blackwell, Oxford, 1989, pp. 360–4.

Quality circles have been introduced for a number of reasons, such as attempts to improve employee relations and enhance various aspects of business performance, and there have been a number of studies of their impact.[6] In general the available research evidence suggests that relatively few strong and enduring effects have resulted from quality circle activities in the matter of employee attitudes and organizational performance. Individual unions, particularly in Britain and the USA, have expressed considerable scepticism, not to say

Table 8.2   *ASTMS on quality circles*

---

1   Quality circles only extend worker participation on management terms.

2   As an alternative channel of workforce–management communication, quality circles can undermine the position of supervisors and challenge existing collective bargaining arrangements.

3   In comparison to collective bargaining, quality circles have a number of disadvantages, namely that members are self-appointed or selected by management, discussion is restricted to the immediate work area, management retains the right to accept, reject or amend proposed solutions and they promote a 'false identification' with management aims.

4   However, as individual employees appear to gain some personal satisfaction from quality circle involvement, their possibilities should not be rejected out of hand. But management's motives for introducing them should be fully examined and the union needs to be in a strong enough position to have the circles operating in a context where there is an expansion of collective bargaining.

5   In situations where quality circles cannot be resisted, there need to be safeguards and *quid pro quos*, including the provision of extensive company information, regular updates on the savings generated through the circles, and union input into the selection of circle volunteers.

Source: Industrial Relations Review and Report No. 385, 1987, pp.15–16.

concern, about the role and value of quality circles. Table 8.2 illustrates the view of one British union.

Outside Japan, the main concern of both HRM practitioners and researchers has been with the question of whether quality circles will survive the test of time. That is, will they survive and become institutionalized in the organizational way of doing things and spread throughout the rest of the organization? The available evidence, particularly from Britain and the United States, points to a very considerable decay in quality circle activities, with many circles being formally or informally abandoned.[7] For example, one study in Britain reported that 25 per cent of the surveyed organizations had suspended their (full) quality circle programmes, while 61 per cent had suspended some individual circles within the programme.[8] There are various individual reasons for the failure of quality circles, although there is frequent reference to the effect that 'the lack of co-operation from middle managers and first line supervisors was especially important'.[9]

However, other researchers have argued that the failure of many quality circles is attributable to more than simply the unfavourable

Table 8.3   *Phases of a quality circle's life*

Phase	Activity	Destructive forces
Start-up	Publicize	Low volunteer rate
	Obtain funds and volunteers	Inadequate funding
	Train	Inability to learn group-process and problem-solving skills
Initial problem-solving	Identify and solve problems	Disagreement on problems
		Lack of knowledge of operations
Approval of initial suggestions	Present and have initial suggestions accepted	Resistance by staff groups and middle management
		Poor presentation and suggestions because of limited knowledge
Implementation	Relevant groups act on suggestions	Prohibitive costs
		Resistance by groups that must implement
Expansion of problem-solving	Form new groups	Member–non-member conflict
	Old groups continue	Raised aspirations
		Lack of problems
		Expense of parallel organization
		Savings not realized
		Rewards wanted
Decline	Fewer groups meet	Cynicism about program
		Burnout

Source: Edward E. Lawler and Susan A. Mohrman, 'Quality Circles after the Fad', *Harvard Business Review*, January–February 1985, p. 67.

attitudes of middle managers.[10] Such individuals have, for instance, emphasized larger organizational design issues (e.g. the problem of circles as parallel structures to normal organizational arrangements) and the technical limitations of the circles themselves (e.g. the limited range of issues addressed). Indeed one widely quoted study has argued that quality circles, by their very nature, carry the seeds of their own destruction, and therefore should always be viewed as a transitional device to other, more broad-ranging participative arrangements.[11] Table 8.3 indicates this view of the life cycle of a quality circle.

Quality circles have not, however, been completely abandoned in all organizations. For example, new initiatives involving quality circles were reported in 5 per cent of manufacturing plants in Britain in 1990.[12] Furthermore there continues to be some research concerning such activities, and among the points made are the following:

- A simple black and white dichotomy of 'success–failure' is not entirely appropriate when analysing such employee involvement initiatives.[13]

- A strong national and industry-level infrastructure is important in explaining the varied record across national boundaries of institutionalizing and diffusing innovations like quality circles.[14]

- Participative arrangements like quality circles require supportive, accompanying measures such as profit-sharing arrangements, commitments to employment security, relatively narrow wage differentials and observance of due process in the workplace.[15]

Moreover, it is increasingly argued that employees and management may learn some useful lessons from the failure of quality circles which will result in the introduction of some form of follow-up programme in which employee participation is emphasized. One such move in this direction is documented in Box 8.1.

Arguably the most important lesson drawn from the experience with quality circles to date is that they have suffered in general from being introduced as a stand-alone, self-contained innovation in a larger, unchanged organizational setting and culture. And according to some commentators, a total quality management (TQM) programme is likely to be considerably more successful than quality circles because it does not suffer from this disadvantage. Accordingly the next section turns to a discussion of TQM, a subject which has captured a great deal of interest among many firms in advanced industrialized economies in the late 1980s and early 1990s.

Box 8.1   *The concern with quality*

The organization concerned is in the electronics industry, has been in operation since late 1981 and currently has 108 employees. It has been attempting to decentralize levels of decision-making within the organization and bring about more of an individual employee sense of commitment, involvement and responsibility for matters concerning the quality of the manufactured product (i.e. 'quality is to be built in, rather than inspected in'); the latter needs to be seen in the context of manufacturing a high precision product, with nearly 13 per cent of the workforce being quality inspectors.

To this end, quality circles were experimented with in the period 1988–9. Two quality circles were formed (six members in each) and given two days of training by outside consultants. One circle in the accounts area worked well and produced a proposal that was adopted and implemented by management, although the other circle was deemed to be unsuccessful, largely as a result of a lack of middle management support on the engineering side. As a consequence it was found difficult to obtain volunteers for the establishment of a third quality circle. Following on this experience, a number of product improvement groups have been established; currently two are in place (six or seven people in each), with another four or five having been previously established. These groups differ from quality circles in a number of ways: membership is compulsory, they are cross-functional and middle managers are represented in them. Initially there was some opposition to establishing them (their existence seemed to indicate the existence of problems in particular areas) and some of the earlier groups were provided with too broad a remit. The current operation of the product improvement groups needs to be seen in the larger context of on-going preparations for the introduction of a total quality management programme.

The increased concern for quality derives from multiple sources. Firstly, the organization was acquired by another company in 1986 and the new chief executive for the company is keen to spread TQM across all sites. Secondly, the product being manufactured has become increasingly sophisticated in nature. Thirdly, their leading customer has become increasingly knowledgeable about the product's capabilities, and, as a consequence, has increased its demands for quality, accuracy, etc. These pressures or incentives for increased quality concern have had to confront two sets of obstacles. First, rapid

Box 8.1 *continued*

organizational growth (70 to 132 employees) in the years 1986–9 brought some 'costs'. The influx of new employees somewhat disrupted the initial strong emphasis on training and job rotation which had meant that many of the original employees could work in at least three of the six functional areas in the production process; in contrast, the more recent hires only worked in a single area and were much more orientated to 'getting the product out of the door'. And secondly, a strong engineering tradition (all the original managers were engineers) and a chief executive officer who kept all key decisions in his personal remit have meant that the experience and confidence to take decisions at the lower levels in the organization is relatively limited.

BEYOND QUALITY CIRCLES AND INTO TQM

The essence of TQM has been described as follows:

Today, TQM is a term which embraces much of current best practice in manufacturing. Its scope has broadened from its early concentration on statistical monitoring of manufacturing processes. Now it can include just-in-time inventory control, the emphasis on customer service (both internal and external customers), and a change in the way people work which emphasizes teamwork, training and greater employee responsibility and involvement in the work process. These are all related devices aimed at reorientating the production process so that it delivers products or services of consistent quality, in a timely fashion, which at least meet customer requirements. Indeed, focus on the customer – as a direct result of competition – is one of the main areas into which TQM has developed over the past few years. (*Financial Times*, 20 March 1991)

The leading features or components of a total quality management programme are typically held to be: (1) continuous problem-solving activity, typically organized around workplace teams; (2) a quality organization or structure to help focus this process, usually through steering teams; (3) statistical control and measurement of quality; (4) identification of 'customers' (internal and external); and (5) extensive training.[16] This being said, a number of different approaches to introducing TQM have been identified in individual organizations. For instance, a recent publication in Britain has distinguished between the following implementation strategies: a visionary model, which tends to be top down, focusing on training and procedures; a planning model, which tends to be off-line, measurement and technology-driven; and a learning model, which tends to be bottom up, attitudinal and involvement-focused.[17] For present purposes, it is important to note that the learning model involves the most substantial and direct HRM element and input.

To date, most of the existing academic literature on TQM has been concerned with discussions of its underlying theory. For example, Hill lists the underlying principles as follows:[18]

1   Quality is a strategic, as opposed to operational, issue for management, and hence senior management needs to be the driving force behind a TQM programme.

2   Cross-functional management (involving the specification of internal customers and the establishment of multi-functional project teams) is an essential feature of TQM, as not all quality improvements can take place within the existing vertical structure of organizations.

3   Most quality problems are held to be due to systems controlled by management, rather than being due to influences within the control of individual employees. As a consequence, improvement is very much a management responsibility.

4   Good underlying measurement and problem identification systems are essential, as is the training of employees in the techniques of issue identification and problem-solving.

5   The improvement process both creates and depends on a larger cultural change in the organization in which particular emphasis is placed on communications, involvement, trust, commitment to the customer, etc.

There is currently little systematic information on the extent of organizational adoption of TQM programmes in most advanced industrialized economies; a recent survey of the Fortune 1000 companies in the USA, however, did report that 77 per cent of the respondent organizations had some of their employees covered by TQM programmes, with on average 41 per cent of employees in organizations with TQM programmes being covered by them.[19] Furthermore, detailed empirical analysis of the outcomes and impact of such programmes are, to say the least, few. There are, however, a few scattered reports on the introduction and operation of TQM in some companies which do contain a few pointers which are worthy of note. The first message is that the introduction of a TQM programme is a relatively slow, drawn-out process which will almost invariably encounter some difficulties on the way; to some commentators this is a virtue of the approach, as it does not promise the 'quick-fix' solution of quality circles, and hence is likely to be less faddish in nature. Box 8.2 provides two illustrative examples of this experience.

As well as the inevitably (and arguably desirable) slow build-up to the introduction of a TQM programme, it is apparent from case studies of individual organizations that a TQM programme is not a self-contained programme of activity. As a consequence, its introduction and operation is likely to have certain 'knock on' effects in other parts of the HRM policy mix, which may necessitate the introduction of changes in the areas affected; this was certainly the experience at Honeywell Control Systems with such a programme.[20]

Table 8.4 sets out the views of two commentators concerning the sort of complementary HRM issues and changes that need to be addressed when introducing a TQM programme.

Although TQM is in its relative infancy, there are already some concerns being expressed in a number of management quarters about the extent of the necessary investment and the lack of an immediate boost to competitive performance. Moreover, newspaper reports are already circulating of individual organizations which have initiated TQM programmes and subsequently scaled them back; Florida Power Light in the USA is frequently mentioned in this regard. According to some practitioners, TQM will only be successful in organizations characterized by an emphasis on tangible results, insistence on performance measurement, an integrated programme and a strong senior management commitment (*Financial Times*, 21 October 1992). At the same time, however, it is apparent that many organizations are exerting (or experiencing) pressure through supply chain relationships for the adoption of TQM programmes. That is, organizations which have adopted TQM are more and more demanding that their suppliers adopt similar programmes (and, in some cases, assisting them). The potential strength of this influence for the adoption and diffusion of TQM needs to be seen in the context of individual organizations substantially reducing their overall number of suppliers (e.g. Xerox in the USA is reported to have reduced its parts vendors from 5,000 to 400 in recent years), and seeking to develop closer, longer-term working relationships with those that remain.

Finally, HRM researchers at the present time are particularly interested in the employee involvement 'roots' of TQM. One recent US study, for instance, has reported that 'if employee involvement

Table 8.4   *TQM and complementary HRM policy changes*

- In selection decisions the willingness of employees to learn new skills needs to be tested; it is important to identify individuals who can function well in group settings, and a realistic preview of expected behaviours needs to be provided.

- Training programmes must reach beyond specific job skills to cover topics such as team work, time management, decision-making skills, etc.

- Career development must seek to provide employees with a systems orientation which means that greater emphasis must be placed on cross-functional experience obtained via horizontal (rather than vertical) work assignments and moves.

- The strong individual orientation and emphasis of the performance appraisal process needs to be changed. More emphasis needs to be given to evaluating contributions to team performance, involving peers in the appraisal process, and making the process less competitive between individuals.

- Pay systems centred around individual job descriptions, job worth and individual merit increases are inconsistent with TQM's emphasis on collective responsibility, horizontal relationships and horizontal learning. Instead, skills-based payment systems, profit-sharing or group based performance pay arrangements are more appropriate.

- Differences in terms and conditions of employment based on hierarchical position need to give way to all-salaried workforce or single status arrangements.

- Adversarial, arm's length collective bargaining needs to be replaced by much more of a joint problem-solving approach.

- Much more emphasis needs to be given to establishing channels of two-way communication concerning strategy and performance.

Source: Adapted from David E. Bowen and Edward E. Lawler, 'Total Quality Orientated Human Resources Management', *Organizational Dynamics*, Spring 1992, pp. 34–40.

and quality are managed as one integrated program or as two co-ordinated programs, they are more likely to achieve desired performance results and to change internal business conditions than if they are run as two separate programs'.[21] A recent case study investigation in Britain has also raised questions about the possible contradictions between the 'hard' (i.e. measurement) and 'soft' (i.e. employee involvement) sides of TQM, arguing that these relationships have not been fully explored in practice.[22] Indeed, Box 8.3 (p. 190) illustrates the contradiction apparent in one management approach to introducing TQM.

Box 8.2   *Building up a TQM programme*

Example 1

The organization concerned is in the electricity supply industry (generation, transmission and distribution), with currently some 9,500 employees. The current moves towards 'total quality management' have their origins in a number of *prior* developments. Firstly, in the early 1980s, some 30 quality circles covering 150–200 employees in the distribution area were set up. These were useful in encouraging some employee participation and team working, but while management were supportive, they were not involved so circles tended to focus on very 'parochial problems'. In the years 1982–4 the quality circle programme effectively 'ran out of steam'. In 1983–4, however, the staff development officer, in an attempt to increase employee motivation, introduced a 'new age thinking' programme which sought to impact on attitudes and values through a process of employee 'self-actualization'. Beginning with employees who interacted directly with the public, some 5,000 staff were put through a series of three-day training sessions. This was an internally run programme (with some 50 internal trainers/facilitators inside the organization) which is still used, but only on an *ad hoc* basis; the staff development officer who initiated the programme and was overwhelmingly its driving force has now retired from the organization. Thirdly, management concerns about the inadequacy of internal communications led to the introduction of team briefing arrangements. These were introduced over eighteen months to two years from 1986 to 1987 right throughout the organization. They still remain in operation, although their effectiveness is judged to be rather uneven.

In 1987 (with privatization looming on the horizon) the productivity services manager investigated a number of 'productivity through quality' initiatives. The three features of such programmes which were particularly attractive to him were (1) their stress on employee involvement and participation (which could usefully build on the earlier experience with the 'new age thinking' programme), (2) the surrounding supportive set of structural (management) arrangements (unlike the case with quality circles); and (3) their emphasis on the measurement of performance. However, it took some considerable time and effort to convince senior management of their potential value. This was because the issue of privatization was occupying the

Box 8.2 *continued*

thoughts of senior management, who needed to be convinced of the value of such a large investment. Within the organization there was, also, a contending school of thought (associated with the strong engineering tradition of the company) which favoured a more conventional (hard measurement), quality assurance approach.

Nevertheless, in the period 1987–9 some six pilot exercises involving 'quality improvement' teams were undertaken. These cross-functional teams (some six or seven members, including a middle management member) worked on a number of problems identified by management, following an in-house, two-day training programme (covering statistical process control (SPC), problem-solving skills etc.) for each team. Furthermore, visits were made to six well-known companies in Britain with well-established quality management programmes. Perhaps the key event in convincing senior management of the potential value of the approach, however, was the visit to two similar (same industry) organizations in the USA, where a very favourable investment return on such programmes was reported. Once 'the green light' had been given, an external consultant for training purposes was selected in late 1989 and a series of one-day seminars for managers took place in early 1990 to explain the essence of the approach.

From May 1990 a training programme in total quality was initiated. This programme had by August 1991 involved (1) six *facilitator* training courses of ten days each (covering team working, team building, problem solving, SPC, etc.) with some 130–140 individuals having gone through these; (2) eight management training courses of four days each, with some 170 individuals having been through these; (3) ten team leaders' training courses of five days' duration (150–160 through these) and (4) 24 team training courses of two days' duration covering 350–400 employees. The training material has been jointly developed with the external consultants, although the latter have been primarily responsible for running the facilitator and management courses, only the remainder being run by 'in-house' staff.

By August 1991 some 60–70 quality improvement teams were in operation, looking at various aspects of the business. More than a dozen teams completed individual assignments and reports on various issues including the nature of bills which are sent to customers, obtaining greater access to homes for meter-reading purposes. Moreover some eighteen teams investigated and reported (over a four-month period) on the matter of improving the effectiveness of the processes of management accountability and responsibility within one business area of the organization. This

Box 8.2 *continued*

resulted in a new organization structure with fewer reporting levels and redefined accountabilities.

The priorities for the future are ensuring the completion of a consistent pattern of training across the organization as a whole, and ensuring that line managers identify with and assume responsibility for the approach via the establishment and maintenance of a supportive infrastructure, the latter involving management teams from director level downwards. The introduction of TQM principles and practices into the natural management processes across the business will be the main focus of attention over the next few years.

Example 2

In this particular organization senior management concern with the level of inventories, extent of product quality and, especially, the speed of delivery to customers led to the launch of a TQM programme in the mid-1980s. An outside consultant was utilized and all 2,000 employees were put through a series of eight training modules for TQM. Over something like five years the results and perceived success of the programme had been judged to be uneven and 'spotty'. Positive results had been reported in some areas, but not in others, with in general the visibility of the results being held to be too long in coming through. This very uneven record was attributed to the fact that continuous improvement can only occur from an existing sound measurement basis, and that this basis did not exist at the time of launch of the programme. As a consequence the organization had to make a sizeable investment in improving the extent and nature of measurement and control systems on the shopfloor. This process has been completed. Moreover the organization moved to a new custom-built site in 1992 which further enhanced the technical capability of its measurement systems. This new site move also enhanced the capacity to introduce a number of organizational changes to complement the TQM programme. For instance there were further, extensive moves in the direction of harmonized terms and conditions of employment, and the quality inspection department was phased out before the occupation of the new site. As a consequence it was proposed to relaunch the TQM programme on the new site in a 'more low key' way with the intention being to build up the process incrementally, starting with a series of small, well-defined projects whose results could be carefully measured and success demonstrated.

Box 8.3   *Introducing TQM: a contradiction in approach*

This US-owned subsidiary in the rubber manufacturing industry proposed, in response to increased customer demands for quality reliability, speed of delivery etc., to introduce a TQM programme into one of its four business areas on site, and then spread it to the other areas over the course of time. The individual business area in which the TQM programme was to be launched was the growing, high-value-added area of its activities. However, prior to launching the programme it was decided to build a new plant (on the existing site) to rehouse this particular part of the business. This decision reflected the view that the physical and technical limitations of the old plant were such as to hinder the effective introduction and operation of the TQM programme. The new plant was designed and brought on stream by a team consisting solely of engineers and senior line managers, with no input being sought from the production employees, union or HRM function. As production started up in the new plant, management faced problems of relatively high absence levels and widespread employee reluctance to carry out any minor variations in day-to-day working. Interviews with employees revealed considerable dissatisfaction with a number of aspects of the working environment of the new plant, aspects which they were never consulted about at the design stage. Management is hopeful that these 'initial teething problems' will wash out over the course of time, as the order book is currently booming and a highly participative training programme in TQM working principles has been introduced in order to facilitate the movement to team working arrangements.

TEAM WORKING ON THE SHOPFLOOR

Team working on the shopfloor has become increasingly common in many organizations in recent years, although in many ways the notion of team working is nothing very new: autonomous or semi-autonomous work groups were central to the theory of socio-technical job design principles in the 1960s and 1970s. The introduction and operation of semi-autonomous work groups, however, never really occurred on any significant scale outside Sweden, although experience with them in selected work settings has provided some insight into the factors that facilitate work group autonomy. The leading factors typically cited in this regard are as follows:[23]

1 when the work is not entirely unskilled;
2 when the work group can be identified as a meaningful unit of the organization, and when inputs and outputs are definite and clearly identifiable and the groups can be separated by stable buffer areas;
3 when turn-over in the group can be kept to a minimum;
4 when there are definite criteria for performance evaluation of the group and group members;
5 when timely feedback is possible;
6 when the group has resources for measuring and controlling its own critical variances in workflow;
7 when the tasks are highly interdependent, so that group members must work together;
8 when cross-training is desired by management;
9 when jobs can be structured to balance group and individual tasks.

In one high-technology organization I have observed, some 30 per cent of the workforce has been moved into semi-autonomous work groups in the last two years, on the basis of some of the factors and considerations listed above. However, the above findings are likely to be of more general interest given that from the 1980s the increasingly favoured work design or redesign principles have involved (1) the use of work teams (admittedly rarely of the semi-autonomous nature), (2) a reduced number of individual job classifications, and (3) the integration of responsibility for quality control into production or operational jobs. These practices are most apparent in new plants or greenfield sites, although a number of well publicized wage agreements in Britain in recent years in existing organizations have involved sizeable wage increases being contingent upon moves in the team working direction. The nature of team working arrangements can vary quite considerably between different organizations. In some cases one is talking about permanent or fixed membership teams in a given work area, whereas in other cases one observes temporary teams established to deal with particular problems or issues. Box 8.4 describes one set of arrangements along the latter lines.

Team-based working arrangements were particularly prominent in the automobile manufacturing industry in the USA in the 1980s. Indeed moves in this direction produced considerable internal controversy within the autoworkers' union. The union

---

Box 8.4   *Team working*

This manufacturing plant, with some 400 employees, had been established for around two and a half years. It is a foreign-owned subsidiary and has a continuous production process involving three crews working a five-shift system. During the course of the last 12–15 months or so it has introduced analytical troubleshooting teams based on the Kepner and Tregoe problem-solving principles. The essence of these principles is the sequential identification of problems, a separation and prioritization of problems (i.e. deal with the biggest one first), the production of a trouble statement on which an individual team focuses, step-by-step breaking down of the problem for analytical purposes, identification of most probable causes, verification of the most probable cause, a fix solution, and finally examination of any possible problems associated with the fix solution.

The training of the production and maintenance workforce in these problem-solving principles has involved groups of twelve employees being put through a three-day participative workshop session. This training was initially provided by consultants from Kepner and Tregoe, although now some in-house expertise has been established with five employees of the plant providing the necessary training.

Analytical troubleshooting teams based on these principles have been a feature of production operations in the parent company for some considerable time, and were deemed to be particularly appropriate for this plant, given its continuous production process and the 'fit' with the larger organizational culture it was seeking to establish (i.e. highly decentralized levels of decision-making with individual employees exhibiting relatively high levels of organizational responsibility and commitment). The perceived advantages of the Kepner and Tregoe problem-solving approach are that individuals avoid rushing to the solution state and that all employees are on the 'same wavelength' in the sense of having a common methodology and language as regards problem-solving.

There are formally designated team leaders who have undergone a somewhat extended programme of training in these principles, although their designation as leaders is not simply a reflection of their position in the organization hierarchy. There are, however, no formally designated teams. These are simply formed as and when problems occur or emerge. In such circumstances the leader in the relevant area will be responsible for determining the size and

Box 8.4 *continued*

composition of the problem-solving team. The majority of problems which have emerged have been dealt with relatively speedily through teams, although one five-person team has been working on one on-going problem for something like eight months.

opponents of such developments (the so-called 'new directions movement') have argued that team working weakens the traditional importance of seniority, increases the workload of individuals by adding new responsibilities (such as quality control), results in team leaders acting as *de facto* foremen, and pits individual workers against each other (via the influence of peer group pressure within teams), all of which works to management's advantage through an increase in the extent of their discretion. Indeed to Parker and Slaughter the team concept is simply 'management by stress'.[24] In contrast, the proponents of team working within the union have argued that moves in this direction are essential for competitive survival, enhance the variety and skill content of jobs and are consistent with the union's long-term goal of increasing the level of worker and union participation in organizational decision-making.[25] As team working arrangements spread further, it is unlikely that such debates will be confined to this particular union. Indeed, in mid-1992 the Union of Communication Workers in Britain voted at its annual conference to oppose the introduction and operation of team working in Royal Mail, the letters arm of the Post Office (*Financial Times*, 20 May 1992). These union concerns, worries and opposition in Britain and the USA stand in marked contrast to the position in some other countries. For instance, IG Metall in (West) Germany had a well-developed, pro-active approach towards 'group working' throughout the 1980s. The key elements of its approach are listed in Table 8.5.

The impact of team working arrangements, *ceteris paribus*, on various measures of organizational performance is of obvious interest to HRM practitioners and researchers. Although systematic empirical research is still in its early days, one study in the US auto industry, for instance, found little evidence of any positive impact on organizational performance.[26] This finding may have reflected the fact that the nature of team working arrangements varied considerably between the plants involved, that team working needed to be considered in conjunction with a complementary set of other arrangements, or that the formal structural measures of team working in the study failed to capture adequately certain more influential, informal processes

Table 8.5   *The IG Metall policy approach to team working*

- A broad assignment of varying tasks for the group (including long cycle times)
- Group competence in decision-making in areas such as job rotation, division of the work, quality control, and training needs
- Decentralization of the plant decision-making structure
- Selection of production organization and technology suitable for group work (based on decentralized technology and production concepts)
- Equal pay for group members
- Equal opportunity for all, including special training where necessary for the disabled and socially disadvantaged, to participate in group work
- Support for the personal and occupational development of individuals and the group
- Regular group meetings, at least one hour per week
- Representation of group interests within the established plant system of interest representation
- Voluntary participation in the groups
- Pilot projects to test the functioning of group work before broader implementation
- A joint steering committee at the firm level, with equal labour and management representation, to oversee and co-ordinate the implementation of group work and the activities of the groups

---

Source: Lowell Turner, *Democracy at Work*, Cornell University Press, Ithaca, 1991, pp.113–14.

associated with the teams. In contrast, a recent study in Britain reported that team working in some organizations had brought sizeable productivity gains as a result of increased output, reduced supervisory support, reduced absenteeism, reduced overtime levels and greater operating awareness.[27] The same report went on to argue that the most appropriate size of teams was 5–12 members, with the more effective teams being characterized by acceptance (by the team) of responsibility for the completion of a full cycle of work activities; possession of the full range of required skills; the ability of the team to regulate its own activities; a team size and structure which facilitated communication and satisfactory working relationships; and the existence of clear criteria for team performance. These findings are clearly similar to some of those cited earlier for semi-autonomous groups.

In statistical studies 'effective' teams are those associated with above-average increments to certain measures of organizational performance. However, one recent publication has suggested a more broad-ranging definition of effective team working, to reflect the fact that not all teams are production-based.[28] In essence it was suggested that there were three dimensions to the notion of effective team working. These were, firstly, the degree to which the team's productive output meets the quality, quantity and timeliness standards of the users of the output; secondly, the degree to which the process involved has enhanced the continued ability of the team to work together; and thirdly, the degree to which the team experience contributed to the job satisfaction of its members. As to the determinants of group or team effectiveness, traditionally discussions along these lines have referred to various factors such as the group (e.g. size), the task (e.g. nature and clarity), the environment (e.g. inter-group relations), leadership style, and procedures. More recently, however, there has been enhanced interest in how HRM policies concerning selection, development, and compensation can facilitate group working;[29] these have added to the traditional approach of how to design jobs for group working purposes.

BEYOND THE SHOPFLOOR WORK TEAMS

One of the most likely HRM developments of the 1990s will be the increased spread of various forms of team working arrangements beyond the shopfloor and into the white collar professional and technical areas of industrial organizations. Indeed, movement along these lines has already occurred in a number of organizations, with the Belbein principles of team selection frequently being referred to, at least in Britain, in this regard.[30]

The leading findings associated with the work of Belbein have been summarized as follows:[31]

1 It is possible to identify and distinguish eight distinct management styles which were labelled 'team roles' (see below).
2 The managers studied tended to adopt one or two of these team roles fairly consistently.
3 Which role they became associated with was capable of prediction through psychometric tests.
4 When team roles were combined in certain ways, they helped to produce more effective teams.
5 Such team roles were not necessarily associated with a person's functional role, but the way in which they were combined seemed to affect job success.

6　Factors which seemed to contribute to effective team work by individuals included correct recognition of their own best role; self-awareness of the best contribution they could make to their team or situation and their ability and preparedness to work out their strengths rather than permitting weaknesses to interfere with their performance.

7　The eight roles (and their functions) identified were:
   (i)　　Chairman: co-ordinating style
   (ii)　　Team leader: directive style
   (iii)　Innovator: creative thinking in the team
   (iv)　Monitor–evaluator: critical thinking in the team
   (v)　　Company worker: getting the work done
   (vi)　Team worker: looking after personal relationships in the team
   (vii)　Completer: keeping the team on its toes
   (viii)　Resource investigator: keeping in touch with other teams.

8　These roles are related to the personality and mental ability of individuals and reflect managerial behaviour in connection with the aims and demands of the manager's job. Since each role contributes to team success, a successful, balanced team will contain all roles.

Box 8.5 shows one organization's application of the Belbein principles.

The appropriate mix of roles in a team may be a necessary, but is arguably not a sufficient, condition for effective team performance. For example, some research in the USA suggests that, over and above issues of team structure, the performance of teams will be influenced (for good or bad) by aspects of the larger organizational context (e.g. reward systems, information systems) and the availability of process assistance.[32]

Within the white collar employment area, team working is particularly likely to become of increased importance in the (new) product development process. The value of a move in this direction in many organizations has been argued on the grounds that Japanese organizations (with their team work emphasis) in the car manufacturing industry take considerably less engineering time to design and bring into production new products compared to their US counterparts.[33] This message is being gradually assimilated in certain organizations. For example, the Rover Group indicated in early 1991 that it was seeking to extend to its full model range the lessons of the

Box 8.5 *Applying the Belbein principles*

The organization concerned has since the late 1980s been undergoing a major restructuring exercise as it seeks to adapt to the demands of its changing product market environment. This organizational and cultural change exercise has particularly emphasized the need for the development of a team working culture right throughout the organization. The process was initiated from the top down, starting at the board level with all appointees (both newcomers and existing internals to be promoted) to the revamped board being screened via, among other things, reference to the Belbein principles. The result was a new senior management team with the following 'mix of roles' (using Belbein's terminology): a chief executive officer (co-ordinator, team worker, resource investigator); a deputy chief executive officer (shaper, monitor–evaluator, co-ordinator); a manufacturing director (shaper, implementor); a finance director (implementor, monitor–evaluator, shaper); a technical director (a resource investigator, monitor–evaluator, plant); a HRM director (co-ordinator, shaper, monitor–evaluator); and a sales director (team worker, co-ordinator, resource investigator).

The board's enthusiasm for the Belbein principles has been and remains, to say the least, very considerable. In their view these principles have provided a common language and frame of reference for discussion which has minimized personality clashes at the board during a period of thorough organizational restructuring. As a consequence an outside consultant specializing in the Belbein principles has been retained and in the last three or four years the principles have been cascaded down throughout the organization. For instance, the top 200 management and technical specialists in the organization have all gone through a process of self-analysis, peer group analysis, superior–subordinate analysis and feedback according to the Belbein principles. These results have been extensively drawn upon when internal task forces have been established to address particular issues and themes confronting the organization; the composition, and often the leadership, of these task forces is more a function of the results of the Belbein analysis than of position in the organizational hierarchy. These results have also been extensively utilized in the process of establishing multi-disciplinary, new product development teams in what is a very R&D-driven organization. The Belbein principles are now incorporated in the selection decision for

Box 8.5 *continued*

both new employees and internal promotions, and have, at least to some extent, been incorporated in the annual appraisal process for the more senior, white collar staff. For such individuals the appraisal process focuses not only on what they have achieved (i.e. results), but also how they have achieved it, with some of the feedback concerning the latter frequently involving guidelines for change using the Belbein principles and terminology.

The stated intention is to spread these principles further throughout the organization in two ways. Firstly, they will try and have the common language and terms of reference of Belbein reduce the extent of the personality clashes in superior–subordinate relationships on a day-to-day basis. The hope here is that wider knowledge of and exposure to the principles will help individuals to adjust their 'management style' according to the nature of the individual they are interacting with. Secondly, the composition or membership of task forces or teams addressing a particular issue or problem will change somewhat according to the particular phase or stage of the problem-solving cycle they have reached.

Land Rover Discovery, a vehicle that was designed, developed and put into production, using a multi-functional team approach, in under three years compared to the average of four to six years in the West European car industry (*Financial Times*, 6 February 1991). The general perception is that the product development process in many organizations is too segmented, specialized and sequential, with product development teams being too inward-looking and overly design-dominated. Indeed Hayes, Wheelwright and Clark have called for the extensive adoption of a new paradigm in the product development process which involves, for example, a project team led by a business manager with broad experience, a project focus which involves a cross-functional team effort throughout and extensive overlapping of the project phases.[34] Box 8.6 indicates one organization's current thinking along these lines.

However, a recent study in the USA usefully illustrates the fact that simply introducing multi-functional new product development teams in an unchanged larger organizational setting is not a recipe for success.[35] The basic conclusion of this study was that larger changes in training, facilitation, evaluation practices and indeed in organizational norms were necessary to ensure that the benefits of diversity outweighed the costs. The current emphasis on the appropriate mix

Box 8.6 *Some new thinking about new product development*

In this organization there are four separate business or product divisions, each of which is at a different stage of the product life cycle, faces a different set of product market circumstances and constraints, and has rather different product market strategies. The development section has the prime responsibility for the development of new products across all four business areas. The section currently has a complement of five staff who in the main are chemists, although physicists and engineers have been employed in the section. The section is responsible for moving a new product through the sequential stages of identifying a market need for a new product, development of the design for a prototype, building and testing a full-scale prototype, in-service testing, development of production methods to full-scale, through to the full commercialization (marketing and sales) of the product.

The senior management of the organization have a commitment to 'keeping the centre lean'. This has meant, firstly, that the development section is staffed solely by technical specialists, with no finance, operations, marketing and sales specialists being employed there. Secondly, the budget of the section has been cut, with the four separate businesses all having product extension budgets. This approach to new product development has generated a number of problems and frustrations in recent years. Firstly, the technical specialists in the development section frequently have to spend as much as 50 per cent of their time on marketing, an area in which they have no particular experience. Secondly, a number of new product development initiatives or launches have been failures, due to the problem of getting the new product satisfactorily 'over the wall' (from the development section) into the individual operating areas. These failures have become increasingly widely recognized throughout the organization, although different perspectives on the reasons for failure are apparent; to the technical section it is the lack of a sense of ownership of (and hence commitment to) the new product in the operating divisions, whereas to the operating divisions it is the 'excessive technical' dominance (relative to practical manufacturing considerations) of the development process.

The appointment of a new MD has opened up the possibility of experimenting with a matrix approach to new product development. This would involve selectively drawing in specialists in finance,

Box 8.6 *continued*

> operations, sales and marketing from the separate operating divisions to be members of new product development teams at particular stages of process (which frequently spans something like a two-year period). The director of development is particularly keen to proceed along these lines, with a proposal to this effect currently being discussed. He is, however, conscious that this process will not automatically guarantee success in an organization with no history of cross-functional team working. He is particularly aware that individuals on the team will need to develop an appreciation of the value of, and willingness to listen to, others' viewpoints and that the line managers in the operating divisions will need to be assured, through experience, that the process does not involve too heavy a time burden on some of their key staff members.

and balance of team roles will hopefully give way in the near future to more of an emphasis on an individual team's interaction with the larger organizational environment. Indeed, as the practice of establishing 'international management teams' gathers pace[36] it will be even more important to look beyond the team as a self-contained entity and to take on board the larger interaction process across multiple organizations.

REFERENCES

1   Michael Beer and Bert Spector (eds.), *Reading in Human Resource Management*, Free Press, New York, 1985, p. 102.
2   Incomes Data Services, *Ever Increasing Circles*, London, 1985.
3   Otto Jacobi and Walther Müller-Jentsch, 'West Germany: Continuity and Structural Change', in Guido Baglioni and Colin Crouch (eds.), *European Industrial Relations*, Sage, London, 1990, p. 132.
4   *People and Productivity: A Challenge to Corporate America*, New York Stock Exchange, New York, 1982.
5   Edward E. Lawler and Susan A. Mohrman, 'Quality Circles after the Fad', *Harvard Business Review*, January–February 1985, p. 66.
6   See, for example, K. Bradley and S. Hill, 'After Japan: The Quality Circle Transplant and Production Efficiency', *British Journal of Industrial Relations*, 21, 1983, pp. 291–311. See also K. Bradley and S. Hill, 'Quality Circles and Managerial Interests', *Industrial Relations*, 26, 1987, pp. 68–82.
7   Robert Drago, 'Quality Circle Survival: An Explanatory Analysis',

Industrial Relations, 27, 1988.

8   Ron Collard and Barrie Dale, 'Quality Circles', in Keith Sisson (ed.), *Personnel Management in Britain*, Basil Blackwell, Oxford, 1989, p. 368.

9   Ibid., p. 368.

10 S. Hill, 'Why Quality Circles Failed but Total Quality Management Might Succeed', *British Journal of Industrial Relations*, 29 (4), December 1991, pp. 541–68.

11 Lawler and Mohrman, 'Quality Circles'.

12 Neil Millward, Mark Stevens, David Smart and W. R. Hawes, *Workplace Industrial Relations in Transition*, Dartmouth, Aldershot, 1992, p. 180.

13 Paul S. Goodman and James W. Dean, 'Creating Long-Term Organizational Change', in Paul S. Goodman and Associates, *Change in Organizations*, Jossey-Bass, San Francisco, 1982, pp. 226–79.

14 Robert Cole, *Strategies for Learning*, University of California Press, Berkeley, 1988.

15 David Levine and Laura D'Andrea Tyson, 'Participation, Productivity and the Firm's Environment', in Alan S. Binder (ed.), *Paying for Productivity*, Brookings Institution, Washington DC, 1990, pp. 183–236.

16 IDS Study No.457, May 1990, p. 1.

17 Susan Whittle, 'Total Quality Management: Redundant Approaches to Culture Change', *QWL News and Abstracts*, 110, Spring 1992.

18 Hill, 'Why Quality Circles Failed', pp. 554–5.

19 Edward E. Lawler, Susan Albers Mohrman and Gerald E. Ledford, *Employee Involvement and Total Quality Management*, Jossey-Bass, San Francisco, 1992, p. 95.

20 *Industrial Relations Review and Report No. 486*, 26 April 1991.

21 Lawler et al., *Employee Involvement*, p. 111.

22 Adrian Wilkinson, Mick Marchington, John Goodman and Peter Ackers, 'Total Quality Management and Employee Involvement', *Human Resource Management Journal*, 2 (4), Summer 1992, pp. 1–20.

23 L. E. Davis and G. J. Wacker, 'Job Design', in G. Salvendy (ed.), *Handbook of Human Factors*, Wiley, New York, 1987.

24 Michael Parker and Jane Slaughter, 'Managing by Stress: The Dark Side of the Team Concept', *ILR Report*, Fall 1988.

25 D. F. Ephlin, 'Devolution by Evolution: The Changing Relationship between GM and the UAW', *Academy of Management Executive*, 2 (1), February 1988, pp. 63–6.

26 Harry C. Katz, Thomas A. Kochan and Jeffery Keefe, 'Industrial Relations and Productivity in the US Automobile Industry', *Brookings Papers on Economic Activity*, 1987, pp. 685–715.

27 Cited in *Industrial Relations Review and Report No. 451*, 7 November 1989, p. 2.

28 J. Richard Hackman (ed.), *Groups That Work (and Those That Don't)*, Jossey-Bass, San Francisco, 1990.

29   Richard A. Guzzo, 'Improving Work-Group Effectiveness', in Randall S. Schuler, Stuart A. Youngblood and Vandra L. Huber (eds.), *Readings in Personnel and Human Resource Management*, West Publishing Co., St Paul, Minn., 3rd edition, 1988, pp. 350–6.

30   R. Meredith Belbein, *Management Teams: Why They Succeed or Fail*, Heinemann, Oxford, 1981.

31   Based on Andrzej Huczynski and David Buchanan, *Organizational Behaviour: An Introductory Text*, Prentice Hall, Hemel Hempstead, 2nd edition, 1991, pp. 244–5.

32   Hackman, *Groups That Work*.

33   Michael L. Dertouzos, Richard K. Lester and Robert M. Solow, *Made in America: Regaining the Productive Edge*, MIT Press, Cambridge, Mass., 1989, pp. 70–1.

34   Robert M. Hayes, Steven C. Wheelwright and Kim B. Clark, *Dynamic Manufacturing*, Free Press, New York, 1985, Chapter 11.

35   Deborah Gladstein Ancona and David E. Caldwell, 'Cross-Functional Teams: Blessing or Curse for New Product Development?', in Thomas A. Kochan and Michael Useem (eds.), *Transforming Organizations*, Oxford University Press, New York, 1992, pp. 154–68.

36   Nicola Phillips, *Managing International Teams*, Pitman, London, 1992.

9

SQUARING THE CIRCLE?

INTRODUCTION

In this book I have examined in turn some of the leading human resource management issues that will be of relevance to line managers. The emphasis so far has been very largely on questions such as what are the appropriate organizational circumstances and interpersonal skills to facilitate the effective operation of certain innovations and techniques in some of the leading functional areas of HRM. This final chapter seeks to step back from the detail of the individual issues discussed in order to provide something of a larger, more rounded perspective on the subject area.

Accordingly in this final chapter I consider in turn some criticisms of the existing human resource management literature, discuss the place of trade unions in the practice of human resource management, and look at the infant field of international HRM.

THE 'QUALITY' OF THE HUMAN RESOURCE MANAGEMENT LITERATURE

In the Introduction to this book I noted that the subject of human resource management is dealt with in an overwhelmingly US-based body of literature which has attracted a considerable number of sceptics and critics both in and outside the USA.[1] It is not, however, always entirely clear whether this criticism is directed at the organizational practice of HRM or the literature on HRM. One suspects that it is a bit of both, although here I initially focus on some of the alleged weaknesses of the relevant body of literature.

To some individuals there is nothing terribly new in the human resource management literature in that it is little more than a body of thought which began with the 'human relations' thinking of the 1930s and has evolved through the organization development and change literature of the 1960s and 1970s. Commentators who subscribe to this sort of view are quite likely to contend that human resource management embodies some of the leading assumptions of the human relations school of thought. For instance, it assumes that high job satisfaction levels lead strongly and directly to high productivity levels, a relationship that empirical research has consistently failed to document.[2] It may also be argued that the stress on the need to integrate human resource and technological developments is little more than the basic message of socio-technical systems theory of the 1960s and 1970s,[3] while the role of a competitive, rapidly changing product market environment in stimulating the need for flexible working practices and a close individual employee–organization identification process is simply rediscovering the wheel as in Burns and Stalker's notion of an organic management system.[4]

A second line of criticism is that the academic literature is running well ahead of actual organizational practice. That is, academics are simply retitling their textbooks (personnel management becomes human resource management), whereas in reality most organizations do not closely integrate (in a two-way fashion) human resource and strategic planning. As a result, so the argument goes, individual human resource management changes in most organizations do not add up to a consistent, integrated package deriving from a long-run, coherent management strategy, and the case studies of sophisticated human resource management policies are based on a very small group of atypical organizations; that is, organizations which operate on greenfield site locations, have above-average levels of 'organizational slack' or resources, or which have had founders or early senior managers who implanted in them a very special organizational culture that assigns a relatively high priority to human resource management development. In short, the basic contention of some individuals is that the potential applicability of a comprehensive human resource management approach is essentially limited to a relatively small, unrepresentative sub-set of individual organizations.

A third line of argument, which draws to some extent on those above, is that human resource management is most applicable in non-union organizations and may be difficult to introduce (as a result of union opposition) in highly unionized firms, but if it is introduced in the latter may have some significant anti-union implications; this line of argument is likely to be largely confined to national systems traditionally characterized by a relatively adversarial, arm's length collective bargaining process (e.g. the USA and Britain). Advocates of this school of thought can variously point to the fact(s) that sophisticated human resource management systems were essentially developed in the non-union sector in the USA in the 1980s and 1990s, are designed to produce a strong individual employee–organization identification process which has the potential to limit the job dissatisfaction which tends to trigger a demand for union representation, and may substitute for, rather than complement, existing collective bargaining arrangements by permitting employers to communicate directly with (and so influence) individual employees rather than communicating indirectly with them through union channels. In short, academic advocates of human resource management may urge the need for senior managers to adopt a multiple-stakeholder perspective (including employees and unions) when formulating their strategy,[5] but its heavy line management orientation and essential aim (i.e. a 'good' human resource management system involves an alignment of the goals and objectives of individual employees with those of the organization) embody strong (if subtle) managerial control and 'unitarist' assumptions and implications.

Another set of criticisms of the human resource management literature concerns its highly descriptive and prescriptive nature. There are in fact two sub-elements to this line of argument. The first is that the literature is very 'politically naive' in the sense that it is based very largely on a rational decision-making paradigm which almost totally ignores the all-important realities of organizational politics and differential sub-unit power within the management hierarchy. As a result, questions concerning the practical means of implementing new, innovative human resource management policies in organizations are very largely neglected. The literature in fact tends to do little more than imply that the very weight of environmental forces, particularly stemming from the product market, will necessarily convince senior management of the need for such a change. The second element of criticism is that the literature claims to be very 'bottom line' orientated, and certainly there are many assertions to the effect that human resource management policies and practices have a considerable positive impact on productivity levels and overall levels of organizational performance. However, claims to this effect need to be seen in the light of the fact that the whole question of just how one measures organizational effectiveness is highly controversial, with relatively little consensus being present in the relevant body of literature.[6] Furthermore, the few existing studies of employee involvement arrangements have tended to reveal relatively few strong relationships with various measures of organizational performance.[7] Moreover there have been remarkably few systematic empirical studies of the relationship between a package of human resource management practices and various measures of larger organizational performance, with the positive findings of Gomez-Mejia's survey in the USA being one of the very few that can be cited in this regard.[8]

One should not automatically leap to the conclusion that all of these reservations about, and criticisms of, the existing human resource management literature are equally valid and strong. Nevertheless there is undoubtedly considerable merit in the number of them, and the very fact that such concerns and criticisms have been expressed should help caution any reader against the belief that the literature consists of a body of prescriptions and recommendations that are well grounded in the results of systematic empirical research.

Fortunately there are some signs of positive change in this regard. The management-driven, strategic human resource management literature very much dominated the scene in the USA in the 1980s, although this is less likely to be true of the 1990s. This is because, firstly, there is growing recognition of, and concern about, the fact that the so-called bottom line orientation of this literature is far from having been well established in practice. As a consequence the nature of this particular stream of literature will need to change considerably, so as to provide more systematic empirical evidence of the positive relationship between human resource management and larger organizational performance; prescription, description and special case study situations will and should be hopefully less acceptable and dominant elements of this literature in the future. Secondly, there is a small, but growing, body of human resource management literature grounded more in the assumptions and values of institutional economists and sociologists (particularly those working on the development of internal labour markets) and mainstream industrial relations researchers. It is to be hoped that this body of work will occupy a much more prominent and influential role in the human resource management literature of the 1990s.

HUMAN RESOURCE MANAGEMENT, INDUSTRIAL RELATIONS AND TRADE UNIONS

Earlier, I referred to the potentially anti-union implications of human resource management and the associated tendency of much of the literature, particularly in the USA, to ignore the presence and role of trade unions. At least three concerns have been expressed (especially in the United States) about the relationship between human resource management and industrial relations.

The first is the concern of industrial relations researchers and teachers that human resource management is increasingly replacing collective bargaining as the popular, core subject matter of industrial relations teaching programmes; allied to this concern is the reduced external funding available for research on collective bargaining. This change, which needs to be seen against the background of the substantial fall in the overall level of union density and collective bargaining coverage in countries like the USA and Britain in recent years, has raised a number of important questions and debates in the industrial relations research community. For example, can industrial relations researchers depart from their traditional concentration on collective bargaining and usefully and legitimately begin to study the employment practices and arrangements of non-union firms? Can industrial relations researchers, relative to labour economists and behavioural scientists, usefully contribute to an understanding of the strategic and workplace (i.e. non-collective bargaining) levels of decision-making, with their increasingly important implications for human resource management developments, in unionized firms? And if the latter does not occur, will the distinctive contribution of industrial relations researchers to an understanding of the employment relationship (i.e. an inherent conflict of interest between employees and employers) be increasingly lost, in both teaching, research and practitioner circles, relative to the 'efficiency' and 'co-operation' themes of economists and behavioural scientists respectively? In other words, will the concerns of 'due process' and 'equity' not figure prominently in the human resource management literature?

A second, related concern of both industrial relations researchers and trade unionists is whether the introduction and diffusion of human resource management practices will increasingly 'substitute' for the union role, and thus help to maintain and increase the size of the non-union employment sector. Those firms which have pioneered human resource management in the USA are invariably non-union ones, and the concern is that the spread of these practices will increasingly limit the ability of unions successfully to organize firms operating with these types of employment packages. There is in fact some survey evidence in the USA which indicates that the presence of certain human resource management arrangements was significantly associated with organizations successfully maintaining their non-union status in the course of the 1980s.[9] In other countries such relationships and alleged effects still remain to be investigated.

The third concern is that management in the unionized sector, in order to try and compete effectively with non-union organizations, will increasingly seek to emulate and introduce the human resource management practices which have been pioneered in the non-union sector. And here the concern in some union circles is that human resource management practices, with their emphasis on team-work, flexibility and individual employee commitment, will increasingly 'individualize' industrial relations, and drive a wedge between the union and its membership. This concern is particularly evident in relation to employee involvement and participation arrangements which increasingly spread throughout the unionized sector in the USA in the 1980s. Although some national unions have positively endorsed such programmes, others remain more cautious and sceptical, while others have been actively opposed to them. Some of the worries expressed about these involvement/participation programmes within the union movement in the USA are that individual employees will increasingly identify with the organization (as opposed to the union), the workforce will become increasingly divided, grievance procedures and shop steward systems will be ignored, and there will be reduced membership interest, commitment and activity in the union.[10] There is, however, variation in union attitudes towards such programmes in the USA, which has been attributed to differing assumptions regarding, for instance, product demand and technological developments, and their different ideological premises.[11]

In summary, human resource management developments are viewed by some commentators in the USA as having a very awkward, essentially negative relationship with industrial relations from the teacher, researcher and union points of view. They are seen as threatening the position of collective bargaining as the traditional centrepiece of industrial relations research, teaching and practice, and raise a variety of potentially difficult questions for unions, namely how to organize new members in the essential absence of job dissatisfaction and how to maintain the loyalty and commitment of existing members.

In the previous chapter we saw that some unions in Britain have issued position statements that are sceptical, not to say critical, of human resource management arrangements such as quality circles. There are, of course, other unions in Britain which seem rather more favourably disposed towards involvement in and co-operation with such practices; it should be emphasized that national position statements and guidelines issued by unions are not necessarily an accurate guide to what is going on in human resource management terms at the level of the individual workplace. Nevertheless it would appear that the general position of the British trade union movement towards human resource management developments, as indicated by the statements of the Trades Union Congress and certain individual unions, can be described as that of a 'decentralized policy with national union guidelines'.[12] In essence this means that British unions: (1) are concerned about HRM developments as potentially 'individualizing' industrial relations, in the sense of having the capacity to undermine union organization and collective bargaining arrangements; but (2) recognize that product and labour market circumstances will inevitably lead some employers to favour such initiatives; (3) feel that the case for membership involvement (or not) should be made at the organizational level on a situation-by-situation basis, and (4) hope that local level negotiators will be wary about such involvement through the inclusion of appropriate safeguards and the obtaining of certain *quid pro quos*. In short, it appears that the union approach towards human resource management in general is relatively similar to that adopted towards other innovations such as the introduction of new technology.

There is no question that human resource management developments are currently the source of much discussion, debate and rethinking within the British trade union movement (*Financial Times*, 11 February 1991). Some union officers view human resource management as a relatively narrowly based movement confined essentially to organizations with above-average levels of 'organizational slack'; others feel that it may be a double-edged weapon from the employer point of view in that if it does not fully deliver on its promises then the result will be an enhanced employee interest in unions. And yet others feel that the unions should borrow some of the relevant techniques and become increasingly member-sensitive through improving, for instance, their own channels of internal communication. Finally, the question needs to be asked whether the vast majority of British trade unions have at best simply reacted to management-led initiatives in HRM? Are there no signs of a more strategic, pro-active approach from the unions? Probably most 'outsiders' would answer 'yes' and 'no' to these two questions. However, there are some signs of an attempt by both the TUC and individual unions to make training the centrepiece of a more pro-active position in relation to HRM; union proposals for joint training councils in individual organizations are clearly, however, making little headway at the present time. Furthermore a TUC consultative document (*Financial Times*, 15 April 1991) urged unions to become more knowledgeable about developments such as total quality management in order to play a more constructive role in human resource management.

These union concerns about the possible adverse implications of HRM and how to respond appropriately to them are very largely, although not exclusively, confined to the USA, Canada and Britain at the present time, countries in which relatively adversarial, arm's length collective bargaining has traditionally been the norm. In contrast, in countries characterized by higher (and more stable) levels of unionization, centralized industrial relations structures, active government involvement in the labour market and a more joint problem-solving collective bargaining orientation, union concerns about the possible negative consequences of HRM are much less apparent. Indeed unions in such systems have developed much more pro-active policy approaches and stances towards individual HRM developments, such as team working (see Table 8.5).

INTERNATIONAL HUMAN RESOURCE MANAGEMENT

If *strategic* human resource management was very much the phrase of the 1980s then it is a reasonably safe bet that *international* human resource management will be the term of the 1990s. The subject matter of international HRM will revolve around the issues associated with the cross-national transfer and management of human resources (e.g. selection of individuals for expatriate assignments), the cross-national interaction of human resources (e.g. establishment of international joint ventures), and comparative HRM (i.e. identifying the nature of, and reasons for, differences in practices across national boundaries); such issues will raise questions such as whether there is increasing divergence (convergence) across national systems, whether practices are culturally determined and to what extent practices in one system can be usefully adopted and modified in other systems. There are already some textbooks on the subject,[13] although it seems a somewhat, to say the least, premature exercise to be synthesizing material in an area that is still in its infancy.[14]

Why is the subject area of international HRM likely to grow? One source of stimulus has undoubtedly been the research of Hofstede which has documented substantial differences in people's work-related values across different countries.[15] These findings have led him to argue that management theories based on the value system of one particular country are basically untenable. Specifically he is highly critical of the fact that the post-war management literature is overwhelmingly US-dominated, which means that much of the received wisdom about, for instance, leadership, motivation, etc. hinges critically on a particular set of cultural values which have limited applicability elsewhere. A similar line of research has been pursued by Laurent, who has concluded 'that deep-seated managerial assumptions are strongly shaped by national cultures and appear quite insensitive to the more transient culture of organizations'.[16] In a subsequent paper, Laurent has argued that a contingent approach to organizational change needs to be developed to take account of the role of national culture, because:

> When a majority of German managers perceive their organizations as a co-ordinated network of individuals taking rational decisions based on their professional knowledge and competence, any process of planned organizational change in Germany will have to take this into consideration. When a majority of British managers view their organization primarily as a network of interpersonal relationships between individuals who get things done by influencing and negotiating with each other, a different approach to organizational change may be needed in England. When a majority of French managers look at their organizations as an authority network where the power to organize and control the actors stems from their positioning in the hierarchy, another change model may be called for in France.[17]

A second source of interest in the field has come not from research, but from actual organizational practice. That is, the increasingly competitive product market environment has stimulated a rethinking of competitive strategy, an important component of which has been to open up the individual organization to forge linkages with organizations in other countries.[18] There are in fact a whole family of strategic alliances or intercorporate linkages which organizations can be and have become increasingly involved in. Examples include licensing agreements, technology transfer arrangements, bidding consortiums and international joint ventures. Even the most casual look at the pages of the *Financial Times* indicates the increased significance of international joint ventures (which involve the creation of a separate organizational entity whose ownership is shared by firms based in different countries) in recent times. For example, in the 1980s, US firms engaged in over 2,000 alliances with firms in European countries;[19] in late 1989, 1,106 joint ventures with western companies had been officially registered in the (then) Soviet Union,[20] while the number of recorded joint ventures in the EC increased by some 80 per cent in the years 1984/5–1988/9.[21]

Box 9.1   *Human resource management in three international joint ventures*

1   This Anglo-German joint venture was established in 1974, and currently has 34 employees. It manufactures electro-mechanical equipment for the North Sea oil industry. It is a non-union organization, with all human resource management matters being dealt with by the managing director and the production manufacturing manager. Their priority concern is to ensure the payment of an hourly wage rate sufficient to recruit labour in a relatively tight local labour market area. They pay considerably above the national engineering agreement, and obtain their information on the going local rate from personal and telephone contacts with other employers in the area. On the procedural side, information from handbooks for small businesses in the UK has been essentially utilized.

2   This Anglo-German joint venture was established in 1972. It is a chemical manufacturing one which currently employs some 200 workers. It is located very close to its British parent company which has meant that there are joint pension arrangements, job vacancies are listed in both the joint venture and the British parent company, terms and conditions of employment are broadly similar, salary survey information is shared and the British parent company's procedural arrangements have provided the basis for those in the joint venture. The joint venture recognizes unions for collective bargaining purposes, and the level of union membership in the joint venture is essentially similar to that in the British parent company. There is a specialist human resource management function and current human resource management developments include the introduction of annual hours arrangements and the negotiation of multi-skilling and functional flexibility arrangements. These developments are on-going throughout the whole of the British parent company's operations.

3   This international joint venture was established in 1987 as a greenfield site. It is in the textile industry, has two Japanese parent companies and a British one and employs 140 workers, a figure expected to rise to 240 in the next twelve months. The human resource management policy mix includes single status arrangements, team-based working arrangements, a strong emphasis on direct, two-way communications (i.e. team briefing) and a system of performance

---

Box 9.1 *continued*

appraisal for all employees. The joint venture is located at a considerable distance from any other plants owned by the British parent company. Indeed its terms and conditions of employment are not linked or related to those anywhere else in the parent company, and it is a non-union establishment in contrast to all other plants owned by the parent company.

The vast majority of research on joint ventures (both national and international ones) has been conducted by business policy and organization strategy researchers. Their work suggests that the single most important decision involved in an international joint venture is that of choosing an appropriate partner. And here the most important considerations have been listed as follows: (1) possession of the desired source of competitive advantage; (2) the need for a complementary or balanced contribution from the firm; (3) a compatible view of international strategy; (4) low risk of becoming a competitor; (5) pre-emptive value as a partner vis-à-vis rivals and (6) organizational compatibility.[22] The importance of taking on board such considerations should be seen in the light of the relatively high 'failure' rates of international joint ventures, with figures of 30–40 per cent frequently being reported.[23]

The 'organizational compatibility' consideration noted above would seem to point to the potential significance of human resource management considerations. Indeed such considerations have figured prominently in media discussions of the problems of, for instance, 'successfully managing' US–Japanese joint ventures (*Financial Times*, 22 February 1991). The increasing number of international joint ventures, together with the publicity of 'organizational incompatibility' problems, is likely to cause human resource management researchers in the 1990s increasingly to switch their attention away from wholly owned, foreign subsidiaries to international joint venture operations. Indeed there are already articles urging work along these lines,[24] and as this process occurs it will be important for researchers to recognize from the outset the quite considerable diversity in the human resource management practices and priorities of international joint ventures. Such diversity and variation is illustrated by the three organizational examples in Box 9.1.

Box 9.1 suggests three basic types of international joint ventures in human resource management terms: (1) the small joint venture partnership in the engineering industry where there is no specialist human resource management function, human resource management issues are few and the organization is essentially similar to a small (domestically owned) single, independent establishment; (2) an international joint venture where the British parent company is, for reasons of physical proximity, the dominant force in human resource management, but there is little in the joint venture in human resource management terms that is different to that elsewhere in the British parent company set-up; and (3) an international joint venture where again the British parent company is the dominant force in the human resource management area, but where a conscious decision has been taken to try and 'break the mould' and depart from the existing parent company HRM practices. It will clearly be an important task for future research to identify the relative proportions of these (and other possible) types in given samples of international joint ventures. Such studies will, however, far from exhaust the potential interest of such organizations to HRM researchers; other issues to be examined will include the identification of the HRM problems that arise in such organizations, and how to provide an HRM package that facilitates the effective performance of individual managers in such organizations.

A FINAL PERSONAL NOTE

At the present time there are numerous books and articles emerging, particularly in Britain, which are concerned with the alleged internal contradictions of human resource management.[25] It is not, however, always clear whether individuals see these contradictions as inherent in the notion of HRM, or whether they arose rather from a poorly thought-out implementation process at the level of the individual organization. However, it is probably true to say that most human resource management researchers have some concerns about both the literature and practice of HRM at present. I am no exception in this regard and as a consequence in this final section wish to highlight some issues in the HRM area which need to be more fully and carefully addressed by researchers, practitioners and policy makers. The issues I have in mind may be briefly highlighted as follows:[26]

- The underlying theory in much of the HRM literature is rather weak. For instance, there is a tendency simply to treat 'human resource potential' (i.e. the motivation, commitment, etc. of individual employees) as an intervening variable between organizational characteristics and organizational outcomes, which if 'managed effectively' will contribute to high performance. In order to demonstrate that the nature of the HRM policy mix positively influences human resource potential which, in turn, feeds through to positive organizational performance, there is a very real need for more explicit theories of employee motivation, commitment, etc. and the need to control for larger influences on such motivation and commitment both within the organization and from the external environment.

- The larger body of organizational theory has increasingly recognized that internal decision-making processes of organizations are more capable of understanding and analysis in 'political', rather than rational, terms in which notions of power, conflict and negotiation are all-important. This insight needs to be increasingly incorporated in the HRM literature in order to try and understand the processes involved in initiating, integrating and institutionalizing individual HRM innovations.

- The unit of analysis involved in the HRM literature is very much that of the individual organization. Such a perspective fails to attach sufficient importance to developments and influences beyond the boundaries of individual organizations that can be particularly important in shaping HRM developments (or the lack of them) in individual organizations. For instance, it is widely contended that the tendency of competing firms to 'poach' trained labour will reduce the incentive of any one firm to engage in training. More generally, it has been suggested that the strength of external financial markets makes for a short-term orientation among British and American management that systematically under-values human resource orientated investments which have definite, short-term costs but longer-term, more uncertain pay-offs.

- The strong management orientation in the HRM literature conveys very much the impression that human resource management innovations are a private affair, in which the government can (and should, at least to some commentators) play a very small role. This is particularly unfortunate given that one of the great challenges in the HRM area is to know how to institutionalize (i.e. ensure the survival of) 'best practice' arrangements in individual organizations and then spread or diffuse such arrangements across a larger cross-section of organizations. And it is the government that can potentially be important in this regard through a variety of mechanisms such as the provision of tax or financial incentives for particular innovations, disseminating information through issuing codes of practice, facilitating the establishment of pilot projects and inter-organizational learning networks, etc. Indeed such initiatives have frequently been undertaken by governments in individual countries and it is important for both practitioners and researchers to learn more about the relative effectiveness of such measures.

Obviously other individuals would want to add to this particular list. But even what has been listed here helps make the basic point that the agenda of both HRM researchers and practitioners should be relatively busy and important for some years to come.

REFERENCES

1　This section draws heavily on P. B. Beaumont, 'The US Human Resource Management Literature: A Review', in Graeme Salaman (ed.), *Human Resource Strategies*, Sage, London, 1992, pp. 20–37.

2　Randall B. Dunham and Frank J. Smith, *Organizational Surveys*, Scott Foresman and Co., Glenview, Ill., 1979.

3　Eric Trist, 'The Evolution of Socio-Technical Systems as a Conceptual Framework and as an Action Research Program', in A. Van de Van and W. Joyce (eds.), *Perspectives on Organizational Design and Behaviour*, Wiley, New York, 1981, pp. 17–75.

4　T. Burns and G. M. Stalker, *The Management of Innovation*, Tavistock, London, 1961.

5　Michael Beer and Bert Spector (eds.), *Reading in Human Resource Management*, Free Press, New York, 1985, p. 5.

6　W. Richard Scott, 'Effectiveness of Organizational Effectiveness Studies', in Paul S. Goodman and Johannes M. Pennings (eds.), *New Perspectives on Organizational Effectiveness*, Jossey-Bass, San Francisco, 1977.

7　David Lewin, 'The Future of Employee Involvement/Participation in the United States', *Proceedings of the Industrial Relations Research Association*, University of Wisconsin, Madison, 1989, pp. 470–5.

8　Luis R. Gomez-Mejia, 'The Role of Human Resources Strategy in Export Performance: A Longitudinal Study', *Strategic Management Journal* 9, 1988, pp. 493–505.

9　Thomas A. Kochan, Harry C. Katz and Robert B. McKersie, *The Transformation of American Industrial Relations*, Basic Books, New York, 1986.

10　Adrienne E. Eaton, 'The Extent and Determinants of Local Union

Control of Participative Programs', *Industrial and Labor Relations Review*, 43 (5), July 1990.

11 Harry C. Katz, 'The Debate over the Reorganization of Work and Industrial Relations within the North American Labor Movement', Mimeographed Paper, ILR School, Cornell University, 1986.

12 P. B. Beaumont, 'Trade Unions and HRM', *Industrial Relations Journal*, 22 (4), Winter 1991.

13 Peter J. Dowling and Randall S. Schuler, *International Dimensions of Human Resource Management*, Plus-Kent, Boston, 1990.

14 André Laurent, 'The Cross-Cultural Puzzle of International Human Resource Management', in Jaydish Sheth and Golpira Eshghi (eds.), *Global Human Resource Perspectives*, South-Western, Cincinnati, 1989, p. 55.

15 Geert Hofstede, 'The Cultural Relativity of Organizational Theories', *Journal of International Business Studies*, 14 (2), 1983, pp. 75–90.

16 Laurent, 'Cross-Cultural Puzzle', p. 58.

17 André Laurent, 'A Cultural View of Organizational Change', in Paul Evans, Yves Doz and André Laurent (eds.), *Human Resource Management in International Firms*, Macmillan, London, 1989.

18 Rosabeth Moss Kanter, *When Giants Learn to Dance*, Simon and Schuster, New York, 1989, Chapter 5.

19 *Fortune*, 27 March 1989, pp. 66–76.

20 Paul R. Lawrence and Charalambos A. Vlachoutsicos (eds.), *Behind the Factory Walls: Decision Making in Soviet and US Enterprises*, Harvard Business School Press, Boston, 1990, p. 4.

21 Figures supplied by Directorate-General for Competition, European Commission.

22 Michael E. Porter and Mark B. Fuller, 'Coalitions and Global Strategy', in Michael E. Porter (ed.), *Competition in Global Industries*, Harvard Business School Press, Boston, 1986, p. 341.

23 J. Peter Killing, *Strategies for Joint Venture Success*, Croom Helm, London, 1983, p. 15.

24 Oded Shenkar and Yoram Zeira, 'Human Resources Management in International Joint Ventures: Directions for Research', *Academy of Management Review*, 12 (3), July 1987.

25 See, for example, Paul Blyton and Peter Turnbull (eds.), *Reassessing Human Resource Management*, Sage, London, 1992.

26 Helpful discussions with Tom Kochan are gratefully acknowledged.

APPENDIX: TEACHING MATERIAL

I have found the following *questions* useful for exam and essay questions and for providing a focus for classroom discussions.

- Is HRM a good thing or bad thing from the point of view of the personnel management function of individual organizations? (Chapter 1)
- Should Britain pursue a low-wage competitive strategy? (Chapter 1)
- What is the essence of 'corporate culture' and how might management seek to change it in an individual organization? (Chapter 2)
- 'Corporate culture is such an elusive term that it has no practical implications for management seeking to bring about organizational change.' Discuss. (Chapter 2)
- What are the major weaknesses of interviews in the selection of employees? How can such weaknesses be overcome? (Chapter 3)
- Given the relative success of assessment centres, why don't more organizations use these for selection purposes? (Chapter 3)
- Can and should performance appraisal interviews be a completely objective exercise? (Chapter 4)
- How can the process of employee appraisals be improved? (Chapter 4)
- What are the leading characteristics or features of a good counselling interview? (Chapter 4 Appendix)
- 'Performance-related pay is the obvious means of stimulating good on-the-job performance.' Discuss. (Chapter 5)
- Performance-related pay arrangements can be variously based on the individual employee, groups of employees or the organization as a whole. Which of these is the most suitable for adoption in most organizations? (Chapter 5)

- 'The good international manager is born not made.' Discuss. (Chapter 6)
- What are the potential benefits and costs of a formal mentoring programme for career development purposes? (Chapter 6)
- 'If employees value face-to-face communication concerning their working environment then there is no substitute for team briefing.' Discuss. (Chapter 7)
- 'Employee attitude surveys generate little real information as employees only tell you what they think you want to hear.' Discuss. (Chapter 7)
- Can organizations usefully build on the lessons of experience with quality circles? (Chapter 8)
- Are team working arrangements the wave of the future? (Chapter 8)

The following *assignment* has proved useful in introducing students to the general subject area and providing line managers with more knowledge of what is happening in their own HRM department. It also provides useful feedback to the teacher (e.g. the thumbnail sketches set in Box 1.1 came from this source).

Basic objective

Recent years have witnessed a great deal of discussion of what is, or should be, happening to the personnel management (human resource) function in individual organizations. Specifically, has the function gained or lost ground, relative to other functions, in terms of resources, influence, status and power in organizations? The basic purpose of the assignment is to document what has happened (if anything) to the PM/HRM function in your organization in recent times (say the last five years). Ideally you should concentrate on your particular workplace, but if you work for a multi-established organization you may want to take on board the nature and influence of developments in the larger organizations.

The basic structure

In essence the assignment should consist of four sections:

(a) A short introductory section designed to familiarize the reader with the nature of your organization. The material covered here should include size of the organization, industry, competitive strategy, recent levels of performance, etc.

(b)   The *subjective* views of individuals in the PM/HRM function, and at least one other functional area of management, as to the extent and nature of any change in the function in recent years.

(c)   Any *objective* indicators of change. For example, changed numbers in the function, title or job description changes, changed reporting relationships, new priorities, etc.

(d)   The major reasons for any observed changes. Changes in labour market conditions, union influence and government legislation are frequently mentioned in this regard. However, there may be other important influences, such as a change in the nature of competitive strategy or a change in the priorities of senior management.

In addition to the Harvard Business School *case studies* there are more and more books of case studies appearing; it is also pleasing to see that some of the more recent case study books are looking beyond the manufacturing sector and some even have an increasingly international flavour. Some of the cases in the books by S. Tyson and A. Kakabadse (eds.) (*Cases in Human Resource Management*, Heinemann, London, 1987), D. Winstanley and J. Woodall (*Case Studies in Personnel*, IPM, London, 1992), A. Mulvie and M. McDougall (*Human Resource Management in Practice*, Chartwell-Bratt, Bromley, 1990), and S. Vickerstaff (*Human Resource Management in Europe*, Chapman and Hall, London, 1992) have proved especially useful.

INDEX